VISITS TO MONASTERIES IN THE LEVANT

Curzon, Robert

www.GeneralBooksClub.com

Publication Data:
Title: Visits to Monasteries in the Levant;
Author: Curzon, Robert
Reprinted: 2010, General Books LLC, Memphis, Tennessee, USA
Contact the publisher: http://generalbooksclub.com/contactus.cfm
Limit of Liability/Disclaimer of Warranty: The publisher makes no representations or warranties with respect to the accuracy or completeness of the book. The information in the book may not be suitable for your situation. You should consult with a professional where appropriate. The publisher is not liable for any damages resulting from the book.

1

VISITS TO MONASTERIES IN THE LEVANT

(This book was
   produced from scanned images of public domain material
   from the Google Print project.)
Book's cover: CURZON'S MONASTERIES
From a Drawing made on the spot by Viscount Eastnor. VIEW OF THE GREAT MONASTERY OF METEORA, FROM THE MONASTERY OF BARLAAM, WITH THE RIVER PENEUS IN THE DISTANCE.From a Drawing made on the spot by Viscount Eastnor.
VIEW OF THE GREAT MONASTERY OF METEORA, FROM THE MONASTERY OF BARLAAM, WITH THE RIVER PENEUS IN THE DISTANCE.
VISITS TO MONASTERIES
IN
THE LEVANT.
BY THE
HONBLE.
ROBERT CURZON, JUN.

From a Sketch by R. Curzon. Interior of the Court of a Greek Monastery. A monk is calling the congregation to prayer, by beating a board called the simandro (σιμανδρο) which is generally used instead of bells.From a Sketch by R. Curzon.

Interior of the Court of a Greek Monastery. A monk is calling the congregation to prayer, by beating a board called the simandro (σιμανδρο) which is generally used instead of bells.

WITH NUMEROUS WOODCUTS.
LONDON:
JOHN MURRAY, ALBEMARLE STREET.
1849.
Contents
List of Illustrations
Footnotes
PREFACE.

In

presenting to the public another book of travels in the East, when it is already overwhelmed with little volumes about palm-trees and camels, and reflections on the Pyramids, I am aware that I am committing an act which requires some better excuse for so unwarrantable an intrusion on the patience of the reader than any that I am able to offer.

The origin of these pages is as follows:—I was staying by myself in an old country-house belonging to my family, but not often inhabited by them, and, having nothing to do in the evening, I looked about for some occupation to amuse the passing hours. In the room where I was sitting there was a large book-case full of ancient manuscripts, many of which had been collected by myself, in various out-of-the-way places, in different parts of the world. Taking some of these ponderous volumes from their shelves, I turned over their wide vellum leaves, and admired the antiquity of one, and the gold and azure which gleamed upon the pages of another. The sight of these books brought before my mind many scenes and recollections of the countries from which they came, and I said to myself, I know what I will do; I will write down some account of the most curious of these manuscripts, and the places in which they were found, as well as some of the adventures which I encountered in the pursuit of my venerable game.

I sat down accordingly, and in a short time accumulated a heap of papers connected more or less with the history of the ancient manuscripts; at the desire of some of my friends I selected the following pages, and it is with great diffidence that I present them to the public. If they have any merits whatever, these must consist in their containing descriptions of localities but seldom visited in modern times; or if they refer to places better known to the general reader, I hope that the peculiar circumstances which occurred during my stay there, or on my journeys through the neighbouring countries, may be found sufficiently interesting to afford some excuse for my presumption in sending them to the press.

I have no further apology to offer. These slight sketches were written for my own diversion when I had nothing better to do, and if they afford any pleasure to the reader under the same circumstances, they will answer as much purpose as was intended in their composition.

CONTENTS.
INTRODUCTORY CHAPTER
Page xix
PART I.
EGYPT IN 1833.
CHAPTER I.
Navarino—The Wrecks of the Turkish and Egyptian Fleets—Alexandria—An Arab Pilot—Intense Heat—Scene from the Hotel Windows—The Water-Carriers—A Procession—A Bridal Party—Violent mode of clearing the Road—Submissive Behaviour of the People—Astonishing Number of Donkeys—Bedouin Arabs; their wild and savage appearance—Early Hours—Visit to the Pasha's Prime Minister, Boghos Bey; hospitable reception—Kawasses and Chaoushes; their functions and powers—The Yassakjis—The Minister's Audience Chamber—Walmas; anecdote of his saving the life of Boghos Bey
1
CHAPTER II.
Rapacity of the Dragomans—The Mahmoudieh Canal—The Nile at Atfeh—The muddy Waters of the Nile—Richness of the Soil—Accident to the Boatmen—Night Sailing—A Collision—A Vessel run down—Escape of the Crew—Solemn Investigation—Final Judgment—Curious Mode of Fishing—Tameness of the Birds—Jewish Malefactors—Moving Pillar of Sand—Arrival at Cairo—Hospitable Reception by the Consul-General
14
CHAPTER III.
National Topics of Conversation—The Rising of the Nile; evil effects of its rising too high; still worse consequences of a deficiency of its waters—The Nilometer—Universal Alarm in August, 1833—The Nile at length rises to the desired Height—Ceremony of cutting the Embankment—The Canal of the Khalidj—Immense Assemblage of People—The State Tent—Arrival of Habeeb Effendi—Splendid Dresses of the Officers—Exertions of the Arab Workmen—Their Scramble for Paras—Admission of the Water—Its sudden Irruption—Excitement of the Ladies—Picturesque Effect of large Assemblies in the East
27
CHAPTER IV.
Early Hours in the Levant—Compulsory Use of Lanterns in Cairo—Separation of the different Quarters of the City—Custom of sleeping in the open air—The Mahomedan Times of Prayer—Impressive Effect of the Morning Call to Prayer from the Minarets—The last Prayer-time, Al Assr—Bedouin Mode of ascertaining this Hour—Ancient Form of the Mosques—The Mosque of Sultan Hassan—Egyptian Mode of "raising the Supplies"—Sultan Hassan's Mosque the Scene of frequent Conflicts—The Slaughter of the Mameluke Beys in the Place of Roumayli—Escape of one Mameluke, and his subsequent Friendship with Mohammed Ali—The Talisman of Cairo—Joseph's Well and Hall—Mohammed Ali's Mosque—His Residence in the Citadel—The Harem—Degraded State of the Women in the East
35
CHAPTER V.

Interview with Mohammed Ali Pasha—Mode of lighting a Room in Egypt—Personal Appearance of the Pasha—His Diamond-mounted Pipe—The lost Handkerchief—An unceremonious Attendant—View of Cairo from the Citadel—Site of Memphis; its immense extent—The Tombs of the Caliphs—The Pasha's Mausoleum—Costume of Egyptian Ladies—The Cobcob, or Wooden Clog—Mode of dressing the Hair—The Veil—Mistaken Idea that the Egyptian Ladies are Prisoners in the Harem; their power of doing as they like—The Veil a complete Disguise—Laws of the Harem—A Levantine Beauty—Eastern Manners—The Abyssinian Slaves—Arab Girls—Ugliness of the Arab Women when old—Venerable Appearance of the old Men—An Arab Sheick
47

CHAPTER VI.
Mohammed Bey, Defterdar—His Expedition to Senaar—His Barbarity and Rapacity—His Defiance of the Pasha—Stories of his Cruelty and Tyranny—The Horseshoe—The Fight of the Mamelukes—His cruel Treachery—His Mode of administering Justice—The stolen Milk—The Widow's Cow—Sale and Distribution of the Thief—The Turkish Character—Pleasures of a Journey on the Nile—The Copts—Their Patriarchs—The Patriarch of Abyssinia—Basileos Bey—His Boat—An American's choice of a Sleeping-place
64

NATRON LAKES.
CHAPTER VII.
Visit to the Coptic Monasteries near the Natron Lakes—The Desert of Nitria—Early Christian Anchorites—St. Macarius of Alexandria—His Abstinence and Penance—Order of Monks founded by him—Great increase of the Number of ascetic Monks in the Fourth Century—Their subsequent decrease, and the present ruined state of the Monasteries—Legends of the Desert—Capture of a Lizard—Its alarming escape—The Convent of Baramous—Night attacks—Invasion of Sanctuary—Ancient Glass Lamps—Monastery of Souriani—Its Library and Coptic MSS.—The Blind Abbot and his Oil-cellar—The persuasive powers of Rosoglio—Discovery of Syriac MSS.—The Abbot's supposed treasure
75

CHAPTER VIII.
View from the Convent Wall—Appearance of the Desert—Its grandeur and freedom—Its contrast to the Convent Garden—Beauty and luxuriance of Eastern Vegetation—Picturesque Group of the Monks and their Visitors—The Abyssinian Monks—Their appearance—Their austere mode of Life—The Abyssinian College—Description of the Library—The mode of Writing in Abyssinia—Immense Labour required to write an Abyssinian book—Paintings and Illuminations—Disappointment of the Abbot at finding the supposed Treasure-box only an old Book—Purchase of the MSS. and Books—The most precious left behind—Since acquired for the British Museum
90

THE CONVENT OF THE PULLEY.
CHAPTER IX.

The Convent of the Pulley—Its inaccessible position—Difficult landing on the bank of the Nile—Approach to the Convent through the Rocks—Description of the Convent and its Inhabitants—Plan of the Church—Books and MSS.—Ancient excavations—Stone Quarries and ancient Tombs—Alarm of the Copts—Their ideas of a Sketch-book
105

RUINED MONASTERY AT THEBES.
CHAPTER X.
Ruined Monastery in the Necropolis of Thebes—"Mr. Hay's Tomb"—The Coptic Carpenter—His acquirements and troubles—He agrees to show the MSS. belonging to the ruined Monastery, which are under his charge—Night visit to the Tomb in which they are concealed—Perils of the way—Description of the Tomb—Probably in former times a Christian Church—Examination of the Coptic MSS.—Alarming interruption—Hurried flight from the Evil Spirits—Fortunate escape—Appearance of the Evil Spirit—Observations on Ghost Stories—The Legend of the Old Woman of Berkeley considered
117

THE WHITE MONASTERY.
CHAPTER XI.
The White Monastery—Abou Shenood—Devastations of the Mamelukes—Description of the Monastery—Different styles of its exterior and interior Architecture—Its ruinous condition—Description of the Church—The Baptistery—Ancient Rites of Baptism—The Library—Modern Architecture—The Church of San Francesco at Rimini—The Red Monastery—Alarming rencontre with an armed party—Feuds between the native Tribes—Faction fights—Eastern Story Tellers—Legends of the Desert—Abraham and Sarah—Legendary Life of Moses—Arabian Story-tellers—Attention of their Audience
130

THE ISLAND OF PHILŒ, c.
CHAPTER XII.
The Island of Philœ—The Cataract of Assouan—The Burial Place of Osiris—The Great Temple of Philœ—The Bed of Pharaoh—Shooting in Egypt—Turtle Doves—Story of the Prince Anas el Ajoud—Egyptian Songs—Vow of the Turtle Dove—Curious fact in Natural History—The Crocodile and its Guardian Bird—Arab notions regarding Animals—Legend of King Solomon and the Hoopoes—Natives of the country round the Cataracts of the Nile—Their appearance and Costume—The beautiful Mouna—Solitary Visit to the Island of Philœ—Quarrel between two native Boys—Singular instance of retributive Justice
141

PART II.
JERUSALEM AND THE MONASTERY AT ST. SABBA.
CHAPTER XIII.

Journey to Jerusalem—First View of the Holy City—The Valley of Gihon—Appearance of the City—The Latin Convent of St. Salvador—Inhospitable Reception by the Monks—Visit to the Church of the Holy Sepulchre—Description of the Interior—The Chapel of the Sepulchre—The Chapel of the Cross on Mount Calvary—The Tomb and Sword of Godfrey de Bouillon—Arguments in favour of the Authenticity of the Holy Sepulchre—The Invention of the Cross by the Empress Helena—Legend of the Cross

165

CHAPTER XIV.

The Via Dolorosa—The Houses of Dives and of Lazarus—The Prison of St Peter—The Site of the Temple of Solomon—The Mosque of Omar—The Hadjr el Sakhara—The Greek Monastery—Its Library—Valuable Manuscripts—Splendid MS. of the Book of Job—Arabic spoken at Jerusalem—Mussulman Theory regarding the Crucifixion—State of the Jews—Richness of their Dress in their own Houses—Beauty of their Women—Their literal Interpretation of Scripture—The Service in the Synagogue—Description of the House of a Rabbi—The Samaritans—Their Roll of the Pentateuch—Arrival of Ibrahim Pasha at Jerusalem

181

CHAPTER XV.

Expedition to the Monastery of St. Sabba—Reports of Arab Robbers—The Valley of Jehoshaphat—The Bridge of Al Sirat—Rugged Scenery—An Arab Ambuscade—A successful Parley—The Monastery of St. Sabba—History of the Saint—The Greek Hermits—The Church—The Iconostasis—The Library—Numerous MSS.—The Dead Sea—The Scene of the Temptation—Discovery—The Apple of the Dead Sea—The Statements of Strabo and Pliny confirmed

192

CHAPTER XVI.

Church of the Holy Sepulchre—Processions of the Copts—The Syrian Maronites and the Greeks—Riotous Behaviour of the Pilgrims—Their immense numbers—The Chant of the Latin Monks—Ibrahim Pasha—The Exhibition of the Sacred Fire—Excitement of the Pilgrims—The Patriarch obtains the Sacred Fire from the Holy Sepulchre—Contest for the Holy Light—Immense sum paid for the privilege of receiving it first—Fatal Effects of the Heat and Smoke—Departure of Ibrahim Pasha—Horrible Catastrophe—Dreadful Loss of Life among the Pilgrims in their endeavours to leave the Church—Battle with the Soldiers—Our Narrow Escape—Shocking Scene in the Court of the Church—Humane Conduct of Ibrahim Pasha—Superstition of the Pilgrims regarding Shrouds—Scallop Shells and Palm Branches—The Dead Muleteer—Moonlight View of the Dead Bodies—The Curse on Jerusalem—Departure from the Holy City

208

PART III.
THE MONASTERIES OF METEORA.
CHAPTER XVII.

Albania—Ignorance at Corfu concerning that Country—Its reported abundance of Game and Robbers—The Disturbed State of the Country—The Albanians—Richness of their Arms—Their free use of them—Comparative Safety of Foreigners—Tragic Fate of a German Botanist—Arrival at Gominitza—Ride to Paramathia—A Night's Bivouac—Reception at Paramathia—Albanian Ladies—Yanina—Albanian Mode of settling a Quarrel—Expected Attack from Robbers—A Body-Guard mounted—Audience with the Vizir—His Views of Criminal Jurisprudence—Retinue of the Vizir—His Troops—Adoption of the European Exercises—Expedition to Berat—Calmness and Self-possession of the Turks—Active Preparations for Warfare—Scene at the Bazaar—Valiant Promises of the Soldiers

235

CHAPTER XVIII.

Start for Meteora—Rencontre with a Wounded Traveller—Barbarity of the Robbers—Albanian Innkeeper—Effect of the Turkish Language upon the Greeks—Mezzovo—Interview with the chief Person in the Village—Mount Pindus—Capture by Robbers—Salutary effects of Swaggering—Arrival under Escort at the Robbers' Head-Quarters—Affairs take a favourable turn—An unexpected Friendship with the Robber Chief—The Khan of Malacash—Beauty of the Scenery—Activity of our Guards—Loss of Character—Arrival at Meteora

257

CHAPTER XIX.

Meteora—The extraordinary Character of its Scenery—Its Caves formerly the Resort of Ascetics—Barbarous Persecution of the Hermits—Their extraordinary Religious Observances—Singular Position of the Monasteries—The Monastery of Barlaam—The difficulty of reaching it—Ascent by a Windlass and Net, or by Ladders—Narrow Escape—Hospitable Reception by the Monks—The Agoumenos, or Abbot—His strict Fast—Description of the Monastery—The Church—Symbolism in the Greek Church—Respect for Antiquity—The Library—Determination of the Abbot not to sell any of the MSS.—The Refectory—Its Decorations—Aërial Descent—The Monastery of Hagios Stephanos—Its Carved Iconostasis—Beautiful View from the Monastery—Monastery of Agia Triada—Summary Justice at Triada—Monastery of Agia Roserea—Its Lady Occupants—Admission refused

279

CHAPTER XX.

The great Monastery of Meteora—The Church—Ugliness of the Portraits of Greek Saints—Greek Mode of Washing the Hands—A Monastic Supper—Morning View from the Monastery—The Library—Beautiful MSS.—Their Purchase—The Kitchen—Discussion among the Monks as to the Purchase Money for the MSS.—The MSS. reclaimed—A last look at their Beauties—Proposed Assault of the Monastery by the Robber Escort

298

CHAPTER XXI.

Return Journey—Narrow Escape—Consequences of Singing—Arrival at the Khan of Malacash—Agreeable Anecdote—Parting from the Robbers at Messovo—A Pilau—Wet Ride to Paramathia—Accident to the Baggage-Mule—Its wonderful Escape—Novel Costume—A Deputation—Return to Corfu

312

PART IV.
THE MONASTERIES OF MOUNT ATHOS.
CHAPTER XXII.

Constantinople—The Patriarch's Palace—The Plague, Anecdotes, Superstitions—The Two Jews—Interview with the Patriarch—Ceremonies of Reception—The Patriarch's Misconception as to the Archbishop of Canterbury—He addresses a Firman to the Monks of Mount Athos—Preparations for Departure—The Ugly Greek Interpreter—Mode of securing his Fidelity

327

CHAPTER XXIII.

Coom Calessi—Uncomfortable Quarters—A Turkish Boat and its Crew—Grandeur of the Scenery—Legend of Jason and the Golden Fleece—The Island of Imbros—Heavy Rain Storm—A Rough Sea—Lemnos—Bad Accommodation—The Old Woman's Mattress and its Contents—Striking View of Mount Athos from the Sea—The Hermit of the Tower

342

CHAPTER XXIV.

Monastery of St. Laura—Kind Reception by the Abbot—Astonishment of the Monks—History of the Monastery—Rules of the Order of St. Basil—Description of the Buildings—Curious Pictures of the Last Judgment—Early Greek Paintings; Richness of their Frames and Decorations—Ancient Church Plate—Beautiful Reliquary—The Refectory—The Abbot's Savoury Dish—The Library—The MSS.—Ride to the Monastery of Caracalla—Magnificent Scenery

356

CHAPTER XXV.

The Monastery of Caracalla—Its beautiful Situation—Hospitable Reception—Description of the Monastery—Legend of its Foundation—The Church—Fine Specimens of Ancient Jewellery—The Library—The Value attached to the Books by the Abbot—He agrees to sell some of the MSS.—Monastery of Philotheo—The Great Monastery of Iveron—History of its Foundation—Its magnificent Library—Ignorance of the Monks—Superb MSS.—The Monks refuse to part with any of the MSS.—Beauty of the Scenery of Mount Athos

377

CHAPTER XXVI.

The Monastery of Stavroniketa—The Library—Splendid MS. of St. Chrysostom—The Monastery of Pantocratoras—Ruinous Condition of the Library—Complete Destruction of the Books—Disappointment—Oration to the Monks—The Great Monastery of Vatopede—Its History—Ancient Pictures in the Church—Legend of the Girdle of the Blessed Virgin—The Library—Wealth and Luxury of the Monks—The Monastery of Sphigmenou—Beautiful Jewelled Cross—The Monastery of Kiliantari—Magnificent MS. in Gold Letters on White Vellum—The Monasteries of Zographou, Castamoneta, Docheirou, and Xenophou—The Exiled Bishops—The Library—Very fine MSS.—Proposals for their Purchase—Lengthened Negotiations—Their successful Issue

391
CHAPTER XXVII.

The Monastery of Russico—Its Courteous Abbot—The Monastery of Xeropotamo—Its History—High Character of its Abbot—Excursion to the Monasteries of St. Nicholas and St. Dionisius—Interesting Relics—Magnificent Shrine—The Library—The Monastery of St. Paul—Respect shown by the Monks—Beautiful MS.—Extraordinary Liberality and Kindness of the Abbot and Monks—A valuable Acquisition at little Cost—The Monastery of Simopetra—Purchase of MS.—The Monk of Xeropotamo—His Ideas about Women—Excursion to Cariez—The Monastery of Coutloumoussi—The Russian Book-Stealer—History of the Monastery—Its reputed Destruction by the Pope of Rome—The Aga of Cariez—Interview in a Kiosk—The She Cat of Mount Athos

413
CHAPTER XXVIII.

Caracalla—The Agoumenos—Curious Cross—The Nuts of Caracalla—Singular Mode of preparing a Dinner Table—Departure from Mount Athos—Packing of the MSS.—Difficulties of the Way—Voyage to the Dardanelles—Apprehended Attack from Pirates—Return to Constantinople

436
Footnotes

INTRODUCTORY CHAPTER.

A more enlarged account of the Monasteries of the Levant would, I think, be interesting for many reasons if the task was undertaken by some one much more competent than myself to do justice to so curious a subject. In these monasteries resided the early fathers of the Church, and within the precincts of their time-hallowed walls were composed those writings which have since been looked up to as the rules of Christian life: from thence also were promulgated the doctrines of the Heresiarchs, which, in the early ages of the Church, were the causes of so much dissension and confusion, rancour and persecution, in the disastrous days of the decline and fall of the Roman empire.

The monasteries of the East are besides particularly interesting to the lovers of the picturesque, from the beautiful situations in which they are almost invariably placed. The monastery of Megaspelion, on the coast of the Gulf of Corinth, is built in the mouth of an enormous cave. The monasteries of Meteora, and some of those on Mount Athos, are remarkable for their positions on the tops of inaccessible rocks; many of the convents in Syria, the islands of Cyprus, Candia, the Archipelago, and the Prince's Islands in the Sea of Marmora, are unrivalled for the beauty of the positions in which they stand; many others in Bulgaria, Asia Minor, Sinope, and other places on the shores of the Black Sea, are most curious monuments of ancient and romantic times. There is one on the road to Persia, about one day's journey inland from Trebizond, which is built half way up the side of a perpendicular precipice; it is ensconced in several fissures of the rock, and various little gardens adjoining the buildings display the industry of the monks; these are laid out on shelves or terraces wherever the nature of the spot affords a ledge of sufficient width to support the soil; the different parts of the monastery are approached by stairs and flights of steps cut in the face of the precipice, leading from one cranny to another; the whole has the appearance of a bas-relief stuck against a wall; this monastery partakes of the nature of a large swallow's nest. But it is for their architecture that the monasteries of the Levant are more particularly deserving of study; for, after the remains of the private houses of the Romans at Pompeii, they are the most ancient specimens extant of domestic architecture. The refectories, kitchens, and the cells of the monks exceed in point of antiquity anything of the kind in Europe. The monastery of St. Katherine at Mount Sinai has hardly been altered since the sixth century, and still contains ornaments presented to it by the Emperor Justinian. The White Monastery and the monastery at Old Cairo, both in Egypt, are still more ancient. The monastery of Kuzzul Vank, near the sources of the Euphrates, is, I believe, as old as the fifth century. The greater number in all the countries where the Greek faith prevails, were built before the year 1000. Most monasteries possess crosses, candlesticks, and reliquaries, many of splendid workmanship, and of the era of the foundation of the buildings which contain them, while their mosaics and fresco paintings display the state of the arts from the most early periods.

It has struck me as remarkable that the architecture of the churches in these most ancient monasteries is hardly ever fine; they are usually small, being calculated only for the monks, and not for the reception of any other congregation. The Greek churches, even those which are not monastic, are far inferior both in size and interest to the Latin basilicas of Rome. With the single exception of the church (now mosque) of St. Sophia, there is no Byzantine church of any magnitude. The student of ecclesiastical antiquities need not extend his architectural researches beyond the shores of Italy: there is nothing in the East so curious as the church of St. Clemente at Rome, which contains all the original fittings of the choir. The churches of St. Ambrogio at Milan, of Sta. Maria Trastevere at Rome, the first church dedicated to the Blessed Virgin; the church of St. Agnese near Rome, the first in which galleries were built over the side aisles for the accommodation of women, who, neither in the Eastern nor Western churches, ever mixed with the men for many centuries; all these and several others in Italy afford more instruction than those of the East—they are larger, more magnificent, and in every respect superior to the ecclesiastical buildings of the Levant. But the poverty of the Eastern church, and its early subjection to Mahometan rulers, while it has kept down the size and splendour of the churches, has at the same time been the means of preserving the monastic establishments in all the rude originality of their ancient forms. In ordinary situations these buildings are of the same character: they resemble small villages, built mostly without much regard to any symmetrical plan, around a church which is constructed in the form of a Greek cross; the roof is covered either with one or five domes; all these buildings are surrounded by a high, strong wall, built as a fortification to protect the brotherhood within, not without reason, even in the present day. I have been quietly dining in a monastery, when shouts have been heard, and shots have been fired against the stout bulwarks of the outer walls, which, thanks to their protection, had but little effect in delaying the transit of the morsel between my fingers into the ready gulf provided by nature for its reception. The monks of the Greek Church have diminished in number and wealth of late years, their monasteries are no longer the schools of learning which they used to be; few can read the Hellenic or ancient Greek; and the following anecdote will suffice to show the estimation in which a conventual library has not unusually been held. A Russian, or I do not know whether he was not a French traveller, in the pursuit, as I was, of ancient literary treasures, found himself in a great monastery in Bulgaria to the north of the town of Cavalla; he had heard that the books preserved in this remote building were remarkable for their antiquity, and for the subjects on which they treated. His dismay and disappointment may be imagined when he was assured by the agoumenos or superior of the monastery, that it contained no library whatever, that they had nothing but the liturgies and church books, and no palaia pragmata or antiquities at all. The poor man had bumped upon a pack-saddle over villainous roads for many days for no other object, and the library of which he was in search had vanished as the visions of a dream. The agoumenos begged his guest to enter with the monks into the choir, where the almost continual church service was going on, and there he saw the double row of long-bearded holy fathers, shouting away at the chorus of χυριε ελεισον

, χριστε ελεισον

(pronounced Kyre eleizon, Christe eleizon), which occurs almost every minute, in the ritual of the Greek Church. Each of the monks was standing, to save his bare legs from the damp of the marble floor, upon a great folio volume, which had been removed from the conventual library and applied to purposes of practical utility in the way which I have described. The traveller on examining these ponderous tomes found them to be of the greatest value; one was in uncial letters, and others were full of illuminations of the earliest date; all these he was allowed to carry away in exchange for some footstools or hassocks, which he presented in their stead to the old monks; they were comfortably covered with ketché or felt, and were in many respects more convenient to the inhabitants of the monastery than the manuscripts had been, for many of their antique bindings were ornamented with bosses and nail heads, which inconvenienced the toes of the unsophisticated congregation who stood upon them without shoes for so many hours in the day. I must add that the lower halves of the manuscripts were imperfect, from the damp of the floor of the church having corroded and eat away their vellum leaves, and also that, as the story is not my own, I cannot vouch for the truth of it, though, whether it is true or not, it elucidates the present state of the literary attainments of the Oriental monks. Ignorance and superstition walk hand in hand, and the monks of the Eastern churches seem to retain in these days all the love for the marvellous which distinguished their Western brethren in the middle ages. Miraculous pictures abound, as well as holy springs and wells. Relics still perform wonderful cures. I will only as an illustration to this statement mention one of the standing objects of veneration which may be witnessed any day in the vicinity of the castle of the Seven Towers, outside of the walls of Constantinople: there a rich monastery stands in a lovely grove of trees, under whose shade numerous parties of merry Greeks often pass the day, dividing their time between drinking, dancing, and devotion.

The unfortunate Emperor Constantine Paleologus rode out of the city alone to reconnoitre the outposts of the Turkish army, which was encamped in the immediate vicinity. In passing through a wood he found an old man seated by the side of a spring cooking some fish on a gridiron for his dinner; the emperor dismounted from his white horse and entered into conversation with the other; the old man looked up at the stranger in silence, when the emperor inquired whether he had heard anything of the movements of the Turkish forces—"Yes," said he, "they have this moment entered the city of Constantinople."

"I would believe what you say," replied the emperor, "if the fish which you are broiling would jump off the gridiron into the spring." This, to his amazement, the fish immediately did, and, on his turning round, the figure of the old man had disappeared. The emperor mounted his horse and rode towards the gate of Silivria, where he was encountered by a band of the enemy and slain, after a brave resistance, by the hand of an Arab or a Negro.

The broiled fishes still swim about in the water of the spring, the sides of which have been lined with white marble, in which are certain recesses where they can retire when they do not wish to receive company. The only way of turning the attention of these holy fish to the respectful presence of their adorers is accomplished by throwing something glittering into the water, such as a handful of gold or silver coin; gold is the best, copper produces no effect; he that sees one fish is lucky, he that sees two or three goes home a happy man; but the custom of throwing coins into the spring has become, from its constant practice, very troublesome to the good monks, who kindly depute one of their community to rake out the money six or seven times a day with a scraper at the end of a long pole. The emperor of Russia has sent presents to the shrine of Baloukli, so called from the Turkish word Balouk, a fish. Some wicked heretics have said that these fishes are common perch: either they or the monks must be mistaken, but of whatever kind they are, they are looked upon with reverence by the Greeks, and have been continually held in the highest honour from the time of the siege of Constantinople to the present day.

I have hitherto noticed those monasteries only which are under the spiritual jurisdiction of the Patriarch of Constantinople, but those of the Copts of Egypt and the Maronites of Syria resemble them in almost every particular. As it has never been the custom of the Oriental Christians to bury the dead within the precincts of the church, they none of them contain sepulchral monuments. The bodies of the Byzantine emperors were enclosed in sarcophagi of precious marbles, which were usually deposited in chapels erected for the purpose—a custom which has been imitated by the sultans of Turkey. Of all these magnificent sarcophagi and chapels or mausoleums where the remains of the imperial families were deposited, only one remains intact; every one but this has been violated, destroyed, or carried away; the ashes of the Cæsars have been scattered to the winds. This is now known by the name of the chapel of St. Nazario e Celso, at Ravenna: it was built by Galla Placidia, the daughter of Theodosius; she died at Rome in 440, but her body was removed to Ravenna and deposited in a sarcophagus in this chapel; in the same place are two other sarcophagi, one containing the remains of Constantius, the second husband of Galla Placidia, and the other holding the body of her son Valentinian III. These tombs have never been disturbed, and are the only ones which remain intact of the entire line of the Cæsars, either of the Eastern or Western empires.

The tombstones or monuments of the Armenians deserve to be mentioned on account of their singularity. They are usually oblong pieces of marble lying flat upon the ground; on these are sculptured representations of the implements of the trade at which the deceased had worked during his lifetime; some display the manner in which the Armenian met his death. In the Petit Champ des Morts at Pera I counted, I think, five tombstones with bas-reliefs of men whose heads had been cut off. In Armenia the traveller is often startled by the appearance of a gigantic stone figure of a ram, far away from any present habitation: this is the tomb of some ancient possessor of flocks and herds whose house and village have disappeared, and nothing but his tomb remains to mark the site which once was the abode of men.

KOORD, OR NATIVE OF KOORDISTAUN. KOORD, OR NATIVE OF KOORDISTAUN.

The Armenian monasteries, with the exception of that of Etchmiazin and one or two others, are much smaller buildings than those of the Greeks; they are constructed after the same model, however, being surrounded with a high blank wall. Their churches are seldom surmounted by a dome, but are usually in the form of a small barn, with a high pitched roof, built like the walls of large squared stones. At one end of the church is a small door, and at the other end a semicircular apsis; the windows are small apertures like loop-holes. These buildings, though of very small size, have an imposing appearance from their air of massive strength. The cells of the Armenian monks look into the courtyard, which is a remarkable fact in that country, where the rest of the inhabitants dwell in burrows underground like rabbits, and keep themselves alive during the long winters of their rigorous climate by the warmth proceeding from the cattle with whom they live, for fire is dear in a land too cold for trees to grow. The monasteries of the various sects of Christians who inhabit the mountains of Koordistaun are very numerous, and all more or less alike. Perched on the tops of crags, in these wild regions are to be seen the monastic fastnesses of the Chaldeans, who of late have been known by the name of Nestorians, the seat of whose patriarchate is at Julamerk. They have now been almost exterminated by Beder Khan Bey, a Koordish chief, in revenge for the cattle which they were alleged to have stolen from the Koordish villages in their vicinity. The Jacobites, the Sabæans, and the Christians of St. John, who inhabit the banks of the Euphrates in the districts of the ancient Susiana, all have fortified monasteries which are mostly of great antiquity. From Mount Ararat to Bagdat, the different sects of Christians still retain the faith of the Redeemer, whom they have worshipped according to their various forms, some of them for more than fifteen hundred years; the plague, the famine, and the sword have passed over them and left them still unscathed, and there is little doubt but that they will maintain the position which they have held so long till the now not far distant period arrives when the conquered empire of the Greeks will again be brought under the dominion of a Christian emperor.

MONASTERIES OF THE LEVANT.
PART I.

EGYPT IN 1833.
CHAPTER I.

Navarino—The Wrecks of the Turkish and Egyptian Fleets—Alexandria—An Arab Pilot—Intense Heat—Scene from the Hotel Windows—The Water-Carriers—A Procession—A Bridal Party—Violent mode of clearing the Road—Submissive Behaviour of the People—Astonishing Number of Donkeys—Bedouin Arabs; their wild and savage appearance—Early Hours—Visit to the Pasha's Prime Minister, Boghos Bey; hospitable reception—Kawasses and Chaoushes; their functions and powers—The Yassakjis—The Minister's Audience Chamber—Walmas; anecdote of his saving the life of Boghos Bey.

It

was towards the end of July, 1833, that I took a passage from Malta to Alexandria in a merchant-vessel called the Fortuna; for in those days there were no steam-packets traversing every sea, with almost the same rapidity and accuracy as railway carriages on shore. We touched on our way at Navarino to sell some potatoes to the splendidly-dressed, and half-starved population of the Morea, numbers of whom we found lounging about in a temporary wooden bazaar, where there was nothing to sell. In various parts of the harbour the wrecks of the Turkish and Egyptian ships of war, stripped of their outer coverings, and looking like the gigantic skeletons of antediluvian animals, gave awful evidence of the destruction which had taken place not very long before in the battle between the Christian and Mahomedan fleets in this calm, land-locked harbour.

On the 31st we found ourselves approaching the castle of Alexandria, and were soon hailed by some people in a curious-looking pilot-boat with a lateen sail. The pilot was an old man with a turban and a long grey beard, and sat cross-legged in the stern of his boat. We looked at him with vast interest, as the first live specimen we had seen of an Arab sailor. He was just the sort of man that I imagine Sindbad the Sailor must have been.

Having by his directions been steered safely into the harbour, we cast anchor not far from the shore, a naked, dusty plain, which the blazing sun seemed to dare any one to cross, on pain of being shrivelled up immediately. The intensity of the heat was tremendous: the tar melted in the seams of the deck: we could scarcely bear it even when we were under the awning. Malta was hot enough, but the temperature there was cool in comparison to the fiery furnace in which we were at present grilling. However, there was no help for it; so, having got our luggage on shore, we sweltered through the streets to an inn called the Tre Anchore—the only hotel in Africa, I believe, in those days. It was a dismal little place, frequented by the captains of merchant-vessels, who, not being hot enough already, raised the temperature of their blood by drinking brandy-and-water, arrack, and other combustibles, in a dark, oven-like room below stairs.

We took possession of all the rooms upstairs, of which the principal one was long and narrow, with two windows at the end, opening on to a covered balcony or verandah: this overlooked the principal street and the bazaar. Here my companion and I soon stationed ourselves and watched the novel and curious scene below; and strange indeed to the eye of an European, when for the first time he enters an Oriental city, is all he sees around him. The picturesque dresses, the buildings, the palm-trees, the camels, the people of various nations, with their long beards, their arms, and turbans, all unite to form a picture which is indelibly fixed in the memory. Things which have since become perfectly familiar to us were then utterly incomprehensible, and we had no one to explain them to us, for the one waiter of the poor inn, who was darting about in his shirt-sleeves after the manner of all waiters, never extended his answers to our questions beyond "Si, Signore," so we got but little information from him; however, we did not make use of our eyes the less for that.

Among the first things we noticed, was the number of half-naked men who went running about, each with something like a dead pig under his arm, shouting out "Mother! mother!"[1] with a doleful voice. These were the sakis or water-carriers, with their goat-skins of the precious element, a bright brass cupful of which they sell for a small coin to the thirsty passengers. An old man with a fan in his hand made of a palm-branch, who was crumpled up in the corner of a sort of booth among a heap of dried figs, raisins, and dates, just opposite our window, was an object of much speculation to us how he got in, and how he would ever manage to get out of the niche into which he was so closely wedged. He was the merchant, as the Arabian Nights would call him, or the shopkeeper as we should say, who sat there cross-legged among his wares waiting patiently for a customer, and keeping off the flies in the meanwhile, as in due time we discovered that all merchants did in all countries of the East. Soon there came slowly by, a long procession of men on horseback with golden bridles and velvet trappings, and women muffled up in black silk wrappers; how they could bear them, hot as it was, astonished us. These ladies sat upon a pile of cushions placed so high above the backs of the donkeys on which they rode that their feet rested on the animal's shoulders. Each donkey was led by one man, while another walked by its side with his hand upon the crupper. With the ladies were two little boys covered with diamonds, mounted on huge fat horses, and ensconced in high-backed Mameluke saddles made of silver gilt. These boys we afterwards found out were being conducted in state to a house of their relations, where the rite of circumcision was to be performed. Our attention was next called to something like a four-post bed, with pink gauze curtains, which advanced with dignified slowness, preceded by a band of musicians, who raised a dire and fearful discord by the aid of various windy engines. This was a canopy, the four poles of which were supported by men, who held it over the heads of a bride and her two bridesmaids or friends, who walked on each side of her. The bride was not veiled in the usual way, as her friends were, but was muffled up in Cashmere shawls from head to foot. Something there was on the top of her head which gleamed like gold or jewels, but the rest of her person was so effectually wrapped up and concealed that no one could tell whether she was pretty or ugly, fat or thin, old or young; and although we gave her credit for all the charms which should adorn a bride, we rejoiced when the villainous band of music which accompanied her turned round a corner and went out of hearing.

NEGRESS WAITING TO BE SOLD IN THE SLAVE BAZAAR, CAIRO NEGRESS WAITING TO BE SOLD IN THE SLAVE BAZAAR, CAIRO

Some miserable-looking black slaves caught our attention, clothed each in a piece of Isabel-coloured canvas and led by a well-dressed man, who had probably just bought them. Then a great personage came by on horseback with a number of mounted attendants and some men on foot, who cleared the way before him, and struck everybody on the head with their sticks who did not get out of the way fast enough. These blows were dealt all round in the most unceremonious manner; but what appeared to us extraordinary was, that all these beaten people did not seem to care for being beat. They looked neither angry nor affronted, but only grinned and rubbed their shoulders, and moved on one side to let the train of the great man pass by. Now if this were done in London, what a ferment would it create! what speeches would be made about tyranny and oppression! what a capital thing some high-minded and independent patriot would make of it! how he would call a meeting to defend the rights of the subject! and how he would get his admirers to vote him a piece of plate for his noble and glorious exertions! Here nobody minded the thing; they took no heed of the indignity; and I verily believe my friend and I, who were safe up at the window, were the only persons in the place who felt any annoyance.

The prodigious multitude of donkeys formed another strange feature in the scene. There were hundreds of them, carrying all sorts of things in panniers; and some of the smallest were ridden by men so tall that they were obliged to hold up their legs that their feet might not touch the ground. Donkeys, in short, are the carts of Egypt and the hackney-coaches of Alexandria.

BEDOUIN ARAB. BEDOUIN ARAB.

In addition to the donkeys long strings of ungainly-looking camels were continually passing, generally preceded by a donkey, and accompanied by swarthy men clad in a short shirt with a red and yellow handkerchief tied in a peculiar way over their heads, and wearing sandals; these savage-looking people were Bedouins, or Arabs of the desert. A very truculent set they seemed to be, and all of them were armed with a long crooked knife and a pistol or two, stuck in a red leathern girdle. They were thin, gaunt, and dirty, and strode along looking fierce and independent. There was something very striking in the appearance of these untamed Arabs: I had never pictured to myself that anything so like a wild beast could exist in human form. The motions of their half-naked bodies were singularly free and light, and they looked as if they could climb, and run, and leap over anything. The appearance of many of the older Arabs, with their long white beard and their ample cloak of camel's hair, called an abba, is majestic and venerable. It was the first time that I had seen these "Children of the Desert," and the quickness of their eyes, their apparent freedom from all restraint, and their disregard of any conventional manners, struck me forcibly. An English gentleman in a round hat and a tight neck-handkerchief and boots, with white gloves and a little cane in his hand, was a style of man so utterly and entirely unlike a Bedouin Arab that I could hardly conceive the possibility of their being only different species of the same animal.

After we had dined, being tired with the heat and the trouble we had had in getting our luggage out of the ship, I resolved to retire to bed at an early hour, and on going to the window to have another look at the crowd, I was surprised to find that there was scarcely anybody left in the streets, for these primitive people all go to bed when it gets dark, as the birds do; and except a few persons walking home with paper lanterns in their hands, the place seemed almost entirely deserted.

The next morning, mounted on donkeys, we shambled across half the city to the residence of Boghos Bey, the Armenian prime minister of Mohammed Ali Pasha; we were received with great kindness and civility, and as at this time there had been but very few European travellers in Egypt, we were treated with distinguished hospitality. The Bey said that although the Pasha was then in Upper Egypt, he would take care that we should have every facility in seeing all the objects of interest, and that he would write to Habeeb Effendi, the Governor of Cairo, to acquaint him of our arrival, and direct him to let us have the use of the Pasha's horses, that kawasses should attend us, and that the Pasha would give us a firman, which would ensure our being well treated throughout the whole of his dominions.

As a kawass is a person mentioned by all Oriental travellers, it may be as well to state that he is a sort of armed servant or body-guard belonging to the government; he bears as his badge of office a thick cane about four feet long, with a large silver head, with which instrument he occasionally enforces his commands and supports his authority as well as his person. Ambassadors, consuls, and occasionally travellers, are attended by kawasses. Their presence shows that the person they accompany is protected by the State, and their number indicates his dignity and rank. Formerly these kawasses were splendidly attired in embroidered dresses, and their arms and the accoutrements of their horses were of silver gilt: the ambassador at Constantinople has, I think, six of these attendants. Of late years their picturesque costume has been changed to a uniform frock-coat of European make, of a whity-brown colour.

Silver head of staff.

There is a higher grade of officer of the same description, who is only to be met with at Court, and whose functions are nearly the same as those of a chamberlain with us. He is called a chaoush. His official staff is surmounted by a silver head, formed like a Greek bishop's staff, from the two horns of which several little round bells are suspended by a silver chain. The chaoush is a personage of great authority in certain things; he is a kind of living firman, before whom every one makes way. As I was desirous of seeing the shrine of the heads of Hassan and Hussein in the mosque of Hassan En, a place of peculiar sanctity at Cairo, into which no Christian had been admitted, the Pasha sent a chaoush with me, who concealed the head of his staff in his clothes, to be ready, in case it had been discovered that I was not a Mahomedan, to protect me from the fury of the devotees, who would probably have torn to pieces any unbeliever who intruded into the temple of the sons of Ali.

Besides these two officers, the chaoush and kawass, there is another attendant upon public men, who is of inferior rank, and is called a yassakji, or forbidder; he looks like a dirty kawass, and has a stick, but without the silver knob. He is generally employed to carry messages, and push people out of the way, to make a passage for you through a crowd; but this kind of functionary is more frequently seen at Constantinople and the northern parts of Turkey than in Egypt.

We found Boghos Bey in a large upper room, seated on a divan with two or three persons to whom he was speaking, while the lower end of the room was occupied by a crowd of chaoushes, kawasses, and hangers-on of all descriptions. We were served with coffee, pipes, and sherbet, and were entertained during the pauses of the conversation by the ticking and chiming of half a dozen clocks which stood about the room, some on the floor, some on the side-tables, and some stuck on brackets against the wall.

One of the persons seated near the prime minister was a shrewd-looking man with one eye, of whom I was afterwards told the following anecdote. His name was Walmas; he had been an Armenian merchant, and was an old acquaintance of Mohammed Ali and of Boghos, before they had either of them risen to their present importance. Soon after the massacre of the Mamelukes, Mohammed Ali desired Boghos to procure him a large sum of money by a certain day, which Boghos declared was impossible at so short a notice. The Pasha, angry at being thwarted, swore that if he had not the money by the day he had named, he would hare Boghos drowned in the Nile. The affrighted minister made every effort to collect the requisite sum, but when the day arrived much was wanting to complete it. Boghos stood before the Pasha, who immediately exclaimed, "Well! where is the money?" "Sir," replied Boghos, "I have not been able to get it all! I have procured all this, but, though I strained every nerve, and took every measure in my power, it was impossible to obtain the remainder." "What," exclaimed the Pasha, "you dog, have you not obeyed my commands? What is the use of a minister who cannot produce all the money wanted by his sovereign, at however short a notice? Here, put this unbeliever in a sack, and fling him into the Nile." This scene occurred in the citadel at Cairo; and an officer and some men immediately put him into a sack, threw it across a donkey, and proceeded to the Nile. As they were passing through the city, they were met by Walmas, who was attended by several servants, and who, seeing something moving in the sack which was laid across the donkey, asked the guards what they had got there. "Oh!" said the officer, "we have got Boghos, the Armenian, and we are going to throw him into the Nile, by his Highness the Pasha's order." "What has he done?" asked Walmas. "What do we know?" replied the officer; "something about money, I believe: no great thing, but his Highness has been in a bad humour lately. He will be sorry for it afterwards. However, we have our orders, and, therefore, please God, we are going to pitch him into the Nile." Walmas determined to rescue his old friend, and, assisted by his servants, immediately attacked the guard, who made little more than a show of resistance. Boghos was carried off, and concealed in a safe place, and the guards returned to the citadel and reported that they had pitched Boghos into the Nile, where he had sunk, as all should do who disobeyed the commands of his Highness. Some time afterwards, the Pasha, overcome by financial difficulties, was heard to say that he wished Boghos was still alive. Walmas, who was present, after some preliminary conversation (for the ground was rather dangerous), said that if his own pardon was insured, he could mention something respecting Boghos which he was sure would be agreeable to his Highness: and at last he owned that he had rescued him from the guards and had kept him concealed in his house in hopes of being allowed to restore so valuable a servant to his master. The Pasha was delighted at the news, instantly reinstated Boghos in all his former honours, and Walmas himself stood higher than ever in his favour; but the guards were executed for disobedience. Ever since that time Boghos Bey has continued to be the principal minister and most confidential adviser of Mohammed Ali Pasha.

CHAPTER II.

Rapacity of the Dragomans—The Mahmoudieh Canal—The Nile at Atfeh—The muddy Waters of the Nile—Richness of the Soil—Accident to the Boatmen—Night Sailing—A Collision—A Vessel run down—Escape of the Crew—Solemn Investigation—Final Judgment—Curious Mode of Fishing—Tameness of the Birds—Jewish Malefactors—Moving Pillar of Sand—Arrival at Cairo—Hospitable Reception by the Consul-General.

So long as there were no hotels in Egypt, the process of fleecing the unwary traveller was conducted on different principles from those followed in Europe. As he seldom understands the language, he requires an interpreter, or dragoman, who, as a matter of course, manages all his pecuniary affairs. The newly-arrived European eats and drinks whatever his dragoman chooses to give him; sees through his dragoman's eyes; hears through his ears; and, although he thinks himself master, is, in fact, only a part of the property of this Eastern servant, to be used by him as he thinks fit, and turned to the best account like any other real or personal estate.

On our landing at Alexandria, my friend and I found ourselves in the same predicament as our predecessors, and straightway fell into the hands of these Philistines, two of whom we hired as interpreters. They were also to act as ciceroni, and were warranted to know all about the antiquities, and everything else in Egypt; they were to buy everything we wanted, to spend our money, and to allow no one to cheat us except themselves. One of these worthies was sent to engage a boat, to carry us down the Mahmoudieh Canal to Atfeh, where the canal is separated from the river by flood-gates, in consequence of which impediment we could not proceed in the same boat, but had to hire a larger one to take us on to Cairo.

The banks of the canal being high, we had no view of the country as we passed along; but on various occasions when I ascended to the top of the bank, while the men who towed the boat rested from their labours, I saw nothing but great sandy flats interspersed with large pools of stagnant, muddy water. This prospect not being very charming, we were glad to arrive the next day on the shores of the Father of Rivers, whose swollen stream, although at Atfeh not more than half a mile in width, rolled by towards the north in eddies and whirlpools of smooth muddy water, in colour closely resembling a sea of mutton-broth.

In my enthusiasm on arriving on the margin of this venerable river, I knelt down to drink some of it, and was disappointed in finding it by no means so good as I had always been told it was. On complaining of its muddy taste, I found that no one drank the water of the Nile till it had stood a day or two in a large earthen jar, the inside of which is rubbed with a paste of bitter almonds. This causes all impurities to be precipitated, and the water, thus treated, becomes the lightest, clearest, and most excellent in the world. At Atfeh, after a prodigious uproar between the men of our two boats, each set claiming to be paid for transporting the luggage, we set sail upon the Nile, and after proceeding a short distance, we stopped at a village, or small town, to buy some fruit. Here the surrounding country, a flat alluvial plain, was richly cultivated. Water-melons, corn, and all manner of green herbs flourished luxuriantly; everything looked delightfully fresh and green; flocks of pigeons were flying about; and multitudes of white spoonbills and other strange birds were stalking among the herbage, and rising around us in every direction. The fertility of the land appeared prodigious, and exceeded anything I had seen before. Numberless boats were passing on the river, and the general aspect of the scene betokened the wealth and plenty which would reward the toils of the agriculturist under any settled form of government. We returned to our boat loaded with fruit, among which were the Egyptian fig, the prickly pear, dates, limes, and melons of kinds that were new to us.

Whilst we were discussing the merits of these refreshing productions, a board, which had been fastened on the outside of the vessel for four or five men to stand on, as they pushed the boat with poles through the shallow water, suddenly gave way, and the men fell into the river: they could, however, all swim like water-rats, and were soon on board again; when, putting out into the middle of the stream, we set two huge triangular lateen sails on our low masts, which raked forwards instead of backwards, and by the help of the wind made our way slowly towards the south. We slept in a small cabin in the stern of our vessel; this had a flat top, and formed the resting-place of the steersman, the captain of the ship, and our servants, who all lay down together on some carpets; the sailors slept upon the deck. We sailed on steadily all night; the stars were wonderfully bright; and I looked out upon the broad river and the flat silent shores, diversified here and there by a black-looking village of mud huts, surrounded by a grove of palms, whence the distant baying of the dogs was brought down upon the wind. Sometimes there was the cry of a wild bird, but soon again the only sound was the gentle ripple of the water against the sides of our boat. If the steersman was not asleep, every one else was; but still we glided on, and nothing occurred to disturb our repose, till the blazing light of the morning sun recalled us to activity, and all the bustling preparations for breakfast.

We had sailed on for some time after this important event, and I was quietly reading in the shade of the cabin, when I was thrown backwards by the sudden stopping of the vessel, which struck against something with prodigious force, and screams of distress arose from the water all around us. On rushing upon deck I found that we had run down another boat, which had sunk so instantly that nothing was to be seen of it except the top of the mast, whose red flag was fluttering just above water, and to which two women were clinging. A few yards astern seven or eight men were swimming towards the shore, and our steersman having in his alarm left the rudder to its own devices, our great sails were swinging and flapping over our heads. There was a cry that our bows were stove in, and we were sinking; but, fortunately, before this could happen, the stream had carried us ashore, where we stuck in the mud on a shoal under a high bank, up which we all soon scrambled, glad to be on terra firma. The country people came running down to satisfy their curiosity, and we procured a small boat, which immediately rowed off to rescue the women who were still clinging to the mast-head of the sunken vessel, which was one of the kind called a djerm, and was laden with thirty tons of corn, besides other goods. No one, luckily, was drowned, though the loss was a serious one to the owners, for there was no chance of recovering either the vessel or the cargo. Whilst we were looking, the red flag to which the women had been clinging toppled over sideways, which completed the entire disappearance of the unfortunate djerm.

Our reis, or captain, now returned to the roof of the cabin, where he sat down upon a mat, and lighting his pipe, smoked away steadily without saying a word, while the wet and dripping sailors, as well as the ladies belonging to the shipwrecked vessel, surrounded him, screaming, vociferating, and shouting all manner of invectives into his ears; in which employment they were effectively joined by a number of half-naked Arabs who had been cultivating the fields hard by. To all this they got no answer, beyond an occasional ejaculation of "God is great, and Mohammed is the prophet of God." His pipe was out before the clamour of the crowd had abated, and then, all of a sudden, he got up and with two or three others embarked in the little boat for a neighbouring village, to report the accident to the sheick, who, we were told, would return with him and inquire into the circumstances of the case.

In about three hours the boat returned with the local authorities, two old villagers, in long blue shirts and dirty turbans, who took their seat upon a mat on the bank and smoked away in a serious manner for some time. Our captain made no more reply to the fresh accusations of the reassembled multitude than he had done before; but lit another pipe, and asserted that God was great. At last the two elders made signs that they intended to speak; and silence being obtained, they, with all due solemnity, declared that they agreed with the captain that God was great, and that undoubtedly Mohammed was the prophet of God. All parties having come to this conclusion, it appeared that there was nothing more to be said, and we returned to our boat, which the sailors, with the help of a rough carpenter, had patched up sufficiently to allow us to sail for a village on the other side of the river.

During the time that we were remaining on the bank I was amused by watching the manœuvres of some boys, who succeeded in catching a quantity of small fish in a very original way. They rolled together a great quantity of tangled weeds and long grass, with one end of which they swam out into the Nile, and bringing it back towards the shore, numerous unsuspecting fish were entangled in the mass of weeds, and were picked out and thrown on the bank by the young fishermen before they had time to get out of the scrape. In this way the boys secured a very respectable heap of small fry.

We arrived safely at the village, where we stayed the night; but the next morning it appeared that the bows of our vessel were so much damaged that she could not be repaired under a delay of some days. Indeed, it appeared that we had been fortunate in accomplishing our passage across the river, for if we had foundered midway, not being able to swim like the amphibious Egyptians, we should probably have been drowned. It was, however, a relief to me to think that there were no crocodiles in this part of the Nile.

The birds at this place appeared to be remarkably tame: some gulls, or waterfowl, hardly troubled themselves to move out of the way when a boat passed them; while those in the fields went on searching among the crops for insects close to the labourers, and without any of the alarm shown by birds in England.

While we were dawdling about in the neighbourhood of the village, one of the servants, an old Maltese, discovered a boat with ten or twelve oars, lying in the vicinity. It belonged to the government, and was conveying two malefactors to Cairo under the guardianship of a kawass, who on learning our mishap gave us a passage in his boat, and to our great joy we bid adieu to our silent captain, and were soon rowing at a great rate, in a fine new canjah, on the way to Cairo. The two prisoners on board were Jews: one was taken up for cheating, and the other for using false weights. They were fastened together by the neck, with a chain about five feet long. One of the two was very restless; they said he had a good chance of being hanged; and he was always pulling the other unfortunate Hebrew about with him by the chain, in a manner which excited the mirth of the sailors, though it must have been anything but amusing to the person most concerned.

The next day there was a hot wind, and the thermometer stood at 98° in the shade. The kawass called our attention to a pillar of sand moving through the air in the desert to the south-east; it had an extraordinary appearance, and its effect upon a party travelling over those burning plains would have been terrific. It was evidently caused by a whirlwind, and men and camels are sometimes suffocated and overwhelmed when they are met by these columns of dry, heated sand, which stalk through the deserts like the evil genii of the storm. I have seen them in other countries, more particularly in Armenia; but this, which I saw on my first journey up the Nile, was the only moving pillar which I met with in Egypt or in any of the surrounding deserts. We passed two men fishing from a small triangular raft, composed of palm-branches fastened on the tops of a number of earthen vases. This raft had a remarkably light appearance; it seemed only just to touch the surface of the water, but was evidently badly calculated for such rude encounters as the one which we had lately experienced. Soon afterwards the tops of the great Pyramids of Giseh caught our admiring gaze, and in the morning of the 12th of August we landed at Boulac, from which a ride of half an hour on donkeys brought our party to the hospitable mansion of the Consul-General, who was good enough to receive us in his house until we could procure quarters for ourselves.

Having arrived at Cairo, a short account of the history of the city may be interesting to some readers. In the sixth and seventh centuries of our era this part of Egypt was inhabited principally by Coptic Christians, whose chief occupation consisted in quarrelling among themselves on polemical points of divinity and ascetic rule. The deserts of Nitria and the shores of the Red Sea were peopled with swarms of monks, some living together in monasteries, some in lavras, or monastic villages, and multitudes hiding their sanctity in dens and caves, where they passed their lives in abstract meditation. In the year 638 the Arabian general Amer ebn el As, with four hundred Arabs (see Wilkinson), advanced to the confines of Egypt, and after thirty days' siege took possession of Pelusium, which had been the barrier of the country on the Syrian side from the earliest periods of the Egyptian monarchy: he advanced without opposition to the city of Babylon, which occupied the site of Masr el Ateekeh, or Old Cairo, on the Nile; but the Roman station, which is now a Coptic monastery, containing a chamber said to have been occupied by the blessed Virgin, was so strong a fortress that the invaders were unable to effect an entrance in a siege of seven months. After this, a reinforcement of four hundred men arriving at their camp, their courage revived, and the castle of Babylon was taken by escalade. On the site of the Arabian encampment at Fostat, Amer founded the first mosque built on Egyptian soil. The town of Babylon was connected with the island of Rhoda by a bridge of boats, by which a communication was kept up with the city of Memphis, on the other side of the Nile. The Copts, whose religious fanaticism occasioned them to hate their masters, the Greeks of the Eastern Empire, more than the Mahomedans, welcomed the moment which promised to free them from their religious adversaries; and the traitor John Mecaukes, governor of Memphis, persuaded them to conclude a treaty with the invaders, by which it was stipulated that two dinars of gold should be paid for every Christian above sixteen years of age, with the exception of old men, women, and monks. From this time Fostat became the Arabian capital of Egypt. In the year 879 Sultan Tayloon, or Tooloon, built himself a palace, to which he added several residences or barracks for his guards, and the great mosque, which still exists, with pointed arches, between Fostat and the present citadel of Cairo. It was not, however, till the year 969 that Goher, the general of El Moez, Sultan of Kairoan, near Tunis, having invaded Egypt, and completely subdued the country, founded a new city near the citadel of Qattaeea, which acquired the name of El Kahira from the following circumstance. The architect having made his arrangements for laying the first stone of the new wall, waited for the fortunate moment, which was to be shown by the astrologers pulling a cord, extending to a considerable distance from the spot. A certain crow, however, who had not been taken into the council of the wise men, perched upon the cord, which was shaken by his weight, and the architect supposing that the appointed signal had been given, commenced his work accordingly. From this unlucky omen, and the vexation felt by those concerned, the epithet of Kahira ("the vexatious" or "unlucky") was added to the name of the city, Masr el Kahira meaning "the unlucky (city of) Egypt." Kahira in the Italian pronunciation has been softened into Cairo, by which name this famous city has been known for many centuries in Europe, though in the East it is usually called Masr only. From this time the Fatemite caliphs of Africa, who brought the bones of their ancestors with them from Kairoan, reigned for ten generations over the land of Egypt. The third in this succession was the Caliph Hakem, who built a mosque near the Bab el Nassr, and who was the founder of the sect of the Druses, and, as some say, of the Assassins. In the year 1171 the famous Saladin usurped the throne from the last of the race of Fatema. His descendant, Moosa el Ashref, was deposed in his turn, in 1250; from which time till the year 1543 Cairo was governed by the curious succession of Mameluke kings, who were mostly Circassian slaves brought up at the court of their predecessors, and arriving at the supreme rule of Egypt by election or intrigue. Toman Bey, the last of the Mameluke kings, was defeated by Selim, Emperor of the Turks, and hanged at Cairo, at the Bab Zooaley. But the aristocracy of the Mamelukes, as it may be called, still remained; and various beys became governors of Egypt under the Turkish sway, till they were all destroyed at one blow by Mohammed Ali Pasha, the now all but independent sovereign of Egypt.

CHAPTER III.

National Topics of Conversation—The Rising of the Nile; evil effects of its rising too high; still worse consequences of a deficiency of its waters—The Nilometer—Universal Alarm in August, 1833—The Nile at length rises to the desired Height—Ceremony of cutting the Embankment—The Canal of the Khalidj—Immense Assemblage of People—The State Tent—Arrival of Habeeb Effendi—Splendid Dresses of the Officers—Exertions of the Arab Workmen—Their Scramble for Paras—Admission of the Water—Its sudden Irruption—Excitement of the Ladies—Picturesque Effect of large Assemblies in the East.

In

England every one talks about the weather, and all conversation is opened by exclamations against the heat or the cold, the rain or the drought; but in Egypt, during one part of the year at least, the rise of the Nile forms the general topic of conversation. Sometimes the ascent of the water is unusually rapid, and then nothing is talked of but inundations; for if the river overflows too much, whole villages are washed away; and as they are for the most part built of sunburned bricks and mud, they are completely annihilated; and when the waters subside, all the boundary marks are obliterated, the course of canals is altered, and mounds and embankments are washed away. On these occasions the smaller landholders have great difficulty in recovering their property; for few of them know how far their fields extend in one direction or the other, unless a tree, a stone, or something else remains to mark the separation of one man's flat piece of mud from that of his neighbour.

But the more frequent and the far more dreaded calamity is the deficiency of water. This was the case in 1833, and we heard nothing else talked of. "Has it risen much to-day?" inquires one.—"Yes, it has risen half a pic since the morning." "What! no more? In the name of the Prophet! what will become of the cotton?"—"Yes; and the doura will be burnt up to a certainty if we do not get four pics more." In short, the Nile has it all its own way; everything depends on the manner in which it chooses to behave, and El Bahar (the river) is in everybody's mouth from morning till night. Criers go about the city several times a day during the period of the rising, who proclaim the exact height to which the water has arrived, and the precise number of pics which are submerged on the Nilometer.

This Nilometer is an ancient octagon pillar of red stone in the island of Rhoda, on the sides of which graduated scales are engraved. It stands in the centre of a cistern, about twenty-five feet square, and more than that in depth. A stone staircase leads down to the bottom, and the side walls are ornamented with Cufic inscriptions beautifully cut. Of this antique column I have seen more than most people; for on the 28th of August, 1833, the water was so low that there was the greatest apprehension of a total failure of the crops, and of the consequent famine. At that time nine feet more water was wanted to ensure an average crop; much of the Indian corn had already failed; and from the Pasha in his palace to the poorest fellah in his mud hovel, all were in consternation; for in this country, where it never rains, everything depends on irrigation,—the revenues of the state, the food of the country, and the life or death of the bulk of the population.

At length the Nile rose to the desired height; and the 6th of September was fixed for the ceremony of cutting the embankment which keeps back the water from entering into the canal of the Khalidj. This canal joins the Nile near the great tower which forms the end of the aqueduct built by Saladin, and through it the water is conveyed for the irrigation of Cairo and its vicinity. One peculiarity of this city is, that several of its principal squares or open spaces are flooded during the inundation; and, in consequence of this, are called lakes, such as Birket el Fil (the Lake of the Elephant), Birket el Esbekieh, c. Many of the principal houses are built upon the banks of the Khalidj canal, which passes through the centre of the town, and which now had the appearance of a dusty, sunken lane; and the annual admission of the water into its thirsty bed is an event looked forward to as a public holiday by all classes. Accordingly, early in the morning, men, women, and children sallied forth to the borders of the Nile, and it seemed as if no one would be left in the city. The worthy citizens of Cairo, on horses, mules, donkeys, and on foot, were seen streaming out of the gates, and making their way in the cool of the morning, all hoping to obtain places from whence they might catch a glimpse of the cutting of the embankment.

We mounted the horses which the Pasha's grooms brought to our door. They were splendidly caparisoned with red velvet and gold; horses were also supplied for all our servants; and we wended our way through happy and excited crowds to a magnificent tent which had been erected for the accommodation of the grandees, on a sort of ancient stone quay immediately over the embankment. We passed through the lines of soldiers who kept the ground in the vicinity of the tent, around which was standing a numerous party of officers in their gala uniforms of red and gold.

On entering the tent we found the Cadi; the son of the sheriff of Mecca, who I believe was kept as a sort of hostage for the good behaviour of his father, the Defterdar, or treasurer, and several other high personages, seated on two carpets, one on each side of a splendid velvet divan, which extended along that side of the tent which was nearest to the river, and which was open. Below the tent was the bank which was to be cut through, with the water of the Nile almost overflowing its brink on the one side, and the deep dry bed of the canal upon the other; a number of half-naked Arabs were working with spades and pick-axes to undermine this bank.

Coffee and sherbet were presented to us while we awaited the arrival of Habeeb Effendi, who was to superintend the ceremony in the absence of the Pasha. No one sat upon the divan which was reserved for the accommodation of the great man, who was vice-viceroy on this occasion. I sat on the carpet by the son of the sheriff of Mecca, who was dressed in the green robes worn by the descendants of the Prophet. We looked at each other with some curiosity, and he carefully gathered up the edge of his sleeve, that it might not be polluted by the touch of such a heathen dog as he considered me to be.

About 9 A.M. the firing of cannon and volleys of musketry, with the discordant noise of several military bands, announced the approach of Habeeb Effendi. He was preceded by an immense procession of beys, colonels, and officers, all in red and gold, with the diamond insignia of their rank displayed upon their breasts. This crowd of splendidly dressed persons, dismounting from their horses, filled the space around the tent; and, opening into two ranks, they made a lane along which Habeeb Effendi rode into the middle of the tent; all bowing low and touching their foreheads as he passed. A horseblock, covered with red cloth, was brought forward for him to dismount upon. His fat grey horse was covered with gold, the whole of the housings of the Wahabee saddle being not embroidered, but so entirely covered with ornaments in goldsmith's work, that the colour of the velvet beneath could scarcely be discerned. The great man was held up under each arm by two officers, who assisted him to the divan, upon which he took his seat, or rather subsided, for the portly proportions of his person prevented his feet appearing as he sat cross-legged upon the cushions, with his back to the canal. Coffee was presented to him, and a diamond-mounted pipe stuck into his mouth; and he puffed away steadily, looking neither right nor left, while the uproar of the surrounding crowd increased every moment. Quantities of rockets and other fireworks were now let off in the broad daylight, cannons fired, and volleys of musketry filled the air with smoke. The naked Arabs in the ditch worked like madmen, tearing away the earth of the embankment, which was rapidly giving way; whilst an officer of the Treasury threw handfuls of new pieces of five paras each (little coins of base silver of the value of a farthing) among them. The immense multitude shouted and swayed about, encouraging the men, who were excited almost to frenzy.

At last there was a tremendous shout: the bank was beginning to give way; and showers of coin were thrown down upon it, which the workmen tried to catch. One man took off his wide Turkish trousers, and stretching them out upon two sticks caught almost a handful at a time. By degrees the earth of the embankment became wet, and large pieces of mud fell over into the canal. Presently a little stream of water made its way down the declivity, but the Arabs still worked up to their knees in water. The muddy stream increased, and all of a sudden the whole bank gave way. Some of the Arabs scrambled out and were helped up the sides of the canal by the crowd; but several, and among others he of the trousers, intent upon the shower of paras, were carried away by the stream. The man struggled manfully in the water, and gallantly kept possession of his trousers till he was washed ashore, and, with the assistance of some of his friends, landed safely with his spoils. The arches of the great aqueduct of Saladin were occupied by parties of ladies; and long lines of women in their black veils sat like a huge flock of crows upon the parapets above. They all waved their handkerchiefs and lifted up their voices in a strange shrill scream as the torrent increased in force; and soon, carrying everything before it, it entirely washed away the embankment, and the water in the canal rose to the level of the Nile.

The desired object having been accomplished, Habeeb Effendi, who had not once looked round towards the canal, now rose to depart; he was helped up the steps of the red horse-block, and fairly hoisted into his saddle; and amidst the roar of cannon and musketry, the shouts of the people, and the clang of innumerable musical instruments, he departed with his splendid train of officers and attendants.

Nothing can be conceived more striking than a great assemblage of people in the East: the various colours of the dresses and the number of white turbans give it a totally different appearance from that of a black and dingy European crowd; and it has been well compared by their poets to a garden of tulips. The numbers collected together on this occasion were immense; and the narrow streets were completely filled by the returning multitude, all delighted with the happy termination of the event of the day; but before noon the whole of the crowd was dispersed, all had returned to their own houses, and the city was as quiet and orderly as if nothing extraordinary had occurred.

CHAPTER IV.

Early Hours in the Levant—Compulsory Use of Lanterns in Cairo—Separation of the different Quarters of the City—Custom of sleeping in the open air—The Mahomedan Times of Prayer—Impressive Effect of the Morning Call to Prayer from the Minarets—The last Prayer-time, Al Assr—Bedouin Mode of ascertaining this Hour—Ancient Form of the Mosques—The Mosque of Sultan Hassan—Egyptian Mode of "raising the Supplies"—Sultan Hassan's Mosque the Scene of frequent Conflicts—The Slaughter of the Mameluke Beys in the Place of Roumayli—Escape of one Mameluke, and his subsequent Friendship with Mohammed Ali—The Talisman of Cairo—Joseph's Well and Hall—Mohammed Ali's Mosque—His Residence in the Citadel—The Harem—Degraded State of the Women in the East.

The
early hours kept in the Levant cannot fail to strike the European stranger. At Cairo every one is up and about at sunrise; all business is transacted in the morning, and some of the bezesteins and principal bazaars are closed at twelve o'clock, at which hour many people retire to their homes and only appear again in the cool of the evening, when they take a ride or sit and smoke a pipe and listen to a storyteller in a coffee-house or under a tree. Soon after sunset the whole city is at rest. Every one who then has any business abroad is obliged to carry a small paper lantern, on pain of being taken up by the guard if he is found without it. Persons of middle rank have a glass lamp carried before them by a servant, and people of consequence are preceded by men who run before their train of horses with a fire of resinous wood, carried aloft on the top of a pole, in an iron grating called a mashlak. This has a picturesque effect, and throws a great light around.

Each different district of the city is separated from the adjoining one by strong gates at the end of the streets: these are all closed at night, and are guarded by a drowsy old man with a long beard, who acts as porter, and who is roused with difficulty by the promise of a small coin when any one wants to pass. These gates contribute greatly to the peace and security of the town; for as the Turks, Arabs, Christians, Jews, Copts, and other religious sects reside each in a different quarter, any disturbance which may arise in one district is prevented from extending to another; and the drunken Europeans cannot intrude their civilization on their quiet and barbarous neighbours. There are here no theatres, balls, parties, or other nocturnal assemblies; and before the hour at which London is well lit up, the gentleman of Cairo ascends to the top of his house and sleeps upon the terrace, and the servants retire to the court-yard; for in the hot weather most people sleep in the open air. Many of the poorer class sleep in the open places and the courts of the mosques, all wrapping up their heads and faces that the moon may not shine upon them.

The Mahomedan day begins at sunset, when the first time of prayer is observed; the second is about two hours after sunset; the third is at the dawn of day, when the musical chant of the muezzins from the thousand minarets of Cairo sounds most impressively through the clear and silent air. The voices of the criers thus raised above the city always struck me as having a holy and beautiful effect. First one or two are heard faintly in the distance, then one close to you, then the cry is taken up from the minarets of other mosques, and at last, from one end of the town to the other, the measured chant falls pleasingly on the ear, inviting the faithful to prayer. For a time it seems as if there was a chorus of voices in the air, like spirits, calling upon each other to worship the Creator of all things. Soon the sound dies away, there is a silence for a while, and then commence the hum and bustle of the awakening city. This cry of man, to call his brother man to prayer, seems to me more appropriate and more accordant to religious feeling than the clang and jingle of our European bells.

The fourth and most important time of prayer is at noon, and it is at this hour that the Sultan attends in state the mosque at Constantinople. The fifth and last prayer is at about three o'clock. The Bedouins of the desert, who, however, are not much given to praying, consider this hour to have arrived when a stick, a spear, or a camel throws a shadow of its own height upon the ground. This time of the day is called "Al Assr." When wandering about in the deserts, I used always to eat my dinner or luncheon at that time, and it is wonderful to what exactness I arrived at last in my calculations respecting the time of the Assr. I knew to a minute when my dromedary's shadow was of the right length.

The minarets of Cairo are the most beautiful of any in the Levant; indeed no others are to be compared to them. Some are of a prodigious height, built of alternate layers of red and white stone. A curious anecdote is told of the most ancient of all the minarets, that attached to the great mosque of Sultan Tayloon, an immense cloister or arcade surrounding a great square. The arches are all pointed, and are the earliest extant in that form, the mosque having been built in imitation of that at Mecca, in the year of the Hegira 265, Anno Domini 879. The minaret belonging to this magnificent building has a stone staircase winding round it outside: the reason of its having been built in this curious form is said to be, that the vizier of Sultan Tayloon found the king one day lolling on his divan and twisting a piece of paper in a spiral form; the vizier remarking upon the trivial nature of the employment of so great a monarch, he replied, "I was thinking that a minaret in this form would have a good effect: give orders, therefore, that such a one be added to the mosque which I am building."[2] In ancient times the mosques consisted merely of large open courts, surrounded by arcades; and frequently, on that side of the court which stood nearest to Mecca, this arcade was double. In later times covered buildings with large domes were added to the court; a style of building which has always been adopted in more northern climates.

The finest mosque of this description is that of Sultan Hassan, in the place of the Roumayli, near the citadel. It is a magnificent structure, of prodigious height; it was finished about the year A.D.

1362. The money necessary for its construction is said to have been procured by the following ingenious device. The good Sultan Hassan was determined to build a mosque and a tomb for himself, but finding a paucity of means in his treasury, he sent out invitations to all the principal people of the country to repair to a grand feast at his court, when he said he would present each of his loving subjects with a robe of honour. On the appointed day they accordingly all made their appearance, dressed in their richest robes of state. There was not one but had a Cashmere shawl round his turban, and another round his waist, with a jewelled dagger stuck in it; besides other ornaments, and caftans of brocade and cloth of gold. They entered the place of the Roumayli each accompanied by a magnificent train of guards and attendants, who, according to the jealous custom of the times, remained below; while the chiefs, with one or two of their personal followers only, ascended into the citadel, and were ushered into the presence of the Sultan. They were received most graciously: how they contrived to pass their time in the fourteenth century, before the art of smoking was invented, I do not know, but doubtless they sat in circles round great bowls of rice, piled over sheep roasted whole, discussed the merits of lambs stuffed with pistachio-nuts, and ate cucumbers for dessert. When the feast was concluded the Sultan announced that each guest at his departure should receive the promised robe of honour; and as these distinguished personages, one by one, left the royal presence, they were conducted to a small chamber near the gate, in which were several armed officers of the household, who, with expressions of the most profound respect and solicitude, divested them of their clothes, which they immediately carried off. The astonished noble was then invested with a long white shirt, and ceremoniously handed out of an opposite door, which led to the exterior of the fortress, where he found his train in waiting. The Sultan kept all that he found worth keeping of the personal effects of his guests, who were afterwards glad to bargain with the chamberlain of the court for the restoration of their robes of state, which were ultimately returned to them—for a consideration. The mosque of Sultan Hassan was built with the proceeds of this original scheme; and the tomb of the founder is placed in a superb hall, seventy feet square, covered with a magnificent dome, which is one of the great features of the city. But he that soweth in the whirlwind shall reap in the storm. In consequence of the great height and thickness of the walls of this stately building, as well as from the circumstance of its having only one great gate of entrance, it was frequently seized and made use of as a fortress by the insurgents in the numerous rebellions and insurrections which were always taking place under the rule of the Mameluke kings. Great stains of blood are still to be seen on the marble walls of the court-yard, and even in the very chamber of the tomb of the Sultan there are the indelible marks of the various conflicts which have taken place, when the guardians of the mosque have been stabbed and cut down in its most sacred recesses. The two minarets of this mosque, one of which is much larger than the other, are among the most beautiful specimens of decorated Saracenic architecture. Of the largest of these minarets the following story is related. There was a man endued with a superabundance of curiosity, who, like Peeping Tom of Coventry, had a fancy for spying at the ladies on the house-tops from the summit of this minaret: at last he made some signals to one of the neighbouring ladies, which were unluckily discovered by the master of the house, who happened to be reposing in the harem. The two muezzins (as they often are) were blind men, and complaint was made to the authorities that the muezzins of Sultan Hassan permitted people to ascend the minarets to gaze into the forbidden precincts of the harems below. The two old muezzins were indignant when they were informed of this accusation, and were determined to watch for the intruder and kill him on the spot, the first time that they should find him ascending the winding staircase of the minaret. In the course of a few days a good-natured person gave the alarm, and told the two blind men that somebody had just entered the doorway on the roof of the mosque by which the minaret is ascended; one of the muezzins therefore ascended the minaret, armed with a sharp dagger, and the other waited at the narrow door below to secure the game whom his companion should drive out of the cover. The young man was surprised by the muezzin while he was looking over the lower gallery of the minaret, but escaping from him he ran up the stairs to the upper gallery: here he was followed by his enemy, who cried to the old man at the bottom to be ready, for he had found the rascal who had brought such scandal on the mosque. The muezzin chased the intruder round the upper gallery, and he slipped through the door and ran down again to the lower one, where he waited till the muezzin passed him on the stairs, then taking off his shoes he followed him lightly and silently till he arrived near the bottom door, when he suddenly pushed the muezzin, who had been up the minaret, against the one who stood guard below; the two blind men, each thinking he had got hold of the villain for whom he was in search, seized each other by the throat and engaged in mortal combat with their daggers, taking advantage of which the other escaped before the blind men had found out their mistake. At the next hour of prayer, their well-known voices not being heard as usual, some of the attendants at the mosque went up upon the roof to see what had happened, when they found the muezzins, who were just able to relate the particulars of their mistake before they died.

It was in the place of the Roumayli that the gallant band of the Mameluke beys were assembled before they were entrapped and killed by the present task-master of Egypt, Mohammed Ali Pasha. They ascended a narrow passage between two high bastions, which led from the lower to the upper gate. The lower gate was shut after they had passed, and they were thus caught as in a trap. All of them were shot except one, who leaped his horse over the battlements and escaped. This man became afterwards a great ally of Mohammed Ali, and I have often seen him riding about on a fine horse caparisoned with red velvet in the old Mameluke style. On the wall in one part of this passage, towards the inner gate, there is a square tablet containing a bas-relief of a spread eagle: this is considered by the superstitious as the talisman of Cairo, and is said to give a warning cry when any calamity is about to happen to the city. Its origin, as well as most things of any antiquity in the citadel, is ascribed to Saladin (Yousef Sala Eddin), who is called here Yousef (Joseph); and Joseph's Well, and Joseph's Hall, are the two great lions of the place.

The well, which is of great depth, is remarkable from its having a broad winding staircase cut in the rock around the shaft: this extends only half way down, where two oxen are employed to draw water by a wheel and buckets from the bottom, which is here poured into a cistern, whence it is raised to the top by another wheel. It is supposed, however, that this well is an ancient work, and that it was only cleaned out by Saladin when he rebuilt the walls of the town and fortified the citadel.

The hall, which was a very fine room, divided into aisles by magnificent antique columns of red granite, has unfortunately been pulled down by Mohammed Ali. He did this to make way for the mosque which he has built of Egyptian alabaster, a splendid material, but its barbarous Armenian architecture offers a sad contrast to the stately edifice which has been so ruthlessly destroyed. It is indeed a sad thing for Cairo that the flimsy architecture of Constantinople, so utterly unsuited to this climate, has been introduced of late years in the public buildings and the palaces of the ministers, which lift up their bald and miserable whitewashed walls above the beautiful Arabian works of earlier days.

The residence of the Pasha is within the walls of the citadel. The long range of the windows of the harem from their lofty position overlook great part of the city, which must render it a more cheerful residence for the ladies than harems usually are. When a number of Eastern women are congregated together, as is frequently the case, without the society of the other sex, it is surprising how helpless they become, and how neglectful of everything excepting their own persons and their food. Eating and dressing are their sole pursuits. If there be a garden attached to the harem they take no trouble about it, and at Constantinople the ladies of the Sultan tread on the flower-beds and destroy the garden as a flock of sheep would do if let loose in it. A Turkish lady is the wild variety of the species. Many of them are beautiful and graceful, but they do not appear to abound in intellectual charms. Until the minds of the women are enlarged by better education, any chance of amelioration among the people of the Levant is hopeless: for it is in the nursery that the seeds of superstition, prejudice, and unreason are sown, the effects of which cling for life to the minds even of superior men.

CHAPTER V.

Interview with Mohammed Ali Pasha—Mode of lighting a Room in Egypt—Personal Appearance of the Pasha—His Diamond-mounted Pipe—The lost Handkerchief—An unceremonious Attendant—View of Cairo from the Citadel—Site of Memphis; its immense extent—The Tombs of the Caliphs—The Pasha's Mausoleum—Costume of Egyptian Ladies—The Coboob, or Wooden Clog—Mode of dressing the Hair—The Veil—Mistaken Idea that the Egyptian Ladies are Prisoners in the Harem; their power of doing as they like—The Veil a complete Disguise—Laws of the Harem—A Levantine Beauty—Eastern Manners—The Abyssinian Slaves—Arab Girls—Ugliness of the Arab Women when old—Venerable Appearance of the old Men—An Arab Sheick.

It

was in the month of February, 1834, that I first had the honour of an audience with Mohammed Ali Pasha. It was during the Mahomedan month of Ramadan, when the day is kept a strict fast, and nothing passes the lips of the faithful till after sunset. It was at night, therefore, that we were received. My companion and myself were residing at that time under the hospitable roof of the Consul-General, and we accompanied him to the citadel. The effect of the crowds of people in the streets, all carrying lanterns, or preceded by men bearing the mashlak, blazing like a beacon on the top of its high pole, was very picturesque. The great hall of the citadel was full of men, arranged in rows with their faces towards the south, going through the forms and attitudes of evening prayer under the guidance of a leader, and with the precision of a regiment on drill.

Passing these, a curtain was drawn aside, and we were ushered at once into the presence of the Viceroy, whom we found walking up and down in the middle of a large room, between two rows of gigantic silver candlesticks, which stood upon the carpet. This is the usual way of lighting a room in Egypt:—Six large silver dishes, about two feet in diameter and turned upside down, are first placed upon the floor, three on each side, near the centre of the room. On each of these stands a silver candlestick, between four and five feet high, containing a wax candle three feet long, and very thick. A seventh candlestick, of smaller dimensions, stands on the floor, separate from these, for the purpose of being moved about; it is carried to any one who wants to read a letter, or to examine an object more closely while he is seated on the divan. Almost every room in the palace has an European chandelier hanging from the ceiling, but I do not remember having ever seen one lit. These large candlesticks, standing in two rows, with the little one before them, always put me in mind of a line of life guards of gigantic stature, commanded by a little officer whom they could almost put in their pockets.

Mohammed Ali desired us to be seated. He was attended by Boghos Bey, who remained standing and interpreted for us. The Pasha at that time was a hale, broad-shouldered, broad-faced man: his short grey beard stuck out on each side of his face; his nostrils were very much opened; and, with his quick sharp eye, he looked like an old grey lion. The expression of his countenance was remarkably intelligent, but excepting this there was nothing particular in his appearance. He was attired in the Nizam dress of blue cloth. This costume consists of a red cap, a jacket with flying sleeves, a waistcoat with tight sleeves under it, a red shawl round the waist, a pair of trousers very full, like trunk hose, down to the knee, from whence to the ankle they were tight. The whole costume is always made of the same coloured cloth, usually black or blue. He had white stockings and yellow morocco shoes.

EGYPTIAN, IN THE NIZAM DRESS. EGYPTIAN, IN THE NIZAM DRESS.

When we were seated on the divan we commenced the usual routine of Oriental compliments; and coffee was handed to us in cups entirely covered with large diamonds. A pipe was then brought to the Pasha, but not to us. This pipe was about seven feet long: the mouthpiece, of light green amber, was a foot long, and a foot more below the mouthpiece, as well as another part of the pipe lower down, was richly set with diamonds of great value, with a diamond tassel hanging to it.

We discoursed for three quarters of an hour about the possibility of laying a railway across the Isthmus of Suez, which was the project then uppermost in the Pasha's mind; but the circumstance which most strongly recalls this audience to my memory, and which struck me as an instance of manners differing entirely from our own, was, in itself, a very trivial one. The Pasha wanted his pocket handkerchief, and looked about and felt in his pocket for it, but could not find it, making various exclamations during his search, which at last were answered by an attendant from the lower end of the room—"Feel in the other pocket," said the servant. "Well, it is not there," said the Pasha. "Look in the other, then." "I have not got a handkerchief," or words to that effect, were replied to immediately,—"Yes, you have;"—"No, I have not;"—"Yes, you have." Eventually this attendant, advancing up to the Pasha, felt in the pocket of his jacket, but the handkerchief was not to be found; then he poked all round the Pasha's waist, to see whether it was not tucked into his shawl: that would not do. So he took hold of his Sovereign and pushed him half over on the divan, and looked under him to see whether he was sitting on the handkerchief; then he pushed him over on the other side. During all which manœuvres the Pasha sat as quietly and passively as possible. The servant then, thrusting his arm up to the elbow in one of the pockets of his Highness's voluminous trousers, pulled out a snuff-box, a rosary, and several other things, which he laid upon the divan. That would not do, either; so he came over to the other pocket, and diving to a prodigious depth he produced the missing handkerchief from the recesses thereof; and with great respect and gravity, thrusting it into the Pasha's hand, he retired again to his place at the lower end of the hall.

After being presented with sherbet, in glass bowls with covers, we took our leave, and rode home through the crowds of persons with paper lanterns, who turn night into day during the month of Ramadan.

The view from that part of the bastions of the citadel which looks over the place of the Roumayli and the great mosque of Sultan Hassan is one of the most extraordinary that can be seen any where. The whole city is displayed at your feet; the numerous domes and minarets, the towers of the Saracenic walls, the flat roofs of the houses, and the narrowness of the streets giving it an aspect very different from that of an European town. You see the Nile and the gardens of Ibrahim Pasha in the island of Rhoda to the left; and the avenue of Egyptian sycamores to the right, leading to the Pasha's country palace of Shoubra. Beyond the Nile, the bare mysterious-looking desert, and the Pyramids standing on their rocky base, lead the mind to dwell upon the mighty deeds of ancient days. The forest of waving palm-trees, around Saccara, stretches away to the south-west, shading the mounds of earth which cover the remains of the vast city of Memphis, in comparison to which London would appear but a secondary town: for if we may judge from the line of pyramids from Giseh to Dashour, which formed the necropolis of Memphis, and the various mounds and dykes and ancient remains which extend along the margin of the Nile for nearly six-and-thirty miles, the extreme length of London being barely eight, and of Paris not much more than four, Memphis must have been larger than London, Paris, and ancient Rome, all united; and judging from the description which Herodotus has given us of the enormous size of the temples and buildings, which are now entirely washed away, in consequence of their having been built on the alluvial plain, which is every year inundated by the waters of the Nile, Memphis in its glory must have exceeded any modern city, as much as the Pyramids exceed any mausoleum which has been erected since those days.

The tombs of the Caliphs, as they are called, although most of them are the burial-place of the Mameluke Sultans of Egypt, are magnificent and imposing buildings. Many of them consist of a mosque built round a court, to which is attached a great hall with a dome, under which is placed the Sultan's tomb. These beautiful specimens of Arabian architecture form a considerable town or city of the dead, on the east and south sides of Cairo, about a mile beyond the walls. I was astonished at their exceeding beauty and magnificence. Most of them were built during the two centuries preceding the conquest of Egypt, by Sultan Selim, in 1517, who tortured the last of the Mameluke Sultans, Toman Bey, and hung him with a rope, which is yet to be seen dangling over the gate called Bab Zuweyleh, in front of which criminals are still executed.

The mausoleum of Sultan Bergook is a triumph of Saracenic architecture.

The minarets of these tombs are most richly ornamented with tracery, sculpture, and variegated marbles. The walls of many of them are built in alternate layers of red and white or black and white marble. The dome of the tomb of Kaitbay is of stone, sculptured all over with an arabesque pattern; and there are several other domes in different mosques at Cairo equally richly ornamented. I have met with none comparable to them either in Europe or in the Levant. It is strange that none of the Italian architects ever thought of domes covered with rich ornamental work in stone or marble; the effect of those at Cairo is indescribably fine. Unfortunately they are now much neglected; but in the clear dry air of Egypt, time falls more lightly on the works of man than in the damp and chilly climates of the north, and the tombs of the Mameluke sovereigns will probably last for centuries to come if they are not pulled down for the materials, or removed to make way for some paltry lath and plaster edifice which will fall in the lifetime of its builder.

Besides these larger structures, many of the smaller tombs, which are scattered over the desert for miles under the hills of Mokattam, are studies for the architect. There are numerous little domes of beautiful design, richly ornamented doors and gateways, tombs and tomb-stones of all sorts and sizes in infinite variety, most of them so well preserved in this glorious climate that the inscriptions on them are as legible as when they were first put up.

The Pasha has built himself a house in this city of the dead, to which many members of his family have gone before him. This mausoleum consists of several buildings covered with low heavy domes, whitewashed or plastered on the outside. Within, if I remember right, are the tombs of Toussoun and Ismael Pashas, and those of several of his wives, grand-children, and relatives; they repose under marble monuments, somewhat resembling altars in shape, with a tall post or column at the head and feet, as is usual in Turkish graves; the column at the head being carved into the form of the head-dress distinctive of the rank or sex of the deceased. These sepulchral chambers are all carpeted, and Cashmere shawls are thrown over many of the tombs, while in arched recesses there are divans with cushions for the use of those who come to mourn over their departed relatives.

We will now return to the living; but so perfect an account of the Arabian population of Cairo is to be found in Mr. Lane's 'Modern Egypt,' that there is little left to say upon that subject, except that since that work was published the presence of numerous Europeans has diminished the originality of the Oriental manners of this city, and numerous vices and modes of cheating, besides a larger variety of drunken scenes, are offered for the observation of the curious, than existed in the more unsophisticated times, before steamers came to Alexandria, and what is called the overland journey to India was established. The population of Cairo consists of the ruling class, who are all Turks, who speak Turkish, and affect to despise all who have never been rowed in a caïque upon the Bosphorus. Then come the Arabs, the former conquerors of the land; they form the bulk of the population—all the petty tradesmen and cultivators of the soil are of Arab origin. Besides these are the Copts, who are descended from the original lords of the country, the ancient Egyptians, who have left such wonderful monuments of their power. After these may be reckoned the motley crew of Jews, Franks, Armenians, Arabs of Barbary and the Hejaz, Syrians, negroes, and Barabra; but these are but sojourners in the land, and, except the Jews, can hardly be counted among the regular subjects of the Pasha. There are besides, the Levantine Christians, who are under the protection of one or other of the European powers. Many of this class are rich and influential merchants; some of them live in the Oriental style, and others are ambitious to assume the tight clothing and manner of life of the Franks. The older merchants among the Levantines keep more to the Oriental ways of life, while the younger gentlemen and ladies follow the ugly fashion of Europe, particularly the men, who leave off the cool and convenient Eastern dress to swelter in the tight bandages of the Franks; the ladies, on the contrary, are apt to retain the Oriental costume, which in its turn is neither so becoming nor so easy as the Paris fashions. It must be the spirit of contradiction, so natural to the human race, which causes this arrangement; for if the men kept to their old costume they would be more comfortable than they can be with tight clothes, coat-collars, and neckcloths, when the thermometer stands at 112° of Fahrenheit in the coolest shade, besides the dignity of their appearance, which is cast away with the folds of the Turkish or Arabian dress. The ladies would be much improved by the artful devices of the Parisian modistes; for although, when young and pretty, all women look well in almost any dress, the elder ladies are sometimes but little to be admired in the shapeless costumes of the Levant, where the richness of the material does not make up for the want of fit and gracefulness which is the character of their dress. This may easily be imagined when it is understood that both men's and women's dresses may be bought ready made in the bazaar, and that any dress will fit anybody unless they are supernaturally fat or of dwarfish stature.

An Egyptian lady's dress consists of a pair of immensely full trousers of satin or brocade, or often of a brilliant cherry-coloured silk: these are tied under the knees, and descending to the ground, have the appearance of a very full petticoat. The Arabic name of this garment is Shintian. Over this is worn a shirt of transparent silk gauze (Kamis). It has long full sleeves, which, as well as the border round the neck, are richly embroidered with gold and bright-coloured silks. The edge of the shirt is often seen like a tunic over the trousers, and has a pretty effect. Over this again is worn a long silk gown, open in front and on each side, called a yelek. The fashion is to have the yelek about a foot longer than the lady who wears it; so that its three tails shall just touch the ground when she is mounted on a pair of high wooden clogs, called cobcobs, which are intended for use in the bath, but in which they often clatter about in the house: the straps over the instep, by which these cobcobs are attached to the feet, are always finely worked, and are sometimes of diamonds. The husband gives his bride on their marriage a pair of these odd-looking things, which are about six or eight inches high, and are always carried on a tray on a man's head in marriage processions. The yelek fits the shape in some degree down to the waist; it comes up high upon the neck, and has tightish sleeves, which are long enough to trail upon the ground. "Oh! thou with the long-sleeved yelek" is a common chorus or ending to a stanza in an Arab song. Not round the waist but round the hips a large and heavy Cashmere shawl is worn over the yelek, and the whole gracefulness of an Egyptian dress consists in the way in which this is put on. In the winter a long gown, called Jubeh, is superadded to all this: it is of cloth or velvet, or a sort of stuff made of the Angora goat's hair, and is sometimes lined with fur.

Young girls do not often wear this nor the yelek, but have instead a waistcoat of silk with long sleeves like those of the yelek. This is called an anteri, and over it they wear a velvet jacket with short sleeves, which is so much embroidered with gold and pearls that the velvet is almost hid. Their hair hangs down in numerous long tails, plaited with silk, to which sequins, or little gold coins, are attached. The plaits must be of an uneven number: it would be unlucky if they were even. Sometimes at the end of one of the plaits hangs the little golden bottle of surmeh with which they black the edges of their eyelids; a most becoming custom when it is well done, and not smeared, as it often is, for then the effect is rather like that of a black eye, in the pugilistic sense of the term. On the head is worn a very beautiful ornament called a koors. It is in the shape of a saucer or shallow basin, and is frequently covered with rose diamonds. I am surprised that it has never been introduced into Europe, as it is a remarkably pretty head-dress, with the long tresses of jet black hair hanging from under it, plaited with the shining coins. Round the head a handkerchief is wound, which spoils the effect of all the rest: but a woman in the East is never seen with the head uncovered, even in the house; and when she goes out, the veil, as we call it, though it has no resemblance to a veil, is used to conceal the whole person. A lady enclosed in this singular covering looks like a large bundle of black silk, diversified only by a stripe of white linen extending down the front of her person, from the middle of her nose to her ungainly yellow boots, into which her stockingless feet are thrust for the occasion. The veils of Egypt, of which the outer black silk covering is called a khabara, and the part over the face a boorkoo, are entirely different from those worn in Constantinople, Persia, or Armenia; these are all various in form and colour, complicated and wonderful garments, which it would take too long to describe, but they, as well as the Egyptian one, answer their intended purpose excellently, for they effectually prevent the display of any grace or peculiarity of form or feature.

There is no greater mistake than to suppose that Eastern ladies are prisoners in the harem, and that they are to be pitied for the want of liberty which the jealousy of their husbands condemns them to. The Christian ladies live from choice and habit in the same way as the Mahomedan women: and, indeed, the Egyptian fair ones have more facilities to do as they choose, to go where they like, and to carry on any intrigue than the Europeans; for their complete disguise carries them safely everywhere. No one knows whether any lady he may meet in the bazaar is his wife, his daughter, or his grandmother: and I have several times been addressed by Turkish and Egyptian ladies in the open street, and asked all sorts of questions in a way that could not be done in any European country. The harem, it is true, is by law inviolable: no one but the Sultan can enter it unannounced, and if a pair of strange slippers are seen left at the outer door, the master of the house cannot enter his own harem so long as this proof of the presence of a visitor remains. If the husband is a bore, an extra pair of slippers will at all times keep him out; and the ladies inside may enjoy themselves without the slightest fear of interruption. It is asserted also that gentlemen, who are not too tall, have gone into all sorts of places under the protection of a lady's veil, so completely does it conceal the person. But this is not the case with the Levantine or Christian ladies: although they live in a harem, like the Mahomedans, it is not protected in the same way: the slippers have not the same effect; for the men of the family go in and out whenever they please; and relations and visitors of the male sex are received in the apartments of the ladies.

On one occasion I accompanied an English traveller, who had many acquaintances at Cairo, to the house of a Levantine in the vicinity of the Coptic quarter. Whilst we were engaged in conversation with an old lady the curtain over the doorway was drawn aside, and there entered the most lovely apparition that can be conceived, in the person of a young lady about sixteen years old, the daughter of the lady of the house. She had a beautifully fair complexion, very uncommon in this country, remarkably long hair, which hung down her back, and her dress, which was all of the same rich material, rose-coloured silk, shot with gold, became her so well, that I have rarely seen so graceful and striking a figure. She was closely followed by two black girls, both dressed in light-blue satin, embroidered with silver; they formed an excellent contrast to their charming mistress, and were very good-looking in their way, with their slight and graceful figures. The young Levantine came and sat by me on the divan, and was much amused at my blundering attempts at conversation in Arabic, of which I then knew scarcely a dozen words. I must confess that I was rather vexed with her for smoking a long jessamine pipe, which, however, most Eastern ladies do. She got up to wait upon us, and handed us the coffee, pipes, and sherbet, which are always presented to visitors in every house. This custom of being waited upon by the ladies is rather distressing to our European notions of devotion to the fair sex: and I remember being horrified shortly after my arrival in Egypt at the manners of a rich old jeweller to whom I was introduced. His wife, a beautiful woman, superbly dressed in brocade, with gold and diamond ornaments, waited upon us during the whole time that I remained in the house. She was the first Eastern lady I had seen, and I remember being much edified at the way she pattered about on a pair of lofty cobcobs, and the artful way in which she got her feet out of them whenever she came up towards where we sat on the divan, at the upper end of the apartment. She stood at the lower end of the room; and whenever the old brute of a jeweller wanted to return anything, some coins which he was showing me, or anything else, he threw them on the floor; and his beautiful wife jumping out of her cobcobs picked them up; and when she had handed them to some of the maids who stood at the door, resumed her station below the step at the further end of the room. She had magnificent eyes and luxuriant black hair, as they all have, and would have been considered a beauty in any country; but she was not to be compared to the bright little damsel in pink, who, besides her beauty, was as cheerful and merry as a bird, and whose lovely features were radiant with archness and intelligence. Many of the Abyssinian slaves are exceedingly handsome: they have very expressive countenances, and the finest eyes in the world, and, withal, so soft and humble a look, that I do not wonder at their being great favourites in Egyptian harems. Many of them, however, have a temper of their own, which comes out occasionally, and in this respect the Arab women are not much behind them. But the fiery passions of this burning climate pass away like a thunderstorm, and leave the sky as clear and serene as it was before.

The Arab girls of the lower orders are often very pretty from the age of about twelve to twenty, but they soon go off; and the astounding ugliness of some of the old women is too terrible to describe. In Europe we have nothing half so hideous as these brown old women, and this is the more remarkable, because the old men are peculiarly handsome and venerable in their appearance, and often display a dignity of bearing which is seldom to be met with in Europe. The stately gravity of an Arab sheick, seated on the ground in the shade of a tree, with his sons and grandsons standing before him, waiting for his commands, is singularly imposing.

CHAPTER VI.

Mohammed Bey, Defterdar—His Expedition to Senaar—His Barbarity and Rapacity—His Defiance of the Pasha—Stories of his Cruelty and Tyranny—The Horseshoe—The Fight of the Mamelukes—His cruel Treachery—His Mode of administering Justice—The stolen Milk—The Widow's Cow—Sale and Distribution of the Thief—The Turkish Character—Pleasures of a Journey on the Nile—The Copts—Their Patriarchs—The Patriarch of Abyssinia—Basileos Bey—His Boat—An American's choice of a Sleeping-place.

Just

before my arrival in Cairo a certain Mohammed Bey, Defterdar, had died rather suddenly, after drinking a cup of coffee, a beverage which occasionally disagrees with the great men in Turkey, although not so much so now as in former days. This Defterdar, or accountant, had been sent by the Sultan to receive the Imperial revenue from the Pasha of Egypt, who had given him his daughter in marriage. As the presence of the Defterdar was probably a check upon the projects of the Pasha, he sent him to Senaar, at the head of an expedition, to revenge the death of Toussoun Pasha, his second son, who had been burned alive in his house by one of the exasperated chiefs of Nubia. This was a mission after Mohammed Bey's own heart: he impaled the chief and several of his family, and displayed a rapacity and cruelty unheard of before even in those blood-stained countries. His talent for collecting spoil, and valuables of every description, was first-rate; chests and bags of the pure gold rings used in the traffic of Central Africa accumulated in his tents; he did not stick at a trifle in his measures for procuring gold, pearls, and diamonds, wherever they were to be heard of; streams of blood accompanied his march, and the vultures followed in his track. He was a sportsman too, and hunted slaves, killing the old ones, and carrying off the children, whom he sent to Egypt to be sold. Many died on the journey; but that did not much matter, as it increased the value of the rest.

At last, alter a most successful campaign, the Defterdar returned to his palace at Cairo, which was reported to be filled with treasure. The habits he had acquired in the upper country stuck to him after he got back to Egypt, and the Pasha was obliged to express his disapprobation of the cruelties which were committed by him on the most trivial occasions. The Defterdar, however, set the Pasha at defiance, told him he was no subject of his, but that he was an envoy from his master the Sultan, to whom alone he was responsible, and that he would do as he pleased with those under his command. The Pasha, it is said, made no further remonstrance, and continued to treat his son-in-law with distinguished courtesy.

Numerous stories are told of the cruelty and tyranny of this man. One day, on his way to the citadel, he found that his horse had cast a shoe. He inquired of his groom, who in Egypt runs by the side of the horse, how it was that his horse had lost his shoe. The groom said he did not know, but that he supposed it had not been well nailed on. Presently they came to a farrier's shop; the Defterdar stopped, and ordered two horseshoes to be brought; one was put upon the horse, and the other he made red hot, and commanded them to nail it firmly to the foot of the groom, whom in that condition he compelled to run by his horse's side up the steep hill which leads to the citadel.

In Turkey it was the custom in the houses of the great to have a number of young men, who in Egypt were called Mamelukes, after that gallant corps had been destroyed. A number of the Mamelukes of Mohammed Bey, Defterdar, driven to desperation by the cruelties of their master, beat or killed one of the superior agas of the household, took some money which they found in his possession, and determined to escape from the service of their tyrant. His guards and kawasses soon found them out, and they retired to a strong tower, which they determined to defend, preferring the remotest chance of successful resistance to the terrors of service under the ferocious Defterdar. The Bey, however, managed to cajole them with promises, and they returned to his palace, expecting to be better treated. They found the Bey seated on his divan in the Manderan or hall of audience, surrounded by the officers and kawasses whom interest had attached to his service. The young Mamelukes had given up the money which they had taken, and the Bey had it on the divan by his side. He now told them that if they would divide themselves into two parties and fight against each other, he would pardon the victorious party, present them with the bag of gold, and permit them to depart; but that if they did not agree to this proposal he would kill them all. The Mamelukes, finding they were entrapped, consented to the conditions of the Bey, and half their number were soon weltering in their blood on the floor of the hall. When the conquerors claimed the promised reward, the Defterdar, who had now far superior numbers on his side, again commanded them to divide and fight against each other. Again they fought in despair, preferring death by their own swords to the tortures which they knew the merciless Defterdar would inflict upon them now that he had got them completely in his power. At length only one Mameluke remained, whom the Bey, with kind and encouraging words, ordered to approach, commending his valour and holding out to him the promised bag of gold as his reward. As he approached, stepping over the bodies of his companions, who all lay dead or dying on the floor, and held out his hands for the money, the Defterdar, with a grim smile, made a sign to one of his kawasses, and the head of the young man rolled at the tyrant's feet "Thus," said he, "shall perish all who dare to offend Mohammed Bey."

The Defterdar was fond of justice, after a fashion, and his mode of administering it was characteristic. A poor woman came before him and complained that one of his kawasses had seized a cup of milk and drunk it, refusing to pay her its value, which she estimated at five paras (a para is the fortieth part of a piastre, which is worth about twopence-halfpenny). The sensitive justice of the Defterdar was roused by this complaint. He asked the woman if she should know the person who had stolen her milk were she to see him again? The woman said she should, upon which the whole household was drawn out before her, and looking round she fixed upon a man as the thief. "Very well," said the Defterdar, "I hope you are sure of your man, and that you have not made a false accusation before me. He shall be ripped open, and if the milk is found in his stomach, you shall receive your five paras; but if there is no milk found, you shall be ripped up in turn for accusing one of my household unjustly." The unfortunate kawass was cut open on the spot; some milk was found in him, and the woman received her five paras.

Another of his judicial sentences was rather an original conception. A man in Upper Egypt stole a cow from a widow, and having killed it, he cut it into twenty pieces, which he sold for a piastre each in the bazaar. The widow complained to the Defterdar, who seized the thief, and having without further ceremony cut him into twenty pieces, forced twenty people who came into the market on that day from the neighbouring villages to buy a piece of thief each for a piastre; the joints of the robber were thus distributed all over the country, and the story told by the involuntary purchasers of these pounds of flesh had a wholesome effect upon the minds of the cattle-stealers: the twenty piastres were given to the woman, whose cows were not again meddled with during the lifetime of the Defterdar. But the character of this man must not be taken as a sample of the habits of the Turks in general. They are a grave and haughty race, of dignified manners; rapacious they often are, but they are generous and brave, and I do not think that, as a nation, they can be accused of cruelty.

Nothing can be more secure and peaceable than a journey on the Nile, as every one knows nowadays. Floating along in a boat like a house, which stops and goes on whenever you like, you have no cares or troubles but those which you bring with you—"cœlum non animum mutant qui trans mare currunt." I can conceive nothing more delightful than a voyage up the Nile with agreeable companions in the winter, when the climate is perfection. There are the most wonderful antiquities for those who interest themselves in the remains of bygone days; famous shooting on the banks of the river, capital dinners, if you know how to make the proper arrangements, comfortable quarters, and a constant change of scene.

The wonders of the land of Ham, its temples and its ruins, have been so well and so often described that I shall not attempt to give any details regarding them, but shall confine myself to some sketches of the Coptic Monasteries which are to be seen on the rocks and deserts, either on the banks of the river or in the neighbourhood of the valley of the Nile.

The ancient Egyptians are now represented by their descendants the Copts, whose ancestors were converted to Christianity in the earliest ages, and whose patriarchs claim their descent, in uninterrupted succession, from St Mark, who was buried at Alexandria, but whose body the Venetians in later ages boast of having transported to their island city.[3]

The Copts look up to their patriarch as the chief of their nation: he is elected from among the brethren of the great monastery of St. Anthony on the borders of the Red Sea, a proceeding which ensures his entire ignorance of all sublunary matters, and his consequent incapacity for his high and responsible office, unless he chance to be a man of very uncommon talents. Like the patriarch of Constantinople, he is usually a puppet in the hands of a cabal who make use of him for their own interested purposes, and when they have got him into a scrape leave him to get out of it as he can. He is called the Patriarch of Alexandria, but for many years his residence has been at Cairo, where he has a large dreary palace. He is surrounded by priests and acolytes; but when I was last at Cairo there was but one remaining Coptic scribe among them, whom I engaged to copy out the Gospel of St Mark from an ancient MS. in the patriarchal library: however, after a very long delay he copied out St. Matthew's Gospel by mistake, and I was told that there was no other person whose profession it was to copy Coptic writings.

The patriarch has twelve bishops under him, whose residences are at Nagadé, Abou Girgé, Aboutig, Siout, Girgé, Manfalout, Maharaka, the Fioum, Atfeh, Behenesé, and Jerusalem: he also consecrates the Abouna or Patriarch of Abyssinia, who by a specific law must not be a native of that country, and who has not the privilege of naming his successor or consecrating archbishops or bishops, although in other respects his authority in religious matters is supreme. The Patriarch of Abyssinia usually ordains two or three thousand priests at once on his first arrival in that country, and the unfitness of the individual appointed to this high office has sometimes caused much scandal. This has arisen from the difficulty there has often been in getting a respectable person to accept the office, as it involves perpetual banishment from Egypt, and a residence among a people whose partiality to raw meat and other peculiar customs are held as abominations by the Egyptians.

The usual trade and occupation of the Copts is that of kateb, scribe, or accountant; they seem to have a natural talent for arithmetic. They appear to be more afflicted with ophthalmia than the Mohamedans, perhaps because they drink wine and spirits, which the others do not.

The person of the greatest consequence among the Copts was Basileos Bey, the Pasha's confidential secretary and minister of finance. This gentleman was good enough to lend me a magnificent dahabieh or boat of the largest size, which I used for many months. It was an old-fashioned vessel, painted and gilt inside in a brilliant manner, which is not usual in more modern boats; but being a person of a fanciful disposition, I preferred the roomy proportions and the quaint arabesque ornaments of this boat, although it was no very fast sailer, to the natty vessels which were more Europeanised and quicker than mine. The principal cabin was about ten feet by twelve, and was ornamented with paintings of peacocks of a peculiar breed and nondescript flowers. The divans, one on each side, were covered with fine carpets, and the cushions were of cloth of gold, with a raised pattern of red velvet. The ceilings were gilt, and we had two red silk flags of prodigious dimensions in addition to streamers forty or fifty feet long at the end of each of the yard-arms: in short, it was full of what is called fantasia in the Levant, and as for its slowness, I consider that rather an advantage in the East. I like to take my time and look about me, and sit under a tree on a carpet when I get to an agreeable place, and I am in no hurry to leave it; so the heavy qualities of the vessel suited me exactly—we did nothing but stop everywhere. But although I confess that I like deliberate travelling, I do not carry my system to the extent of an American friend with whom I once journeyed from the shores of the Black Sea to Hungary. We were taking a walk together in the mountains near Mahadia, when seeing him looking about among the rocks I asked him what he wanted. "Oh," said he, "I am looking out for a good place to go to sleep in, for there is a beautiful view here, and I like to sleep where there is a fine prospect, that I may enjoy it when I awake; so good afternoon, and if you come back this way mind you call me." Accordingly an hour or two afterwards I came back and aroused my friend, who was still fast asleep. "I hope you enjoyed your nap," said I; "we had a glorious walk among the hills." "Yes," said he, "I had a famous nap." "And what did you think of the view when you awoke?" "The view!" exclaimed he, "why, I forgot to look at it!"

NATRON LAKES.

CHAPTER VII.

Visit to the Coptic Monasteries near the Natron Lakes—The Desert of Nitria—Early Christian Anchorites—St. Macarius of Alexandria—His Abstinence and Penance—Order of Monks founded by him—Great increase of the Number of ascetic Monks in the Fourth Century—Their subsequent decrease, and the present ruined state of the Monasteries—Legends of the Desert—Capture of a Lizard—Its alarming escape—The Convent of Baramous—Night attacks—Invasion of Sanctuary—Ancient Glass Lamps—Monastery of Souriani—Its Library and Coptic MSS.—The Blind Abbot and his Oil-cellar—The persuasive powers of Rosoglio—Discovery of Syriac MSS.—The Abbot's supposed treasure.

In

the month of March, 1837, I left Cairo for the purpose of visiting the Coptic monasteries in the neighbourhood of the Natron lakes, which are situated in the desert to the north-west of Cairo, on the western side of the Nile. I had some difficulty in procuring a boat to take me down the river—indeed there was not one to be obtained; but two English gentlemen, on their way from China to England, were kind enough to give me a passage in their boat to the village of Terrané, the nearest spot upon the banks of the Nile to the monasteries which I proposed to visit.

The Desert of Nitria is famous in the annals of monastic history as the first place to which the Anchorites, in the early ages of Christianity, retired from the world in order to pass their lives in prayer and contemplation, and in mortification of the flesh. It was in

Egypt where monasticism first took its rise, and the Coptic monasteries of St. Anthony and St. Paul claim to be founded on the spots where the first hermits established their cells on the shores of the Red Sea. Next in point of antiquity are the monasteries of Nitria, of which we have authentic accounts dated as far back as the middle of the second century; for about the year 150 A.D.

Fronto retired to the valleys of the Natron lakes with seventy brethren in his company. The Abba Ammon (whose life is detailed in the 'Vitæ Patrum' of Rosweyd, Antwerp, 1628, a volume of great rarity and dulness, which I only obtained after a long search among the mustiest of the London book-stalls) flourished, or rather withered, in this desert in the beginning of the fourth century. At this time also the Abba Bischoi founded the monastery still called after his name, which, it seems, was Isaiah or Esa: the Coptic article Pe or Be makes it Besa, under which name he wrote an ascetic work, a manuscript of which, probably almost if not quite as old as his time, I procured in Egypt. It is one of the most ancient manuscripts now extant.

But the chief and pattern of all the recluses of Nitria was the great St. Macarius of Alexandria, whose feast-day—a day which he never observed himself—is still kept by the Latins on the 2nd, and by the Greeks on the 19th of January. This famous saint died A.D. 394, after sixty years of austerities in various deserts: he first retired into the Thebaid in the year 335, and about the year 373 established himself in a solitary cell on the borders of the Natron lakes. Numerous anchorites followed his example, all living separately, but meeting together on Sundays for public prayer. Self-denial and abstinence were their great occupations; and it is related that a traveller having given St. Macarius a bunch of grapes, he sent it to another brother, who sent it to a third, and at last, the grapes having passed through the hands of some hundreds of hermits, came back to St. Macarius, who rejoiced at such a proof of the abstinence of his brethren, but refused to eat of it himself. This same saint having thoughtlessly killed a gnat which was biting him, he was so unhappy at what he had done, that to make amends for his inadvertency, and to increase his mortifications, he retired to the marshes of Scete, where there were flies whose powerful stings were sufficient to pierce the hide of a wild boar; here he remained six months, till his body was so much disfigured that his brethren on his return only knew him by the sound of his voice. He was the founder of the monastic order which, as well as the monastery still existing on the site of his cell, was called after his name. By their rigid rule the monks are bound to fast the whole year, excepting on Sundays and during the period between Easter and Whitsuntide: they were not to speak to a stranger without leave. During Lent St. Macarius fasted all day, and sometimes ate nothing for two or three days together; on Sundays, however, he indulged in a raw cabbage-leaf, and in short set such an example of abstinence and self-restraint to the numerous anchorites of the desert, that the fame of his austerities gained him many admirers. Throughout the middle ages his name is mentioned with veneration in all the collections of the lives of the saints: he is represented pointing out the vanities of life in the great fresco of the Triumph of Death, by Andrea Orcagna, in the Campo Santo at Pisa. In his Life in Caxton's 'Golden Legende,' and in 'The Lives of the Fathers,' by Wynkyn de Worde, a detailed account will be found of a most interesting conversation which Macarius had with the devil, touching divers matters. Several of his miracles are also put into modern English, in Lord Lindsay's book of Christian Art. I have a MS. of the Gospels in Coptic, written by the hand of one

Zapita Leporos, under the rule of the great Macarius, in the monastery of Laura, about the year 390, and which may have been used by the Saint himself.

After the time of Macarius the number of ascetic monks increased to a surprising amount. Rufinus, who visited them in the year 372, mentions fifty of their convents; Palladius, who was there in the year 387, reckons the devotees at five thousand. St Jerome also visited them, and their number seems to have been kept up without much diminution for several centuries.[4] After the conquest of Egypt by the Arabians, and about the year 967, a Mahomedan author, Aboul Faraj of Hispahan, wrote a book of poems, called the 'Book of Convents,' which is in praise of the habits and religious devotion of the Christian monks. The dilapidated monastery of St. Macarius was repaired and fortified by Sanutius, Patriarch of Alexandria, at which good work he laboured with his own bands: this must have been about the year 880, as he died in 881. In more recent times the multitude of ascetics gradually decreased, and but few travellers have extended their researches to their arid haunts. At present only four monasteries remain entire, although the ruins of many others may still be traced in the desert tracts on the west side of the line of the Natron lakes, and the valley of the waterless river, which, at some very remote period, is supposed to have formed the bed of one of the branches of the Nile.

At the village of Terrané I was most hospitably received by an Italian gentleman, who was superintending the export of the natron. Here I procured camels; I had brought a tent with me; and the next day we set off across the plain, with the Arabs to whom the camels belonged, and who, having been employed in the transport of the natron, were able to show us the way, which it would have been very difficult to trace without their help. The memory of the devils and evil spirits who, according to numerous legends, used formerly to haunt this desert, seemed still to awake the fears of these Arab guides. During the first day's journey I talked to them on the subject, and found that their minds were full of superstitious fancies.

It is said that tailors sometimes stand up to rest themselves, and on that principle I had descended from my huge, ungainly camel, who had never before been used for riding, and whose swinging paces were very irksome, and was resting myself by walking in his shade, when seeing something run up to a large stone which lay in the way, I moved it to see what it was. I found a lizard, six or eight inches long, of a species with which I was unacquainted. I caught the reptile by the nape of the neck, which made him open his ugly mouth in a curious way, and he wriggled about so much that I could hardly hold him. Judging that he might be venomous, I looked about for some safe place to put him, and my eye fell upon the large glass lantern which was used in the tent; that, I thought, was just the thing for my lizard, so I put him into the lantern, which hung at the side of the baggage camel, intending to examine him at my leisure in the evening. When the sun was about to set, the tent was pitched, and a famous fire lit for the cook. It was in a bare, open place, without a hill, stock, or stone in sight in any direction all around. The camels were tethered together, near the baggage, which was piled in a heap to the windward of the fire; and, as it was getting dark, one of the Arabs took the lantern to the fire to light it. He got a blazing stick for this purpose, and held up the lantern close to his face to undo the hasp, which he had no sooner accomplished than out jumped the lizard upon his shoulder and immediately made his escape. The Arab, at this unexpected attack, gave a fearful yell, and dashing the lantern to pieces on the ground, screamed out that the devil had jumped upon him and had disappeared in the darkness, and that he was certain he was waiting to carry us all off. The other Arabs were seriously alarmed, and for a long while paid no attention to my explanation about the lizard, which was the cause of all the disturbance. The worst of the affair was that the lantern being broken to bits, we could have no light; for the wind blew the candles out, notwithstanding our most ingenious efforts to shelter them. The Arabs were restless all night, and before sunrise we were again under way, and in the course of the day arrived at the convent of Baramous. This monastery consisted of a high stone wall, surrounding a square enclosure, of about an acre in extent. A large square tower commanded the narrow entrance, which was closed by a low and narrow iron door. Within there was a good-sized church in tolerable preservation, standing nearly in the centre of the enclosure, which contained nothing else but some ruined buildings and a few large fig-trees, growing out of the disjointed walls. Two or three poor-looking monks still tenanted the ruins of the abbey. They had hardly anything to offer us, and were glad to partake of some of the rice and other eatables which we had brought with us. I wandered about among the ruins with the half-starved monks following me. We went into the square tower, where, in a large vaulted room with open unglazed windows, were forty or fifty Coptic manuscripts on cotton paper, lying on the floor, to which several of them adhered firmly, not having been moved for many years. I only found one leaf on vellum, which I brought away. The other manuscripts appeared to be all liturgies; most of them smelling of incense when I opened them, and well smeared with dirt and wax from the candles which had been held over them during the reading of the service.

I took possession of a half-ruined cell, where my carpets were spread, and where I went to sleep early in the evening; but I had hardly closed my eyes before I was so briskly attacked by a multitude of ravenous fleas, that I jumped up and ran out into the court to shake myself and get rid if I could of my tormentors. The poor monks, hearing my exclamations, crept out of their holes and recommended me to go into the church, which they said would be safe from the attacks of the enemy. I accordingly took a carpet which I had well shaken and beaten, and lay down on the marble floor of the church, where I presently went to sleep. Again I was awakened by the wicked fleas, who, undeterred by the sanctity of my asylum, renewed their attack in countless legions. The slaps I gave myself were all in vain; for, although I slew them by dozens in my rage, others came on in their place. There was no withstanding them, and, fairly vanquished, I was forced to abandon my position, and walk about and look at the moon till the sun rose, when my villainous tormentors slunk away and allowed me a short snatch of the repose which they had prevented my enjoying all night.

There were several curious lamps in this church formed of ancient glass, like those in the mosque of Sultan Hassan at Cairo, which are said to be of the same date as the mosque, and to be of Syrian manufacture. These, which were in the shape of large open vases, were ornamented with pious sentences in Arabic characters, in blue on a white ground.[5] They were very handsome, and, except one of the same kind, which is now in England, in the possession of Mr. Magniac, I never saw any like them. They are probably some of the most ancient specimens of ornamental glass existing, excepting, of course, the vases and lachrymatories of the classic times.

Quitting the monastery of Baramous, we went to that of Souriani, where we left our baggage and tent, and proceeded to visit the monasteries of Amba Bischoi and Abou Magar, or St. Macarius, both of which were in very poor condition. These monasteries are so much alike in their plan and appearance, that the description of one is the description of all. I saw none but the church books in either of them, and at the time of my visit they were apparently inhabited only by three or four monks, who conducted the services of their respective churches.

On this journey we passed many ruins and heaps of stones nearly level with the ground, the remains of some of the fifty monasteries which once flourished in the wilderness of Scete.

In the evening I returned to Souriani, where I was hospitably received by the abbot and fourteen or fifteen Coptic monks. They provided me with an agreeable room looking into the garden within the walls. My servants were lodged in some other small cells or rooms near mine, which happily not being tenanted by fleas or any other wild beasts of prey, was exceedingly comfortable when my bright-coloured carpets and cushions were spread upon the floor; and, after the adventures of the two former nights, I rested in great comfort and peace.

In the morning I went to see the church and all the other wonders of the place, and on making inquiries about the library, was conducted by the old abbot, who was blind, and was constantly accompanied by another monk, into a small upper room in the great square tower, where we found several Coptic manuscripts. Most of these were lying on the floor, but some were placed in niches in the stone wall. They were all on paper, except three or four. One of these was a superb manuscript of the Gospels, with commentaries by the early fathers of the church; two others were doing duty as coverings to a couple of large open pots or jars, which had contained preserves, long since evaporated. I was allowed to purchase these vellum manuscripts, as they were considered to be useless by the monks, principally I believe because there were no more preserves in the jars. On the floor I found a fine Coptic and Arabic dictionary. I was aware of the existence of this volume, with which they refused to part. I placed it in one of the niches in the wall; and some years afterwards it was purchased for me by a friend, who sent it to England after it had been copied at Cairo. They sold me two imperfect dictionaries, which I discovered loaded with dust upon the ground. Besides these, I did not see any other books but those of the liturgies for various holy days. These were large folios on cotton paper, most of them of considerable antiquity, and well begrimed with dirt.

The old blind abbot had solemnly declared that there were no other books in the monastery besides those which I had seen; but I had been told, by a French gentleman at Cairo, that there were many ancient manuscripts in the monks' oil cellar; and it was in pursuit of these and the Coptic dictionary that I had undertaken the journey to the Natron lakes. The abbot positively denied the existence of these books, and we retired from the library to my room with the Coptic manuscripts which they had ceded to me without difficulty; and which, according to the dates contained in them, and from their general appearance, may claim to be considered among the oldest manuscripts in existence, more ancient certainly than many of the Syriac MSS. which I am about to describe.

The abbot, his companion, and myself sat down together. I produced a bottle of rosoglio from my stores, to which I knew that all Oriental monks were partial; for though they do not, I believe, drink wine because an excess in its indulgence is forbidden by Scripture, yet ardent spirits not having been invented in those times, there is nothing said about them in the Bible; and at Mount Sinai and all the other spots of sacred pilgrimage the monks comfort themselves with a little glass or rather a small coffee cup of arrack or raw spirits when nothing better of its kind is to be procured. Next to the golden key, which masters so many locks, there is no better opener of the heart than a sufficiency of strong drink,—not too much, but exactly the proper quantity judiciously exhibited (to use a chemical term in the land of Al Chémé, where alchemy and chemistry first had their origin). I have always found it to be invincible; and now we sat sipping our cups of the sweet pink rosoglio, and firing little compliments at each other, and talking pleasantly over our bottle till some time passed away, and the face of the blind abbot waxed bland and confiding; and he had that expression on his countenance which men wear when they are pleased with themselves and bear goodwill towards mankind in general. I had by the bye a great advantage over the good abbot, as I could see the workings of his features and he could not see mine, or note my eagerness about the oil-cellar, on the subject of which I again gradually entered. "There is no oil there," said he. "I am curious to see the architecture of so ancient a room," said I; "for I have heard that yours is a famous oil-cellar." "It is a famous cellar," said the other monk. "Take another cup of rosoglio," said I. "Ah!" replied he, "I remember the days when it overflowed with oil, and then there were I do not know how many brethren here with us. But now we are few and poor; bad times are come over us: we are not what we used to be." "I should like to see it very much," said I; "I have heard so much about it even at Cairo. Let us go and see it; and when we come back we will have another bottle; and I will give you a few more which I have brought with me for your private use."

This last argument prevailed. We returned to the great tower, and ascended the steep flight of steps which led to its door of entrance. We then descended a narrow staircase to the oil-cellar, a handsome vaulted room, where we found a range of immense vases which formerly contained the oil, but which now on being struck returned a mournful, hollow sound. There was nothing else to be seen: there were no books here: but taking the candle from the hands of one of the brethren (for they had all wandered in after us, having nothing else to do), I discovered a narrow low door, and, pushing it open, entered into a small closet vaulted with stone which was filled to the depth of two feet or more with the loose leaves of the Syriac manuscripts which now form one of the chief treasures of the British Museum. Here I remained for some time turning over the leaves and digging into the mass of loose vellum pages; by which exertions I raised such a cloud of fine pungent dust that the monks relieved each other in holding our only candle at the door, while the dust made us sneeze incessantly as we turned over the scattered leaves of vellum. I had extracted four books, the only ones I could find which seemed to be tolerably perfect, when two monks who were struggling in the corner pulled out a great big manuscript of a brown and musty appearance and of prodigious weight, which was tied together with a cord. "Here is a box!" exclaimed the two monks, who were nearly choked with the dust; "we have found a box, and a heavy one too!" "A box!" shouted the blind abbot, who was standing in the outer darkness of the oil-cellar—"A box! Where is it? Bring it out! bring out the box! Heaven be praised! We have found a treasure! Lift up the box! Pull out the box! A box! A box! Sandouk! sandouk!" shouted all the monks in various tones of voice. "Now then let us see the box! bring it out to the light!" they cried. "What can there be in it?" and they all came to help and carried it away up the stairs, the blind abbot following them to the outer door, leaving me to retrace my steps as I could with the volumes which I had dug out of their literary grave.

CHAPTER VIII.

View from the Convent Wall—Appearance of the Desert—Its grandeur and freedom—Its contrast to the Convent Garden—Beauty and luxuriance of Eastern Vegetation—Picturesque Group of the Monks and their Visitors—The Abyssinian Monks—Their appearance—Their austere mode of Life—The Abyssinian College—Description of the Library—The mode of Writing in Abyssinia—Immense Labour required to write an Abyssinian book—Paintings and Illuminations—Disappointment of the Abbot at finding the supposed Treasure-box only an old Book—Purchase of the MSS. and Books—The most precious left behind—Since acquired for the British Museum.

On

leaving the dark recesses of the tower I paused at the narrow door by which we had entered, both to accustom my eyes to the glare of the daylight, and to look at the scene below me. I stood on the top of a steep flight of stone steps, by which the door of the tower was approached from the court of the monastery: the steps ran up the inside of the outer wall, which was of sufficient thickness to allow of a narrow terrace within the parapet; from this point I could look over the wall on the left hand upon the desert, whose dusty plains stretched out as far as I could see, in hot and dreary loneliness to the horizon. To those who are not familiar with the aspect of such a region as this, it may be well to explain that a desert such as that which now surrounded me resembles more than anything else a dusty turnpike-road in England on a hot summer's day, extended interminably, both as to length and breadth. A country of low rounded hills, the surface of which is composed entirely of gravel, dust, and stones, will give a good idea of the general aspect of a desert. Yet, although parched and dreary in the extreme from their vastness and openness, there is something grand and sublime in the silence and loneliness of these burning plains; and the wandering tribes of Bedouins who inhabit them are seldom content to remain long in the narrow inclosed confines of cultivated land. There is always a fresh breeze in the desert, except when the terrible hot wind blows; and the air is more elastic and pure than where vegetation produces exhalations which in all hot climates are more or less heavy and deleterious. The air of the desert is always healthy, and no race of men enjoy a greater exemption from weakness, sickness, and disease than the children of the desert, who pass their lives in wandering to and fro in search of the scanty herbage on which their flocks are fed, far from the cares and troubles of busy cities, and free from the oppression which grinds down the half-starved cultivators of the fertile soil of Egypt.

Whilst from my elevated position I looked out on my left upon the mighty desert, on my right how different was the scene! There below my feet lay the convent garden in all the fresh luxuriance of tropical vegetation. Tufts upon tufts of waving palms overshadowed the immense succulent leaves of the banana, which in their turn rose out of thickets of the pomegranate rich with its bright green leaves and its blossoms of that beautiful and vivid red which is excelled by few even of the most brilliant flowers of the East. These were contrasted with the deep dark green of the caroub or locust-tree; and the yellow apples of the lotus vied with the clusters of green limes with their sweet white flowers which luxuriated in a climate too hot and sultry for the golden fruit of the orange, which is not to be met with in the valley of the Nile. Flowers and fair branches exhaling rich perfume and bearing freshness in their very aspect became more beautiful from their contrast to the dreary arid plains outside the convent walls, and this great difference was owing solely to there being a well of water in this spot from which a horse or mule was constantly employed to draw the fertilizing streams which nourished the teeming vegetation of this monastic garden.

I stood gazing and moralizing at these contrasted scenes for some time; but at length when I turned my eyes upon my companions and myself, it struck me that we also were somewhat remarkable in our way. First there was the old blind grey-bearded abbot, leaning on his staff, surrounded with three or four dark robed Coptic monks, holding in their hands the lighted candles with which we had explored the secret recesses of the oil-cellar; there was I dressed in the long robes of a merchant of the East, with a small book in the breast of my gown and a big one under each arm; and there were my servants armed to the teeth and laden with old books; and one and all we were so covered with dirt and wax from top to toe, that we looked more as if we had been up the chimney than like quiet people engaged in literary researches. One of the monks was leaning in a brown study upon the ponderous and gigantic volume in its primæval binding, in the interior of which the blind abbot had hoped to find a treasure. Perched upon the battlements of this remote monastery we formed as picturesque a group as one might wish to see; though perhaps the begrimed state of our flowing robes as well as of our hands and faces would render a somewhat remote point of view more agreeable to the artist than a closer inspection.

While we had been standing on the top of the steps, I had heard from time to time some incomprehensible sounds which seemed to arise from among the green branches of the palms and fig-trees in a corner of the garden at our feet. "What," said I to a bearded Copt, who was seated on the steps, "is that strange howling noise which I hear among the trees? I have heard it several times when the rustling of the wind among the branches has died away for a moment. It sounds something like a chant, or a dismal moaning song: only it is different in its cadence from anything that I have heard before." "That noise," replied the monk, "is the sound of the service of the church which is being chanted by the Abyssinian monks. Come down the steps and I will show you their chapel and their library. The monastery which they frequented in this desert has fallen to decay; and they now live here, their numbers being recruited occasionally by pilgrims on their way from Abyssinia to Jerusalem, some of whom pass by each year; not many now, to be sure; but still fewer return to their own land."

Giving up my precious manuscripts to the guardianship of my servants and desiring them to put them down carefully in my cell, I accompanied my Coptic friend into the garden, and turning round some bushes, we immediately encountered one of the Abyssinian monks walking with a book in his hand under the shade of the trees. Presently we saw three or four more; and very remarkable looking persons they were. These holy brethren were as black as crows; tall, thin, ascetic looking men of a most original aspect and costume. I have seen the natives of many strange nations, both before and since, but I do not know that I ever met with so singular a set of men, so completely the types of another age and of a state of things the opposite to European, as these Abyssinian Eremites. They were black, as I have already said, which is not the usual complexion of the natives of Habesh; and they were all clothed in tunics of wash leather made, they told me, of gazelle skins. This garment came down to their knees, and was confined round their waist with a leathern girdle. Over their shoulders they had a strap supporting a case like a cartridge-box, of thick brown leather, containing a manuscript book; and above this they wore a large shapeless cloak or toga, of the same light yellow wash leather as the tunic; I do not think that they wore anything on the head, but this I do not distinctly remember. Their legs were bare, and they had no other clothing, if I may except a profuse smearing of grease; for they had anointed themselves in the most lavish manner, not with the oil of gladness, but with that of castor, which however had by no means the effect of giving them a cheerful countenance; for although they looked exceedingly slippery and greasy, they seemed to be an austere and dismal set of fanatics: true disciples of the great Macarius, the founder of these secluded monasteries, and excellently calculated to figure in that grim chorus of his invention, or at least which is called after his name, "La danse Macabre," known to us by the appellation of the Dance of Death. They seemed to be men who fasted much and feasted little; great observers were they of vigils, of penance, of pilgrimages, and midnight masses; eaters of bitter herbs for conscience' sake. It was such men as these who lived on the tops of columns, and took up their abodes in tombs, and thought it was a sign of holiness to look like a wild beast—that it was wicked to be clean, and superfluous to be useful in this world; and who did evil to themselves that good might come. Poor fellows! they meant well, and knew no better; and what more can be said for the endeavours of the best of men?

Accompanied by a still increasing number of these wild priests we traversed the shady garden, and came to a building with a flat roof, which stood in the south-east corner of the enclosure and close to the outer wall. This was the college or consistory of the Abyssinian monks, and the accompanying sketch made upon the spot will perhaps explain the appearance of this room better than any written description. The round thing upon the floor is a table upon which the dishes of their frugal meal were set; by the side of this low table we sat upon the ground on the skin of some great wild beast, which did duty as a carpet. This room was also their library, and on my remarking the number of books which I saw around me they seemed proud of their collection, and told me that there were not many such libraries as this in their country. There were perhaps nearly fifty volumes, and as the entire literature of Abyssinia does not include more than double that number of works, I could easily imagine that what I saw around me formed a very considerable accumulation of manuscripts, considering the barbarous state of the country from which they came.

INTERIOR OF THE ABYSSINIAN LIBRARY, IN THE MONASTERY OF SOURIANI ON THE NATRON LAKES.

INTERIOR OF THE ABYSSINIAN LIBRARY, IN THE MONASTERY OF SOURIANI ON THE NATRON LAKES.Abyssinian monk clothed in leather. The dining table. The blind abbot leaning over the Author. Abyssinian monk. Coptic monk. The books hanging from wooden pegs let into the wall. The Author's Egyptian servants.

The disposition of the manuscripts in this library was very original. I have had no means of ascertaining whether all the libraries of Abyssinia are arranged in the same style. The room was about twenty-six feet long, twenty wide, and twelve high; the roof was formed of the trunks of palm trees, across which reeds were laid, which supported the mass of earth and plaster, of which the terrace roof was composed; the interior of the walls was plastered white with lime; the windows, at a good height from the ground, were unglazed, but were defended with bars of iron-wood or some other hard wood; the door opened into the garden, and its lock, which was of wood also, was of that peculiar construction which has been used in Egypt from time immemorial. A wooden shelf was carried in the Egyptian style round the walls, at the height of the top of the door, and on this shelf stood sundry platters, bottles, and dishes for the use of the community. Underneath the shelf various long wooden pegs projected from the wall; they were each about a foot and a half long, and on them hung the Abyssinian manuscripts, of which this curious library was entirely composed.

The books of Abyssinia are bound in the usual way, sometimes in red leather and sometimes in wooden boards, which are occasionally elaborately carved in rude and coarse devices: they are then enclosed in a case, tied up with leather thongs; to this case is attached a strap for the convenience of carrying the volume over the shoulders, and by these straps the books were hung to the wooden pegs, three or four on a peg, or more if the books were small: their usual size was that of a small, very thick quarto. The appearance of the room, fitted up in this style, together with the presence of various long staves, such as the monks of all the Oriental churches lean upon at the time of prayer, resembled less a library than a barrack or guard-room, where the soldiers had hung their knapsacks and cartridge-boxes against the wall.

All the members of this church militant could read fluently out of their own books, which is more than the Copts could do in whose monastery they were sojourning. Two or three, with whom I spoke, were intelligent men, although not much enlightened as to the affairs of this world: the perfume of their leather garments and oily bodies was, however, rather too powerful for my olfactory nerves, and after making a slight sketch of their library I was glad to escape into the open air of the beautiful garden, where I luxuriated in the shade of the palms and the pomegranates. The strange costumes and wild appearance of these black monks, and the curious arrangement of their library, the uncouth sounds of their singing and howling, and the clash of their cymbals in the ancient convent of the Natron lakes, formed a scene such as I believe few Europeans have witnessed.

The labour required to write an Abyssinian book is immense, and sometimes many years are consumed in the preparation of a single volume. They are almost all written upon skins; the only one not written upon vellum that I have met with is in my own possession; it is on charta bombycina. The ink which they use is composed of gum, lampblack, and water. It is jet black, and keeps its colour for ever: indeed in this respect all Oriental inks are infinitely superior to ours, and they have the additional advantage of not being corrosive or injurious either to the pen or paper. Their pen is the reed commonly used in the East, only the nib is made sharper than that which is required to write the Arabic character. The ink-horn is usually the small end of a cow's horn, which is stuck into the ground at the feet of the scribe. In the most ancient Greek frescos and illuminations this kind of ink-horn is the one generally represented, and it seems to have been usually inserted in a hole in the writing-desk: no writing-desk, however, is in use among the children of Habesh. Seated upon the ground, the square piece of thick greasy vellum is held upon the knee or on the palm of the left hand.

The Abyssinian alphabet consists of 8 times 26 letters, 208 characters in all, and these are each written distinctly and separately like the letters of an European printed book. They have no cursive writing; each letter is therefore painted, as it were, with the reed pen, and as the scribe finishes each he usually makes a horrible face and gives a triumphant flourish with his pen. Thus he goes on letter by letter, and before he gets to the end of the first line he is probably in a perspiration from his nervous apprehension of the importance of his undertaking. One page is a good day's work, and when he has done it he generally, if he is not too stiff, follows the custom of all little Arab boys, and swings his head or his body from side to side, keeping time to a sort of nasal recitative, without the help of which it would seem that few can read even a chapter of the Koran, although they may know it by heart.

Some of these manuscripts are adorned with the quaintest and grimmest illuminations conceivable. The colours are composed of various ochres. In general the outlines of the figures are drawn first with the pen. The paint brush is made by chewing the end of a reed till it is reduced to filaments and then nibbling it into a proper form: the paint brushes of the ancient Egyptians were made in the same way, and excellent brooms for common purposes are made at Cairo by beating the thick end of a palm-branch till the fibres are separated from the pith, the part above, which is not beaten, becoming the handle of the broom. The Abyssinian having nibbled and chewed his reed till he thinks it will do, proceeds to fill up the spaces between the inked outlines with his colours. The Blessed Virgin is usually dressed in blue; the complexion of the figures is a brownish red, and those in my possession have a curious cast of the eyes, which gives them a very cunning look. St John, in a MS. which I have now before me, is represented with woolly hair, and has two marks or gashes on each side of his face, in accordance with the Abyssinian or Galla custom of cutting through the skin of the face, breast, and arms, so as to leave an indelible mark. This is done in youth, and is said to preserve the patient from several diseases. The colours are mixed up with the yolk of an egg, and the numerous mistakes and slips of the brush are corrected by a wipe from a wet finger or thumb, which is generally kept ready in the artist's mouth during the operation; and it is lucky if he does not give it a bite in the agony of composition, when with an unsteady hand the eye of some famous saint is smeared all over the nose by an unfortunate swerve of the nibbled reed.

It is not often, however, that the arts of drawing and painting are thus ruthlessly mangled on the pages of their books, and notwithstanding the disadvantages under which the writers labour, some of these manuscripts are beautifully written, and are worthy of being compared with the best specimens of calligraphy in any language. I have a MS. containing the book of Enoch, and several books of the Old Testament, which is remarkable for the perfection of its writing, the straightness of the lines, and the equal size and form of the characters throughout: probably many years were required to finish it. The binding is of wooden boards, not sawn or planed, but chopped apparently out of a tree or a block of hard wood, a task of patience and difficulty which gives evidence of the enthusiasm and goodwill which have been displayed in the production of a work, in toiling upon which the pious man in the simplicity of his heart doubtless considered that he was labouring for the honour of the church, ad majorem Dei gloriam. It was this feeling which in the middle ages produced all those glorious works of art which are the admiration of modern times, and its total absence now is deeply to be deplored in our own country.

Having satiated my curiosity as to the Abyssinian monks and their curious library, I returned to my own room, where I was presently joined by the abbot and his companion, who came for the promised bottle of rosoglio, which they now required the more to keep up their spirits on finding that the box of treasure was only a large old book. They murmured and talked to themselves between the cups of rosoglio, and so great was their disappointment that it was some time before they recovered the equilibrium of their minds. "You found no treasure," I remarked, "but I am a lover of old books; let me have the big one which you thought was a box and the others which I have brought out with me, and I will give you a certain number of piastres in exchange. By this arrangement we shall be both of us contented, for the money will be useful to you, and I should be glad to carry away the books as a memorial of my visit to this interesting spot." "Ah!" said the abbot. "Another cup of rosoglio," said I; "help yourself." "How much will you give?" asked the abbot. "How much do you want?" said I; "all the money I have with me is at your service." "How much is that?" he inquired. Out came the bag of money, and the agreeable sound of the clinking of the pieces of gold or dollars, I forget which they were, had a soothing effect upon the nerves of the blind man, and in short the bottle and the bargain were concluded at the same moment.

The Coptic and Syriac manuscripts were stowed away in one side of a great pair of saddle-bags. "Now," said I, "we will put these in the other side, and you shall take it out and see the Arabs place it on the camel." We could not by any packing or shifting get all the books into the bag, and the two monks would not let me make another parcel, lest, as I understood, the rest of the brethren should discover what it was, and claim their share of the spoil. In this dreadful dilemma I looked at each of the books, not knowing which to leave behind, but seeing that the quarto was the most imperfect, I abandoned it, and I have now reason to believe, on seeing the manuscripts of the British Museum, that this was the famous book with the date of A.D.

411, the most precious acquisition to any library that has been made in modern times, with the exception, as I conceive, of some in my own collection. It is, however, a satisfaction to think that this book, which contains some lost epistles of St. Ignatius, has not been thrown away, but has fallen into better hands than mine.

THE CONVENT OF THE PULLEY.
CHAPTER IX.

The Convent of the Pulley—Its inaccessible position—Difficult landing on the bank of the Nile—Approach to the Convent through the Rocks—Description of the Convent and its Inhabitants—Plan of the Church—Books and MSS.—Ancient excavations—Stone Quarries and ancient Tombs—Alarm of the Copts—Their ideas of a Sketch-book.

The

Coptic monasteries were usually built in desert or inaccessible places, with a view to their defence in troubled times, or in the hope of their escaping the observation of marauding parties, who were not likely to take the trouble of going much out of their way unless they had assured hopes of finding something better worth sacking than a poor convent. The access to Der el Adra, the Convent of the Virgin, more commonly known by the name of the Convent of the Pulley, is very singular. This monastery is situated on the top of the rocks of Gebel el terr, where a precipice above 200 feet in height is washed at its base by the waters of the Nile. When I visited this monastery on the 19th of February, 1838, there was a high wind, which rendered the management of my immense boat, above 80 feet long, somewhat difficult; and we were afraid of being dashed against the rocks if we ventured too near them in our attempt to land at the foot of the precipice. The monks, who were watching our manœuvres from above, all at once disappeared, and presently several of them made their appearance on the shore, issuing in a complete state of nudity from a cave or cleft in the face of the rock. These worthy brethren jumped one after another into the Nile, and assisted the sailors to secure the boat with ropes and anchors from the force of the wind. They swam like Newfoundland dogs, and, finding that it was impossible for the boat to reach the land, two of the reverend gentlemen took me on their shoulders and, wading through a shallow part of the river, brought me safely to the foot of the rock. When we got there I could not perceive any way to ascend to the monastery, but, following the abbot, I scrambled over the broken rocks to the entrance of the cave. This was a narrow fissure where the precipice had been split by some convulsion of nature, the opening being about the size of the inside of a capacious chimney. The abbot crept in at a hole at the bottom: he was robed in a long dark blue shirt, the front of which he took up and held in his teeth; and, telling me to observe where he placed his feet, he began to climb up the cleft with considerable agility. A few preliminary lessons from a chimney-sweep would now have been of the greatest service to me; but in this branch of art my education had been neglected, and it was with no small difficulty that I climbed up after the abbot, whom I saw striding and sprawling in the attitude of a spread eagle above my head. My slippers soon fell off upon the head of a man under me, whom, on looking down, I found to be the reis, or captain of my boat, whose immense turban formed the whole of his costume. At least twenty men were scrambling and puffing underneath him, most of them having their clothes tied in a bundle on their heads, where they had secured them when they swam or waded to the shore. Arms and legs were stretched out in all manner of attitudes, the forms of the more distant climbers being lost in the gloom of the narrow cavern up which we were advancing, the procession being led by the unrobed ecclesiastics. Having climbed up about 120 feet, we emerged in a fine perspiration upon a narrow ledge of the rock on the face of the precipice, which had an unpleasant slope towards the Nile. It was as slippery as glass; and I felt glad that I had lost my shoes, as I had a firmer footing without them. We turned to the right, and climbing a projection of the rock seven or eight feet high—rather a nervous proceeding at such a height to those who were unaccustomed to it—we gained a more level space, from which a short steep pathway brought us to the top of the precipice, whence I looked down with much self-complacency upon my companion who was standing on the deck of the vessel.

The convent stands about two hundred paces to the north of the place where we ascended. It had been originally built of small square stones of Roman workmanship; but, baring fallen into decay, it had been repaired with mud and sunburnt bricks. Its ground plan was nearly a square, and its general appearance outside was that of a large pound or a small kitchen garden, the walls being about 20 feet high and each side of the square extending about 200 feet, without any windows or architectural decoration. I entered by a low doorway on the side towards the cliff, and found myself in a yard of considerable size full of cocks, hens, women, and children, who were all cackling and talking together at the top of their shrill voices. A large yellow-coloured dog, who was sleeping in the sunshine in the midst of all this din, was awakened by its cessation as I entered. He greeted my arrival with a growl, upon which he was assailed with a volley of stones and invectives by the ladies whom he had intended to protect. Every man, woman, and child came out to have a peep at the stranger, but when my numerous followers, many in habiliments of the very slightest description, crowded into the court, the ladies took fright, and there was a general rush into the house, the old women hiding their faces without a moment's delay, but the younger ones taking more time in the adjustment of their veils. When peace was in some measure restored, and the poor dog had been pelted into a hole, the abbot, who had now permitted his long shirt to resume its usual folds, conducted me to the church, which was speedily filled with the crowd. It was interesting from its great antiquity, having been founded, as they told me, by a rich lady of the name of Halané, who was the daughter of a certain Kostandi, king of Roum. The church is partly subterranean, being built in the recesses of an ancient stone-quarry; the other parts of it are of stone plastered over. The roof is flat and is formed of horizontal beams of palm trees, upon which a terrace of reeds and earth is laid. The height of the interior is about 25 feet. On entering the door we had to descend a flight of narrow steps, which led into a side aisle about ten feet wide, and which is divided from the nave by octagon columns of great thickness supporting the walls of a sort of clerestory. The columns were surmounted by heavy square plinths almost in the Egyptian style.

As I consider this church to be interesting from its being half a catacomb, or cave, and one of the earliest Christian buildings which has preserved its originality, I subjoin a plan of it, by which it will be seen that it is constructed on the principle of a Latin basilica, as the buildings of the Empress Helena usually were; the Byzantine style of architecture, the plan of which partook of the form of a Greek cross, being a later invention; for the earliest Christian churches were not cruciform, and seldom had transepts, nor were they built with any reference to the points of the compass.[8]

Plan of the church, the convent of the Pulley.
Plan of the church, the convent of the Pulley.1.   Altar.   6.   Two three-quarter columns.
2.   Apsis, apparently cut out of the rock.   7.   Eight columns.[6]
3.   Two Corinthian columns.   8.   Dark room cut out of the rock
(there is another corresponding to it under the steps).[7]
4.   Wooden partitions of lattice-work, about 10 ft. high.   9.   Steps leading down into the church.
5.   Steps leading up to the sanctuary.   10.   Screen before the Altar.

The ancient divisions of the church are also more strictly preserved in this edifice than in the churches of the West; the priests or monks standing above the steps (marked No. 5), the celebrant of the sacrament only going behind the screen (No. 10); the bulk of the congregation stand, there are no seats below the steps (No. 5), and the place for the women is behind the screen marked No. 4. The church is very dimly lighted by small apertures in the walls of the clerestory, above the columns, and the part about the absis is nearly dark in the middle of the day, candles being always necessary during the reading of the service. The two Corinthian columns are of brick, plastered; they are not fluted, but are of good proportions and appear to be original. The absis is of regular Grecian or Roman architecture, and is ornamented with six pilasters, and three niches in which are kept the books, cymbals, candlesticks, and other things which are used for the daily service. Here I found twenty-three manuscript books, fifteen in Coptic with Arabic translations, for the Coptic language is now understood by few, and eight Arabic manuscripts. The Coptic books were all liturgies: one of them, a folio, was ornamented with a large illumination, intended to represent the Virgin and the infant Saviour; it is almost the only specimen of Coptic art that I ever met with in a book, and its style and execution are so poor, that, perhaps, it is fortunate that they should be so rare. The Arabic books, which, as well as the Coptic, were all on cotton-paper, consisted of extracts from the New Testament and lives of the saints.

I had been told that there was a great chest bound with iron, which was kept in a vault in this monastery, full of ancient books on vellum, and which was not to be opened without the consent of the Patriarch; I could, however, make out nothing of this story, but it does not follow that this chest of ancient manuscripts does not exist; for, surrounded as I was by crowds of gaping Copts and Arabs, I could not expect the abbot to be very communicative; and they have from long oppression acquired such a habit of denying the fact of their having anything in their possession, that, perhaps, there may still be treasures here which some future traveller may discover.

While I was turning over the books, the contents of which I was able to decypher, from the similarity of the Coptic to the Greek alphabet, the people were very much astonished at my erudition, which appeared to them almost miraculous. They whispered to each other, and some said I must be a foreign Copt, who had returned to the land of his fathers. They asked my servant all manner of questions; but when he told them that he did not believe I knew a word of Coptic, their astonishment was increased to fear. I must be a magician, they said, and some kept a sharp look-out for the door, to which there was an immediate rush when I turned round. The whole assembly were puzzled, for in their simplicity they were not aware that people sometimes pore over books, and read them too, without understanding them, in other languages besides Coptic.

We emerged from the subterranean church, which, being half sunk in the earth and surrounded by buildings, had nothing remarkable in its exterior architecture, and ascended to the terrace on the roof of the convent, whence we had a view of numerous ancient stone quarries in the desert to the east. They appeared to be of immense extent; the convent itself and two adjoining burial-grounds were all ensconced in the ancient limestone excavations.

I am inclined to think, that although all travellers in Egypt pass along the river below this convent, few have visited its interior. It is now more a village than a monastery, properly speaking, as it is inhabited by numerous Coptic families who are not connected with the monks. These poor people were so surprised at my appearance, and watched all my actions with such intense curiosity, that I imagine they had scarcely ever seen a stranger before. They crowded every place where I was likely to pass, staring and gaping, and chattering to each other. Being much pressed with the throng in the court-yard, I made a sudden spring towards one of the little girls who was foremost in the crowd, uttering a shout at the same time as if I was going to seize her as she stood gazing openmouthed at me. She screamed and tumbled down with fright, and the whole multitude of women and children scampered off as fast as their legs could carry them. Some fell down, others tumbled over them, making an indescribable confusion; but being reassured by the laughter of my party, they soon stopped and began laughing and talking with greater energy than before. At length I took refuge in the room of the superior, who gave me some coffee, with spices in it; and soon afterwards I took leave of this singular community.

We walked to some quarries about two miles off to the north-east, which well repaid our visit The rocks were cut into the most extraordinary forms. There were several grottos, and also an ancient tomb with hieroglyphics sculptured on the rock. Among these I saw the names of Rameses II. and some other kings. Near this tomb is a large tablet on which is a bas-relief of a king making an offering to a deity with the head of a crocodile, whose name, according to Wilkinson, was Savak: he was worshipped at Ombos and Thebes, but was held in such small respect at Dendera that the inhabitants of that place made war upon the men of Ombos, and ate one of their prisoners, in emulation probably of the god he worshipped. Indeed, they appear to have considered the inhabitants of that city to have been a sort of vermin which it was incumbent upon all sensible Egyptians to destroy whenever they had an opportunity.

In one place among the quarries a large rock has been left standing by itself with two apertures, like doorways, cut through it, giving it the resemblance of a propylon or the front of a house. It is not more than ten feet thick, although it is eighty or ninety feet long, and fifty high. Near it a huge slab projects horizontally from the precipice, supported at its outer edge by a single column. Some of the Copts, whose curiosity appeared to be insatiable, had followed us to these quarries, for the mere pleasure of staring at us. One of them, observing me making a sketch, came and peeped over my shoulder. "This Frank," said he to his friends, "has got a book that eats all these stones, and our monastery besides." "Ah!" said the other, "I suppose there are no stones in his country, so he wants to take some of ours away to show his countrymen what fine things we have here in Egypt; there is no place like Egypt, after all. Mashallah!"

RUINED MONASTERY AT THEBES.
CHAPTER X.

Ruined Monastery in the Necropolis of Thebes—"Mr. Hay's Tomb"—The Coptic Carpenter—His acquirements and troubles—He agrees to show the MSS. belonging to the ruined Monastery, which are under his charge—Night visit to the Tomb in which they are concealed—Perils of the way—Description of the Tomb—Probably in former times a Christian Church—Examination of the Coptic MSS.—Alarming interruption—Hurried flight from the Evil Spirits—Fortunate escape—Appearance of the Evil Spirit—Observations on Ghost Stories—The Legend of the Old Woman of Berkeley considered.

On

a rocky hill, perforated on all sides by the violated sepulchres of the ancient Egyptians, in the great Necropolis of Thebes, not far from the ruins of the palace and temple of Medinet Habou, stand the crumbling walls of an old Coptic monastery, which I was told had been inhabited, almost within the memory of man, by a small community of Christian monks. I was living at this period in a tomb, which was excavated in the side of the precipice, above Sheick Abd el Gournoo. It had been rendered habitable by some slight alterations, and a little garden was made on the terrace in front of it, whence the view was very remarkable. The whole of the vast ruins of Thebes were stretched out below it; whilst, beyond the mighty Nile, the huge piles of Luxor and Carnac loomed dark and mysterious in the distance, which was bounded by the arid chain of the Arabian mountains, the outline of their wild tops showing clear and hard against the cloudless sky. This habitation was known by the name of "Mr. Hay's tomb." The memory of this gentleman is held in the highest honour and reverence by the villagers of the surrounding districts, who look back to the time of his residence among them as the only satisfactory period of their miserable existence.

One of the numerous admirers of Mr. Hay, among the poorer inhabitants of the neighbourhood, was a Coptic carpenter, a man of no small natural genius and talent, who in any other country would have risen above the sphere of his comrades if any opportunity of distinguishing himself had offered. He could read and write Coptic and Arabic; he had some knowledge of astronomy, and some said of magic also; and he was a very tolerable carpenter, although the only tools which he was able to procure were of the roughest sort. In all these accomplishments he was entirely self-taught; while his poverty was such that his costume consisted of nothing but a short shirt, or tunic, made of a homespun fabric of goat's hair, or wool, and a common felt skull-cap, with some rags twisted round it for a turban. With higher acquirements than the governor of the district, the poor Copt was hardly able to obtain bread to eat; and indeed it was only from the circumstance of his being a Christian that he and the other males of his family were not swept away in the conscription which has depopulated Egypt under the present government more than all the pillage and massacres and internal feuds of the followers of the Mameluke Beys.

On those numerous occasions when the carpenter had nothing else to do, he used to come and talk to me; and endeavour to count up, upon his fingers, how often he had "eat stick;" that is, had been beaten by one Turkish officer or another for his inability to pay the tax to the Pasha, the tooth-money to some kawass, the forced contribution to the Nazir, or some other expected or unexpected call upon his empty pocket,—an appendage to his dress, by the by, which he did not possess; for having nothing in the world to put in it, a pocket was clearly of no use to him. The carpenter related to me the history of the ruined Coptic monastery; and I found that its library was still in existence. It was carefully concealed from the Mahomedans, as a sacred treasure; and my friend the carpenter was the guardian of the volumes belonging to his fallen church. After some persuasion he agreed, in consideration of my being a Christian, to let me see them; but he said I must go to the place where they were concealed at night, in order that no one might follow our steps; and he further stipulated that none of the Mahomedan servants should accompany us, but that I should go alone with him. I agreed to all this; and on the appointed night I sallied forth with the carpenter after dark. There were not many stars visible; and we had only just light enough to see our way across the plain of Thebes, or rather among the low hills and narrow valleys above the plain, which are so entirely honeycombed with ancient tombs and mummy pits that they resemble a rabbit warren on a large scale. Skulls and bones were strewed on our path; and often at the mouths of tombs the night wind would raise up fragments of the bandages which the sacrilegious hand of the Frankish spoilers of the dead had torn from the bodies of the Egyptian mummies in search of the scarabæi, amulets, and ornaments which are found upon the breast of the deceased subjects of the Pharaohs.

Away we went stumbling over ruins, and escaping narrowly the fate of those who descend into the tomb before their time. Sometimes we heard a howl, which the carpenter said came from a hyena, prowling like ourselves among the graves, though on a very different errand. We kept on our way, by many a dark ruin and yawning cave, breaking our shins against the fallen stones until I was almost tired of the journey, which in the darkness seemed interminable; nor had I any idea where the carpenter was leading me. At last, after a fatiguing walk, we descended suddenly into a place something like a gravel pit, one side of which was closed by the perpendicular face of a low cliff, in which a doorway half filled up with rubbish betokened the existence of an ancient tomb. By the side of this doorway sat a little boy, whom I discovered by the light of the moon, which had just risen, to be the carpenter's son, an intelligent lad, who often came to pay me a visit in company with his father. It was here that the Coptic manuscripts were concealed, and it was a spot well chosen for the purpose; for although I thought I had wandered about the Necropolis of Thebes in every direction, I had never stumbled upon this place before, neither could I ever find it afterwards, although I rode in that direction several times.

I now produced from my pocket three candles, which the carpenter had desired me to bring, one for him, one for his son, and one for myself. Having lit them, we entered into the doorway of the tomb, and passing through a short passage, found ourselves in a great sepulchral hall. The earth and sand which had been blown into the entrance formed an inclined plane, sloping downwards to another door sculptured with hieroglyphics, through which we passed into a second chamber, on the other side of which was a third doorway, leading into a magnificent subterranean hall, divided into three aisles by four square columns, two on each side. There may have been six columns, but I think there were only four. The walls and columns, or rather square piers which supported the roof, retained the brilliant white which is so much to be admired in the tombs of the kings and other stately sepulchres. On the walls were various hieroglyphics, and on the square piers tall figures of the gods of the infernal regions—Kneph, Khonso, and Osiris—were portrayed in brilliant colours, with their immense caps or crowns, and the heads of the jackal and other beasts. At the further end of this chamber was a stone altar, standing upon one or two steps, in an apsis or semicircular recess. As this is not usual in Egyptian tombs, I have since thought that this had probably been altered by the Copts in early times, and that, like the Christians of the West in the days of their persecution, they had met in secret in the tombs for the celebration of their rites, and had made use of this hall as a church, in the same way as we see the remains of chapels and places of worship in the catacombs of Rome and Syracuse. The inner court of the Temple of Medinet Habou has also been converted into a Christian church; and the worthy Copts have daubed over the beautifully executed pictures of Rameses II. with a coat of plaster, upon which they have painted the grim figures of St. George, and various old frightful saints and hermits, whose uncouth forms would almost give one the idea of their having served for a system of idolatry much less refined than the worship of the ancient gods of the heathen, whose places they have usurped in these gigantic temples.

The Coptic manuscripts, of which I was in search, were lying upon the steps of the altar, except one, larger than the rest, which was placed upon the altar itself. They were about eight or nine in number, all brown and musty looking books, written on cotton paper, or charta bombycina, a material in use in very early times. An edict or charter, on paper, exists, or at least did exist two years ago, in the museum of the Jesuits' College, called the Colleggio Romano, at Rome: its date was of the sixth century; and I have a Coptic manuscript written on paper of this kind, which was finished, as appears by a note at the end, in the year 1018: these are the oldest dates that I have met with in any manuscripts on paper.

Having found these ancient books we proceeded to examine their contents, and to accomplish this at our ease, we stuck the candles on the ground, and the carpenter and I sat down before them, while his son brought us the volumes from the steps of the altar, one by one.

The first which came to hand was a dusty quarto, smelling of incense, and well spotted with yellow wax, with all its leaves dogs-eared or worn round with constant use: this was a MS. of the lesser festivals. Another appeared to be of the same kind; a third was also a book for the church service. We puzzled over the next two or three, which seemed to be martyrologies, or lives of the saints; but while we were poring over them, we thought we heard a noise. "Oh! father of hammers," said I to the carpenter, "I think I heard a noise: what could it be?—I thought I heard something move." "Did you, hawaja?" (O merchant), said the carpenter; "it must have been my son moving the books, for what else could there be here?—No one knows of this tomb or of the holy manuscripts which it contains. Surely there can be nothing here to make a noise, for are we not here alone, a hundred feet under the earth, in a place where no one comes?—It is nothing: certainly it is nothing;" and so saying, he lifted up one of the candles and peered about in the darkness; but as there was nothing to be seen, and all was silent as the grave, he sat down again, and at our leisure we completed our examination of all the books which lay upon the steps.

They proved to be all church books, liturgies for different seasons, or homilies; and not historical, nor of any particular interest, either from their age or subject. There now remained only the great book upon the altar, a ponderous quarto, bound either in brown leather or wooden boards; and this the carpenter's son with difficulty lifted from its place, and laid it down before us on the ground; but, as he did so, we heard the noise again. The carpenter and I looked at each other: he turned pale—perhaps I did so too; and we looked over our shoulders in a sort of anxious, nervous kind of way, expecting to see something—we did not know what. However, we saw nothing; and, feeling a little ashamed, I again settled myself before the three candle-ends, and opened the book, which was written in large black characters of unusual size. As I bent over the huge volume, to see what it was about, suddenly there arose a sound somewhere in the cavern, but from whence it came I could not comprehend; it seemed all round us at the same moment. There was no room for doubt now: it was a fearful howling, like the roar of a hundred wild beasts. The carpenter looked aghast: the tall and grisly figures of the Egyptian gods seemed to stare at us from the walls. I thought of Cornelius Agrippa, and felt a gentle perspiration coming on which would have betokened a favourable crisis in a fever. Suddenly the dreadful roar ceased, and as its echoes died away in the tomb, we felt considerably relieved, and were beginning to try and put a good face upon the matter, when, to our unutterable horror, it began again, and waxed louder and louder, as if legions of infernal spirits were let loose upon us. We could stand this no longer: the carpenter and I jumped up from the ground, and his son in his terror stumbled over the great Coptic manuscript, and fell upon the candles, which were all put out in a moment; his screams were now added to the uproar which resounded in the cave: seeing the twinkling of a star through the vista of the two outer chambers, we all set off as hard as we could run, our feelings of alarm being increased to desperation when we perceived that something was chasing us in the darkness, while the roar seemed to increase every moment. How we did tear along! The devil take the hindmost seemed about to be literally fulfilled; and we raised stifling clouds of dust, as we scrambled up the steep slope which led to the outer door. "So then," thought I, "the stories of gins, and ghouls, and goblins, that I have read of and never believed, must be true after all, and in this city of the dead it has been our evil lot to fall upon a haunted tomb!"

Breathless and bewildered, the carpenter and I bolted out of this infernal palace into the open air, mightily relieved at our escape from the darkness and the terrors of the subterranean vaults. We had not been out a moment, and had by no means collected our ideas, before our alarm was again excited to its utmost pitch.

The evil one came forth in bodily shape, and stood revealed to our eyes distinctly in the pale light of the moon.

While we were gazing upon the appearance, the carpenter's son, whom we had quite forgotten in our hurry, came creeping out of the doorway of the tomb upon his hands and knees.

"Why, father!" said he, after a moment's silence, "if that is not old Fatima's donkey, which has been lost these two days! It is lucky that we have found it, for it must have wandered into this tomb, and it might have been starved if we had not met with it to-night."

The carpenter looked rather ashamed of the adventure; and as for myself, though I was glad that nothing worse had come of it, I took comfort in the reflection that I was not the first person who had been alarmed by the proceedings of an ass.

I have related the history of this adventure because I think that, on some foundation like this, many well-accredited ghost stories may have been founded. Numerous legends and traditions, which appear to be supernatural or miraculous, and the truth of which has been attested and sworn to by credible witnesses, have doubtless arisen out of facts which actually did occur, but of which some essential particulars have been either concealed, or had escaped notice; and thus many marvellous histories have gone abroad, which are so well attested, that although common sense forbids their being believed, they cannot be proved to be false. In this case, if the donkey had not fortunately come out and shown himself, I should certainly have returned to Europe half impressed with the belief that something supernatural had occurred, which was in some mysterious manner connected with the opening of the magic volume which we had taken from the altar in the tomb. The echoes of the subterranean cave so altered the sound of the donkey's bray, that I never should have discovered that these fearful sounds had so undignified an origin; a story never loses by telling, and with a little gradual exaggeration it would soon have become one of the best accredited supernatural histories in the country.

The well-known story of the old woman of Berkeley has been read with wonder and dread for at least four hundred years: it is to be found in early manuscripts; it is related by Olaus Magnus, and is to be seen illustrated by a woodcut, both in the German and Latin editions of the 'Nuremberg Chronicle,' which was printed in the year 1493. There is no variation in the legend, which is circumstantially the same in all these books. Without doubt it was partly founded upon fact, or, as in the case of the story of the Theban tomb, some circumstances have been omitted which make all the difference; and a natural though perhaps extraordinary occurrence has been handed down for centuries, as a fearful instance of the power of the evil one in this world over those who have given themselves up to the practice of tremendous crimes.

There are many supernatural stories, which we are certain cannot by any possibility be true; but which nevertheless are as well attested, and apparently as fully proved, as any facts in the most veracious history. Under circumstances of alarm or temporary hallucination people frequently believe that they have had supernatural visitations. Even the tricks of conjurers, which have been witnessed by a hundred persons at a time, are totally incomprehensible to the uninitiated; and in the middle ages, when these practices were resorted to for religious or political ends, it is more than probable that many occurrences which were supposed to be supernatural might have been explained, if all the circumstances connected with them had been fairly and openly detailed by an impartial witness.

THE WHITE MONASTERY.
CHAPTER XI.

The White Monastery—Abou Shenood—Devastations of the Mamelukes—Description of the Monastery—Different styles of its exterior and interior Architecture—Its ruinous condition—Description of the Church—The Baptistery—Ancient Rites of Baptism—The Library—Modern Architecture—The Church of San Francesco at Rimini—The Red Monastery—Alarming rencontre with an armed party—Feuds between the native Tribes—Faction fights—Eastern Story Tellers—Legends of the Desert—Abraham and Sarah—Legendary Life of Moses—Arabian Story-tellers—Attention of their Audience.

Mounting
our noble Egyptian steeds, or in other words having engaged a sufficient number of little braying donkeys, which the peasants brought down to the river side, and put our saddles on them, we cantered in an hour and a half from the village of Souhag to the White Monastery, which is known to the Arabs by the name of Derr abou Shenood. Who the great Abou Shenood had the honour to be, and what he had done to be canonized, I could meet with no one to tell me. He was, I believe, a Mahomedan saint, and this Coptic monastery had been in some sort placed under the shadow of his protection, in the hopes of saving it from the persecutions of the faithful. Abou Shenood, however, does not appear to have done his duty, for the White Monastery has been ruined and sacked over and over again. The last outrage upon the unfortunate monastery occurred about 1812, when the Mamelukes who had encamped upon the plains of Itfou, having no better occupation, amused themselves by burning all the houses, and killing all the people in the neighbourhood. Since that time the monks having returned one by one, and finding that no one took the trouble to molest them, began to repair the convent, the interior of which had been gutted by the Mamelukes; but the immense strength of the outer walls had resisted all their efforts to destroy them.

The peculiarity of this monastery is, that the interior was once a magnificent basilica, while the exterior was built by the Empress Helena, in the ancient Egyptian style. The walls slope inwards towards the summit, where they are crowned with a deep overhanging cornice. The building is of an oblong shape, about two hundred feet in length by ninety wide, very well built, of fine blocks of stone; it has no windows outside larger than loopholes, and these are at a great height from the ground. Of these there are twenty on the south side and nine at the east end. The monastery stands at the foot of the hill, on the edge of the Libyan desert, where the sand encroaches on the plain. It looks like the sanctuary, or cella, of an ancient temple, and is not unlike the bastion of an old-fashioned fortification; except one solitary doom tree, it stands quite alone, and has a most desolate aspect, backed, as it is, by the sandy desert, and without any appearance of a garden, either within or outside its walls. The ancient doorway of red granite, on the south side, has been partially closed up, leaving an opening just large enough to admit one person at a time.

The door was closed, and we shouted in vain for admittance. We then tried the effect of a double knock in the Grosvenor Square style with a large stone, but that was of no use; so I got one still larger, and banged away at the door with all my might, shouting at the same time that we were friends and Christians. After some minutes a small voice was heard inside, and several questions being satisfactorily answered, we were let in by a monk; and passing through the narrow door, I found myself surrounded by piles of ruined buildings of various ages, among which the tall granite columns of the ancient church reared themselves like an avenue on either side of the desecrated nave, which is now open to the sky, and is used as a promenade for a host of chickens. Some goats also were perched upon fragments of ruined walls, and looked cunningly at us as we invaded their domain. I saw some Coptic women peeping at me from the windows of some wretched hovels of mud and brick, which they had built up in corners among the ancient ruins like swallows' nests.

There were but three poor priests. The principal one led us to the upper part of the church, which had lately been repaired and walled off from the open nave; and enclosed the apsis and transepts, which had been restored in some measure, and fitted for the performance of divine service. The half domes of the apsis and two transepts, which were of well-built masonry, were still entire, and the original frescos remain upon them. Those in the transepts are stiff figures of saints; and in the one over the altar is the great figure of the Redeemer, such as is usually met with in the mosaics of the Italian basilicas. These apsides are above fifty feet from the ground, which gives them a dignity of appearance, and leaves greater cause to regret the destruction of the nave, which, with its clerestory, must have been still higher. There appear to have been fifteen columns on each side of the centre aisle, and two at the end opposite the altar, which in this instance I believe is at the west end. The roof over the part of the east end, which has been fitted up as a church, is supported by four square modern piers of plastered brick or rubble work. On the side walls, above the altar, there are some circular compartments containing paintings of the saints; and near these are two tablets with inscriptions in black on a white ground. That on the left appeared to be in Abyssinian: the one on the other side was either Coptic or uncial Greek; but it was too dark, and the tablet was too high, to enable me to make it out There is also a long Greek inscription in red letters on one of the modern square piers, which looks as if it was of considerable antiquity; and the whole interior of the building bears traces of having been repaired and altered, more than once, in ancient times. The richly ornamented recesses of the three apsides have been smeared over with plaster, on which some tremendously grim saints have been portrayed, whose present threadbare appearance shows that they have disfigured the walls for several centuries. Some comparatively modern capitals, of bad design, have been placed upon two or three of the granite columns of the nave; and others, which were broken, have been patched with brick, plastered and painted to look like granite. The principal entrance was formerly at the west end; where there is a small vestibule, immediately within the door of which, on the left hand, is a small chapel, perhaps the baptistery, about twenty-five feet long, and still in tolerable preservation. It is a splendid specimen of the richest Roman architecture of the latter empire, and is truly an imperial little room. The arched ceiling is of stone; and there are three beautifully ornamented niches on each side. The upper end is semicircular, and has been entirely covered with a profusion of sculpture in panels, cornices, and every kind of architectural enrichment When it was entire, and covered with gilding, painting, or mosaic, it must have been most gorgeous. The altar on such a chapel as this was probably of gold, set full of gems; or if it was the baptistery, as I suppose, it most likely contained a bath, of the most precious jasper, or of some of the more rare kinds of marble, for the immersion of the converted heathen, whose entrance into the church was not permitted until they had been purified with the waters of baptism in a building without the door of the house of God; an appropriate custom, which was not broken in upon for ages; and even then the infant was only brought just inside the door, where the font was placed on the left hand of the entrance; a judicious practice, which is completely set at nought in England, where the squalling imp often distracts the attention of the congregation; and is finally sprinkled, instead of being immersed, the whole ceremony having been so much altered and pared down from its original symbolic form, that were a Christian of the early ages to return upon the earth, he would be unable to recognise its meaning.

The conventual library consisted of only half-a-dozen well-waxed and well-thumbed liturgies; but one of the priests told me that they boasted formerly of above a hundred volumes written on leather (gild razali), gazelle skins, probably vellum, which were destroyed by the Mamelukes during their last pillage of the convent.

The habitations of the monks, according to the original design of this very curious building, were contained in a long slip on the south side of the church, where their cells were lit by the small loopholes seen from the outside. Of these cells none now remain: they must have been famously hot, exposed as they were all day long to the rays of the southern sun; but probably the massive thickness of the walls and arched ceilings reduced the temperature. There was no court or open space within the convent; the only place where its inhabitants could have walked for exercise in the open air was upon the flat terrace of the roof, the deck of this ship of St Peter; for the White Monastery in some respects resembled a dismasted man-of-war, anchored in a sea of burning sand.

In modern times we are not surprised on finding a building erected at an immense expense, in which the architecture of the interior is totally different from that of the exterior. A Brummagem Gothic house is frequently furnished and ornamented within in what is called "a chaste Greek style," and vice versâ. A Grecian house—that is to say, a square white block, with square holes in it for windows, and a portico in front—is sometimes inhabited by an antiquarian, who fits it up with Gothic furniture, and a Gothic paper designed by a crafty paper-hanger in the newest style. But in ancient days it was very rare to see such a mixture. I am surprised that the architect of the enthusiastic empress did not go on with the interior of this building as he had begun the exterior. The great hall of Carnac would have afforded him a grand example of an aisle with a clerestory, and side windows, with stone mullions, which would have answered his purpose, in the

Egyptian style. The only other instance of this kind, where two distinct styles of architecture were employed in the middle ages on the inside and outside of the same building, is in the church of St. Francesco, at Rimini, which was built by Sigismond Malatesta as a last resting-place for himself and his friends. He lies in a Gothic shrine within; and the bodies of the great men of his day repose in sarcophagi of classic forms outside; each of which stands in the recess of a Roman arch, in which style of architecture the exterior of the building is erected.

About two miles to the north of the White Monastery, in a small village sheltered by a grove of palms, stands another ancient building called the Red Monastery.

On our return to Souhag we met a party of men on foot, who were armed with spears, shields, and daggers, and one or two with guns. They were led by a man on horseback, who was completely armed with all sorts of warlike implements. They stopped us, and began to talk to our followers, who were exceedingly civil in their behaviour, for the appearance of the party was of a doubtful character; and we felt relieved when we found that we were not to be robbed, but that our friends were on an expedition against the men of Tahta, who some time ago had killed a man belonging to their village, and they were going to avenge his death. This was only one detachment of many that had assembled in the neighbouring villages, each headed by its sheick, or the sheick's son, if the father was an old man. The numbers engaged in this feud amounted, they told us, to between two and three hundred men on each side. Every now and then, it seems, when they have got in their harvest, they assemble to have a fight. Several are wounded, and sometimes a few are killed; in which case, if the numbers of the slain are not equal, the feud continues; and so it goes on from generation to generation, like a faction fight in Ireland, or the feudal wars of the barons of the middle ages,—a style of things which appears to belong to the nature of the human race, and not to any particular country, age, or faith.

Parting from this warlike band with mutual compliments and good wishes, and our guides each seizing the tail of one of our donkeys to increase his onward speed, we trotted away back to the boat, which was waiting for us at Souhag. There we found our boatmen and a crowd of villagers, listening to one of those long stories with which the inhabitants of Egypt are wont to enliven their hours of inactivity. This is an amusement peculiar to the East, and it is one in which I took great delight during many a long journey through the deserts on the way to Mount Sinai, Syria, and other places. The Arabs are great tellers of stories; and some of them have a peculiar knack in rendering them interesting and exciting the curiosity of their audience. Many of these stories were interesting from their reference to persons and occurrences of Holy Writ, particularly of the Old Testament. There are many legends of the patriarch Abraham and his beautiful wife Sarah, who, excepting Eve, is said to have been the fairest of all the daughters of the earth. King Solomon is the hero of numerous strange legends; and his adventures with the gnomes and genii who were subjected to his sway are endless. The poem of Yousef and Zuleica is well known in Europe. And the traditions relating to the prophet Moses are so numerous, that, with the help of a very curious manuscript of an apocryphal book ascribed to the great leader of the Jews, I have been enabled to compile a connected biography, in which many curious circumstances are detailed that are said to have taken place during his eventful life, and which concludes with a highly poetical legend of his death. Many of the stories told by the Arabs resemble those of the Arabian Nights; and a large proportion of these are not very refined.

MENDICANT DERVISH. MENDICANT DERVISH.

I have often been greatly amused with watching the faces of an audience who were listening to a well-told story, some eagerly leaning forward, others smoking their pipes with quicker puffs, when something extraordinary was related, or when the hero of the story had got into some apparently inextricable dilemma. These story-telling parties are usually to be seen seated in a circle on the ground in a shady place. The donkey-boy will stop and gape open-mouthed on overhearing a few words of the marvellous adventures of some enchanted prince, and will look back at his four-footed companion, fearing lest he should resume his original form of a merchant from the island of Serendib. The greatest tact is required on the part of the narrator to prevent the dispersion of his audience, who are sometimes apt to melt away on his stopping at what he considers a peculiarly interesting point, and taking that opportunity of sending round his boy with a little brass basin to collect paras. I know of few subjects better suited for a painter than one of these story-tellers and his group of listeners.

THE ISLAND OF PHILŒ, c.

CHAPTER XII.

The Island of Philœ—The Cataract of Assouan—The Burial Place of Osiris—The Great Temple of Philœ—The Bed of Pharaoh—Shooting in Egypt—Turtle Doves—Story of the Prince Anas el Ajoud—Egyptian Songs—Vow of the Turtle Dove—Curious fact in Natural History—The Crocodile and its Guardian Bird—Arab notions regarding Animals—Legend of King Solomon and the Hoopoes—Natives of the country round the Cataracts of the Nile—Their appearance and Costume—The beautiful Mouna—Solitary Visit to the Island of Philœ—Quarrel between two native Boys—Singular instance of retributive Justice.

Every

part of Egypt is interesting and curious, but the only place to which the epithet of beautiful can be correctly applied is the island of Philœ, which is situated immediately to the south of the cataract of Assouan. The scenery around consists of an infinity of steep granite rocks, which stand, some in the water, others on the land, all of them of the wildest and most picturesque forms. The cataract itself cannot be seen from the island of Philœ, being shut out by an intervening rock, whose shattered mass of red granite towers over the island, rising straight out of the water. From the top of this rock are seen the thousand islands, some of bare rock, some covered with palms and bushes, which interrupt the course of the river and give rise to those eddies, whirlpools, and streams of foaming water which are called the cataracts of the Nile, but which may be more properly designated as rapids, for there is no perpendicular fall of more than two or three feet, and boats of the largest size are drawn with ropes against the stream through certain channels, and are shot down continually with the stream on their return without the occurrence of serious accidents.

Several of these rocks are sculptured with tablets and inscriptions, recording the offerings of the Pharaohs to the gods; and the sacred island of Philœ, the burial-place of Osiris, is covered with buildings, temples, colonnades, gateways, and terrace walls, which are magnificent even in their ruin, and must have been superb when still entire, and filled with crowds of priests and devotees, accompanied by all the flags and standards, gold and glitter, of the ceremonies of their emblematical religion.

Excepting the Pyramids, nothing in Egypt struck me so much as when on a bright moonlit night I first entered the court of the great temple of Philœ. The colours of the paintings on the walls are as vivid in many places as they were the day they were finished: the silence and the solemn grandeur of the immense buildings around me were most imposing; and on emerging from the lofty gateway between the two towers of the propylon, as I wandered about the island, the tufts of palms, which are here of great height, with their weeping branches, seemed to be mourning over the desolation of the stately palaces and temples to which in ancient times all the illustrious of Egypt were wont to resort, and into whose inner recesses none might penetrate; for the secret and awful mysteries of the worship of Osiris were not to be revealed, nor were they even to be spoken of by those who were not initiated into the highest orders of the priesthood. Now all may wander where they choose, and speculate on the uses of the dark chambers hidden in the thickness of the walls, and trace out the plans of the courts and temples with the long lines of columns which formed the avenue of approach from the principal landing-place to the front of the great temple.

The whole island is encumbered with piles of immense squared stones, the remains of buildings which must have been thrown down by an earthquake, as nothing else could shake such solid works from their foundations.[9] The principal temple, and several smaller ones, are still almost entire. One of these, called by the natives the Bed of Pharaoh, is a remarkably light and airy-looking structure, differing, in this respect, from the usual character of Egyptian architecture. On the terrace overhanging the Nile, in front of this graceful temple, I had formed my habitation, where there are some vaults of more recent construction, which are usually taken possession of by travellers and fitted up with the carpets, cushions, and the sides of the tents which they bring with them.

Every one who travels in Egypt is more or less a sportsman, for the infinity of birds must tempt the most idle or contemplative to go "a birding," as the Americans term it. I had shot all sorts of birds and beasts, from a crocodile to a snipe; and among other game I had shot multitudes of turtle doves; these pretty little birds being exceedingly tame, and never flying very far, I sometimes got three or four at a shot, and a dozen or so of them made a famous pie or a pilau, with rice and a tasty sauce; but a somewhat singular incident put an end to my warfare against them. One day I was sitting on the terrace before the Bed of Pharaoh, surrounded by a circle of Arabs and negroes, and we were all listening to a story which an old gentleman with a grey beard was telling us concerning the loves of the beautiful Ouardi, who was shut up in an enchanted palace on this very island to secure her from the approaches of her lover, Prince Anas el Ajoud, the son of the Sultan Esshamieh, who had married seven wives before he had a son. The first six wives, on the birth of Anas el Ajoud, placed a log in his cradle, and exposed the infant in the desert, where he was nursed by a gazelle, and whence he returned to punish the six cruel step-mothers, who fully believed he was dead, and to rejoice the heart of his father, who had been persuaded by these artful ladies that his sultana by magic art had presented him with a log instead of a son, who was to be the heir of his dominions, c. Prince Anas, who was in despair at being separated from his lady love, used to sing dismal songs as he passed in his gilded boat under the walls of the island palace. These, at last, were responded to from the lattice by the fair Ouardi, who was soon afterwards carried off by the enamoured prince. The story, which was an interminable rigmarole, as long as one of those spun on from night to night by the Princess Sherezade, was diversified every now and then by the fearful squealing of an Arab song. The old storyteller, shutting his eyes and throwing back his head that his mind might not be distracted by any exterior objects, uttered a succession of sounds which set one's teeth on edge.[10]

AMAAN.

(musical notation) AMAAN.

Whilst the old gentleman was shooting out one of these amatory ditties, and I was sitting still listening to these heart-rending sounds, a turtle-dove—who was probably awakened from her sleep by the fearful discord, or might, perhaps, have been the beautiful Princess Ouardi herself transformed into the likeness of a dove—flew out of one of the palm-trees which grow on the edge of the bank, and perched at a little distance from us. We none of us moved, and the turtle-dove, after pausing for a moment, ran towards me and nestled under the full sleeve of my benisch. It stayed there till the story and the songs were ended, and when I was obliged to arise, in order to make my compliments to the departing guests, the dove flew into the palm-tree again, and went to roost among the branches, where several others were already perched with their heads under their wings. Thereupon I made a vow never to shoot another turtle-dove, however much pie or pilau might need them, and I fairly kept my vow. Luckily turtle-doves are not so good as pigeons, so it was no great loss. Although not to be compared to the Roman bird, the Egyptian pigeon is very good eating when he is tender and well dressed.

As I am on the subject of birds I will relate a fact in natural history which I was fortunate enough to witness, and which, although it is mentioned so long ago as the times of Herodotus, has not, I believe, been often observed since; indeed I have never met with any traveller who has himself seen such an occurrence.

I had always a strong predilection for crocodile shooting, and had destroyed several of these dragons of the waters. On one occasion I saw, a long way off, a large one, twelve or fifteen feet long, lying asleep under a perpendicular bank about ten feet high, on the margin of the river. I stopped the boat at some distance; and noting the place as well as I could, I took a circuit inland, and came down cautiously to the top of the bank, whence with a heavy rifle I made sure of my ugly game. I had already cut off his head in imagination, and was considering whether it should be stuffed with its mouth open or shut. I peeped over the bank. There he was, within ten feet of the sight of the rifle. I was on the point of firing at his eye, when I observed that he was attended by a bird called a ziczac. It is of the plover species, of a greyish colour, and as large as a small pigeon.

The bird was walking up and down close to the crocodile's nose. I suppose I moved, for suddenly it saw me, and instead of flying away, as any respectable bird would have done, he jumped up about a foot from the ground, screamed "Ziczac! ziczac!" with all the powers of his voice, and dashed himself against the crocodile's face two or three times. The great beast started up, and immediately spying his danger, made a jump up into the air, and dashing into the water with a splash which covered me with mud; he dived into the river and disappeared. The ziczac, to my increased admiration, proud apparently of having saved his friend, remained walking up and down, uttering his cry, as I thought, with an exulting voice, and standing every now and then on the tips of his toes in a conceited manner, which made me justly angry with his impertinence. After having waited in vain for some time, to see whether the crocodile would come out again, I got up from the bank where I was lying, threw a clod of earth at the ziczac, and came back to the boat, feeling some consolation for the loss of my game in having witnessed a circumstance, the truth of which has been disputed by several writers on natural history.

The Arabs say that every race of animals is governed by its chief, to whom the others are bound to pay obeisance. The king of the crocodiles holds his court at the bottom of the Nile near Siout. The king of the fleas lives at Tiberias, in the Holy Land; and deputations of illustrious fleas, from other countries, visit him on a certain day in his palace, situated in the midst of beautiful gardens, under the Lake of Genesareth. There is a bird which is common in Egypt called the hoopoe (Abou hood-hood), of whose king the following legend is related. This bird is of the size and shape as well as the colour of a woodcock; but has a crown of feathers on its head, which it has the power of raising and depressing at will. It is a tame, quiet bird; usually to be found walking leisurely in search of its food on the margin of the water. It seldom takes long flights; and is not harmed by the natives, who are much more sparing of the life of animals than we Europeans are:—

In the days of King Solomon, the son of David, who, by the virtue of his cabalistic seal, reigned supreme over genii as well as men, and who could speak the languages of animals of all kinds, all created beings were subservient to his will. Now when the king wanted to travel, he made use, for his conveyance, of a carpet of a square form. This carpet had the property of extending itself to a sufficient size to carry a whole army, with the tents and baggage; but at other times it could be reduced so as to be only large enough for the support of the royal throne, and of those ministers whose duty it was to attend upon the person of the sovereign. Four genii of the air then took the four corners of the carpet, and carried it with its contents wherever King Solomon desired. Once the king was on a journey in the air, carried upon his throne of ivory over the various nations of the earth. The rays of the sun poured down upon his head, and he had nothing to protect him from its heat. The fiery beams were beginning to scorch his neck and shoulders, when he saw a flock of vultures flying past. "Oh, vultures!" cried King Solomon, "come and fly between me and the sun, and make a shadow with your wings to protect me, for its rays are scorching my neck and face." But the vultures answered, and said, "We are flying to the north, and your face is turned towards the south. We desire to continue on our way; and be it known unto thee, O king! that we will not turn back on our flight, neither will we fly above your throne to protect you from the sun, although its rays may be scorching your neck and face. "Then King Solomon lifted up his voice, and said, "Cursed be ye, O vultures!—and because you will not obey the commands of your lord, who rules over the whole world, the feathers of your necks shall fall off; and the heat of the sun, and the cold of the winter, and the keenness of the wind, and the beating of the rain, shall fall upon your rebellious necks, which shall not be protected with feathers, like the necks of other birds. And whereas you have hitherto fared delicately, henceforward ye shall eat carrion and feed upon offal; and your race shall be impure till the end of the world." And it was done unto the vultures as King Solomon had said.

Now it fell out that there was a flock of hoopoes flying past; and the king cried out to them, and said, "O hoopoes! come and fly between me and the sun, that I may be protected from its rays by the shadow of your wings." Whereupon the king of the hoopoes answered, and said, "O king, we are but little fowls, and we are not able to afford much shade; but we will gather our nation together, and by our numbers we will make up for our small size." So the hoopoes gathered together, and, flying in a cloud over the throne of the king, they sheltered him from the rays of the sun.

When the journey was over, and King Solomon sat upon his golden throne, in his palace of ivory, whereof the doors were emerald, and the windows of diamonds, larger even than the diamond of Jemshid, he commanded that the king of the hoopoes should stand before his feet. "Now," said King Solomon, "for the service that thou and thy race have rendered, and the obedience thou hast shown to the king, thy lord and master, what shall be done unto thee, O hoopoe? and what shall be given to the hoopoes of thy race, for a memorial and a reward?" Now the king of the hoopoes was confused with the great honour of standing before the feet of the king; and, making his obeisance, and laying his right claw upon his heart, he said, "O king, live for ever! Let a day be given to thy servant, to consider with his queen and his councillors what it shall be that the king shall give unto us for a reward." And King Solomon said, "Be it so." And it was so.

But the king of the hoopoes flew away; and he went to his queen, who was a dainty hen, and he told her what had happened, and he desired her advice as to what they should ask of the king for a reward; and he called together his council, and they sat upon a tree, and they each of them desired a different thing. Some wished for a long tail; some wished for blue and green feathers; some wished to be as large as ostriches; some wished for one thing, and some for another; and they debated till the going down of the sun, but they could not agree together. Then the queen took the king of the hoopoes apart and said to him, "My dear lord and husband, listen to my words; and as we have preserved the head of King Solomon, let us ask for crowns of gold on our heads, that we may be superior to all other birds." And the words of the queen and the princesses her daughters prevailed; and the king of the hoopoes presented himself before the throne of Solomon, and desired of him that all hoopoes should wear golden crowns upon their heads. Then Solomon said, "Hast thou considered well what it is that thou desirest?" And the hoopoe said, "I have considered well, and we desire to have golden crowns upon our heads." So Solomon replied, "Crowns of gold shall ye have: but, behold, thou art a foolish bird; and when the evil days shall come upon thee, and thou seest the folly of thy heart, return here to me, and I will give thee help." So the king of the hoopoes left the presence of King Solomon, with a golden crown upon his head. And all the hoopoes had golden crowns; and they were exceeding proud and haughty. Moreover, they went down by the lakes and the pools, and walked by the margin of the water, that they might admire themselves as it were in a glass. And the queen of the hoopoes gave herself airs, and sat upon a twig; and she refused to speak to the merops her cousin, and the other birds who had been her friends, because they were but vulgar birds, and she wore a crown of gold upon her head.

Now there was a certain fowler who set traps for birds; and he put a piece of a broken mirror into his trap, and a hoopoe that went in to admire itself was caught. And the fowler looked at it, and saw the shining crown upon its head; so he wrung off its head, and took the crown to Issachar, the son of Jacob, the worker in metal, and he asked him what it was. So Issachar, the son of Jacob, said, "It is a crown of brass." And he gave the fowler a quarter of a shekel for it, and desired him, if he found any more, to bring them to him, and to tell no man thereof. So the fowler caught some more hoopoes, and sold their crowns to Issachar, the son of Jacob; until one day he met another man who was a jeweller, and he showed him several of the hoopoes' crowns. Whereupon the jeweller told him that they were of pure gold; and he gave the fowler a talent of gold for four of them.

Now when the value of these crowns was known, the fame of them got abroad, and in all the land of Israel was heard the twang of bows and the whirling of slings; bird-lime was made in every town; and the price of traps rose in the market, so that the fortunes of the trap-makers increased. Not a hoopoe could show its head but it was slain or taken captive, and the days of the hoopoes were numbered. Then their minds were filled with sorrow and dismay, and before long few were left to bewail their cruel destiny.

At last, flying by stealth through the most unfrequented places, the unhappy king of the hoopoes went to the court of King Solomon, and stood again before the steps of the golden throne, and with tears and groans related the misfortunes which had happened to his race.

So King Solomon looked kindly upon the king of the hoopoes, and said unto him, "Behold, did I not warn thee of thy folly, in desiring to have crowns of gold? Vanity and pride have been thy ruin. But now, that a memorial may remain of the service which thou didst render unto me, your crowns of gold shall be changed into crowns of feathers, that ye may walk unharmed upon the earth." Now when the fowlers saw that the hoopoes no longer wore crowns of gold upon their heads, they ceased from the persecution of their race; and from that time forth the family of the hoopoes have flourished and increased, and have continued in peace even to the present day.

And here endeth the veracious history of the king of the hoopoes.

But to return to the island of Philœ. The neighbourhood of the cataracts is inhabited by a peculiar race of people, who are neither Arabs, nor negroes, like the Nubians, whose land joins to theirs. They are of a clear copper colour; and are slightly but elegantly formed. They have woolly hair; and are not encumbered with much clothing. The men wear a short tunic of white cotton; but often have only a petticoat round their loins. The married women have a piece of stuff thrown over their heads which envelopes the whole person. Under this they wear a curious garment made of fine strips of black leather, about a foot long, like a fringe. This hangs round the hips, and forms the only clothing of unmarried girls, whose forms are as perfect as that of any ancient statue. They dress their hair precisely in the same way as we see in the pictures of the ancient Egyptians, plaited in numerous tresses, which descend about half way down the neck, and are plentifully anointed with castor-oil; that they may not spoil their head-dresses, they use, instead of a pillow to rest their heads upon at night, a stool of hard wood like those which are found in the ancient tombs, and which resemble in shape the handle of a crutch more than anything else that I can think of. The women are fond of necklaces and armlets of beads; and the men wear a knife of a peculiar form, stuck into an armlet above the elbow of the left arm. When they go from home they carry a spear, and a shield made of the skin of the hippopotamus or crocodile, with which they are very clever in warding off blows, and in defending themselves from stones or other missiles.

Of this race was a girl called Mouna, whom I had known as a child when I was first at Philœ. She grew up to be the most beautiful bronze statue that can be conceived. She used to bring eggs from the island on which she lived to Philœ: her means of conveyance across the water was a piece of the trunk of a doom-tree, upon which she supported herself as she swam across the Nile ten times a-day. I never saw so perfect a figure as that of Mouna. She was of a lighter brown than most of the other girls, and was exactly the colour of a new copper kettle. She had magnificent large eyes; and her face had but a slight leaning towards the Ethiopian contour. Her bands and feet were wonderfully small and delicately formed. In short, she was a perfect beauty in her way; but the perfume of the castor-oil with which she was anointed had so strong a savour that, when she brought us the eggs and chickens, I always admired her at a distance of ten yards to windward. She had an ornamented calabash to hold her castor-oil, from which she made a fresh toilette every time she swam across the Nile.

I have been three times at Philœ, and indeed I had so great an admiration of the place that on my last visit, thinking it probable that I should never again behold its wonderful ruins and extraordinary scenery, I determined to spend the day there alone, that I might meditate at my leisure and wander as I chose from one well-remembered spot to another without the incumbrance of half a dozen people staring at whatever I looked at, and following me about out of pure idleness. Greatly did I enjoy my solitary day, and whilst leaning over the parapet on the top of the great Propylon, or seated on one of the terraces which overhung the Nile, I in imagination repeopled the scene, with the forms of the priests and worshippers of other days, restored the fallen temples to their former glory, and could almost think I saw the processions winding round their walls, and heard the trumpets, and the harps, and the sacred hymns in honour of the great Osiris. In the evening a native came over with a little boat to take me off the island, and I quitted with regret this strange and interesting region.

I landed at the village of rude huts on the shore of the river and sat down on a stone, waiting for my donkey, which I purposed to ride through the desert in the cool of the evening to Assouan, where my boat was moored. While I was sitting there, two boys were playing and wrestling together; they were naked and about nine or ten years old. They soon began to quarrel, and one of them drew the dagger which he wore upon his arm and stabbed the other in the throat. The poor boy fell to the ground bleeding; the dagger had entered his throat on the left side under the jawbone, and being directed upwards had cut his tongue and grazed the roof of his mouth. Whilst he cried and writhed about upon the ground with the blood pouring out of his mouth, the villagers came out from their cabins and stood around talking and screaming, but affording no help to the poor boy. Presently a young man, who was, I believe, a lover of Mouna's, stood up and asked where the father of the boy was, and why he did not come to help him. The villagers said he had no father. "Where are his relations, then?" he asked. The boy had no relations, there was no one to care for him in the village. On hearing this he uttered some words which I did not understand, and started off after the boy who had inflicted the wound. The young assassin ran away as fast as he could, and a famous chase took place. They darted over the plain, scrambled up the rocks, and jumped down some dangerous-looking places among the masses of granite which formed the background of the village. At length the boy was caught, and, screaming and struggling, was dragged to the spot where his victim lay moaning and heaving upon the sand. The young man now placed him between his legs, and in this way held him tight whilst he examined the wound of the other, putting his finger into it and opening his mouth to see exactly how far it extended. When he had satisfied himself on the subject he called for a knife; the boy had thrown his away in the race, and he had not one himself. The villagers stood silent around, and one of them having handed him a dagger, the young man held the boy's head sideways across his thigh and cut his throat exactly in the same way as he had done to the other. He then pitched him away upon the ground, and the two lay together bleeding and writhing side by side. Their wounds were precisely the same; the second operation had been most expertly performed, and the knife had passed just where the boy had stabbed his playmate. The wounds, I believe, were not dangerous, for presently both the boys got up and were led away to their homes. It was a curious instance of retributive justice, following out the old law of blood for blood, an eye for an eye, a tooth for a tooth.

MONASTERIES OF THE LEVANT.
PART II.

JERUSALEM AND THE MONASTERY
OF ST. SABBA.
1834.
PLAN OF THE CHURCH OF THE HOLY SEPULCHRE.The Holy maltese cross Sepulchre.
1. Entrance to the Church. 15. Where Mary Magdalene stood.
2. The Stone of Unction. 16. Where our Lord appeared to Mary Magdalene.
3. Where our Saviour was nailed to the Cross. 17. The Pillar of Flagellation.
4. Mount Calvary triple cross 18. Rooms of the Latin Convent.
5. Chapel of the Sacrifice of Isaac. 19. Chapel of the Maronites.
6. Chapel of the Altar of Melchisedec. 20. Chapel of the Georgians.
7. Stairs up to Mount Calvary. 21. Sepulchre of Joseph of Arimathea.
8. Stairs down to the Chapel of St. Helena. 22. Chapel of the Copts.
9. Stairs down to the Chapel of the Invention of the Cross. 23. Chapel of the Jacobites.
10. Place where the three Crosses were discovered. 24. Chapel of the Abyssinians, over which is the Chapel of the Armenians.
11. Chapel of the Division of the Garments. 25. The spot where the Blessed Virgin and St. John stood during the Crucifixion.
12. Prison of our Lord. 26. Steps before the entrance of the Holy Sepulchre.
13. Greek Choir, in it center of the world
, the center of the world; on each side are the Stalls for the Monks. 27. Ante-room to the Holy Sepulchre.
In the center is the stone where the Angel sat;
on either side the two windows from whence the
Holy Fire is delivered to the multitude.
14. Latin Choir. 28. The Iconostasis, or Screen before the Greek Altar, which, as in English Churches, is called the Holy Table—ικονοσταοις
.

CHAPTER XIII.
Journey to Jerusalem—First View of the Holy City—The Valley of Gihon—Appearance of the City—The Latin Convent of St. Salvador—Inhospitable Reception by the Monks—Visit to the Church of the Holy Sepulchre—Description of the In-

terior—The Chapel of the Sepulchre—The Chapel of the Cross on Mount Calvary—The Tomb and Sword of Godfrey de Bouillon—Arguments in favour of the Authenticity of the Holy Sepulchre—The Invention of the Cross by the Empress Helena—Legend of the Cross.

"Ecco apparir Gerusalem si vede,
Ecco additar Gerusalem si scorge,
Ecco da mile voce unitamente,
Gerosalemme salutar si sente.
* * *
E l'uno all'altro il mostra e in tanto oblia,
La noja e il mal della passata via.
* * *
Al gran placer che quella prima vista,
Dolcemente spirò nell'altrui petto,
Alta contrizion succese mista,
Di timoroso e riverente affetto,
Ossano appena d'inalzar la vista
Ver la città, di Christo albergo eletto:
Dove mori, dove sepolto fue;
Dove poi riveste le membre sue."
Tasso
, Gerusalemme Liberata, Canto 3.

We left our camels and dromedaries, and wild Arabs of the desert, at Gaza; and being now provided with horses, and a tamer sort of Yahoo to attend upon them, we took our way across the hills towards Jerusalem.

The road passes over a succession of rounded rocky hills, almost every step being rendered interesting by its connexion with the events of Holy Writ. On our left we saw the village of Kobab, and on our right the ruins of a castle said to have been built by the Maccabees, and not far from it the remains of an ancient Christian church.

As our train of horses surmounted each succeeding eminence, every one was eager to be the first who should catch a glimpse of the Holy City. Again and again we were disappointed; another rocky valley yawned beneath us, and another barren stony hill rose up beyond. There seemed to be no end to the intervening hills and dales; they appeared to multiply beneath our feet. At last, when we had almost given up the point and had ceased to contend for the first view by galloping ahead; as we ascended another rocky brow we saw the towers of what seemed to be a Gothic castle; then, as we approached nearer, a long line of walls and battlements appeared crowning a ridge of rock which rose from a narrow valley to the right. This was the valley of the pools of Gihon, where Solomon was crowned, and the battlements which rose above it were the long looked-for walls of Jerusalem. With one accord our whole party drew their bridles, and stood still to gaze for the first time upon this renowned and sacred city.

It is not easy to describe the sensations which fill the breast of a Christian when, after a long and toilsome journey, he first beholds this, the most interesting and venerated spot upon the whole surface of the globe. Every one was silent for a while, absorbed in the deepest contemplation. The object of our pilgrimage was accomplished, and I do not think that anything we saw afterwards during our stay in Jerusalem made a more profound impression on our minds than this first distant view.

It was curious to observe the different effect which our approach to Jerusalem had upon the various persons who composed our party. A Christian pilgrim, who had joined us on the road, fell down upon his knees and kissed the holy ground; two others embraced each other, and congratulated themselves that they had lived to see Jerusalem. As for us Franks, we sat bolt upright upon our horses, and stared and said nothing; whilst around us the more natural children of the East wept for joy, and, as in the army of the Crusaders, the word Jerusalem! Jerusalem! was repeated from mouth to mouth; but we, who consider ourselves civilized and superior beings, repressed our emotions; we were above showing that we participated in the feelings of our barbarous companions. As for myself, I would have got off my horse and walked bare-footed towards the gate, as some did, if I had dared: but I was in fear of being laughed at for my absurdity, and therefore sat fast in my saddle. At last I blew my nose, and, pressing the sharp edges of my Arab stirrups on the lank sides of my poor weary jade, I rode on slowly towards the Bethlehem gate.

On the sloping sides of the valley of Gihon numerous groups of people were lying under the olive-trees in the cool of the evening, and parties of grave Turks, seated on their carpets by the road-side, were smoking their long pipes in dignified silence. But what struck me most were some old white-bearded Jews, who were holding forth to groups of their friends or disciples under the walls of the city of their fathers, and dilating perhaps upon the glorious actions of their race in former days.

Jerusalem has been described as a deserted and melancholy ruin, filling the mind with images of desolation and decay, but it did not strike me as such. It is still a compact city, as it is described in Scripture; the Saracenic walls have a stately, magnificent appearance; they are built of large and massive stones. The square towers, which are seen at intervals, are handsome and in good repair; and there is an imposing dignity in the appearance of the grim old citadel, which rises in the centre of the line of walls and towers, with its batteries and terraces one above another, surmounted with the crimson flag of Turkey floating heavily over the conquered city of the cross.

We entered by the Bethlehem gate: it is commanded by the citadel, which was built by the people of Pisa, and is still called the castle of the Pisans. There we had some parleying with the Egyptian guards, and, crossing an open space famous in monastic tradition as the garden where Bathsheba was bathing when she was seen by King David from the roof of his palace, we threaded a labyrinth of narrow streets, which the horses of our party completely blocked up; and as soon as we could, we sent a man with our letters of introduction to the superior of the Latin convent. I had letters from Cardinal Weld and Cardinal Pedicini, which we presumed would ensure us a warm and hospitable reception; and as travellers are usually lodged in the monastic establishments, we went on at once to the Latin convent of St. Salvador, where we expected to enjoy all the comforts and luxuries of European civilization after our weary journey over the desert from Egypt. We, however, quickly discovered our mistake; for, on dismounting at the gate of the convent, we were received in a very cool way by the monks, who appeared to make the reception of travellers a mere matter of interest, and treated us as if we were dust under their feet. They put us into a wretched hole in the Casa Nuova, a house belonging to them near the convent, where there was scarcely room for our baggage; and we went to bed not a little mortified at our inhospitable reception by our Christian brethren, so different from what we had always experienced from the Mahometans. The convent of St. Salvador belongs to a community of Franciscan friars; they were most of them Spaniards, and, being so far away from the superior officers of their order, they were not kept in very perfect discipline. It was probably owing to our being heretics that we were not better received. Fortunately we had our own beds, tents, cooking-utensils, carpets, c.; so that we soon made ourselves comfortable in the bare vaulted rooms which were allotted to us, and for which, by-the-bye, we had to pay pretty handsomely.

The next morning early we went to the church of the Holy Sepulchre, descending the hill from the convent, and then down a flight of narrow steps into a small paved court, one side of which is occupied by the Gothic front of the church. The court was full of people selling beads and crucifixes and other holy ware. We had to wait some time, till the Turkish doorkeepers came to unlock the door, as they keep the keys of the church, which is only open on certain days, except to votaries of distinction. There is a hole in the door, through which the pilgrims gave quantities of things to the monks inside to be laid upon the sepulchre. At last the door was opened, and we went into the church.

On entering these sacred walls the attention is first directed to a large slab of marble on the floor opposite the door, with several lamps suspended over it, and three enormous waxen tapers about twenty feet in height standing at each end. The pilgrims approach it on their knees, touch and kiss it, and, prostrating themselves before it, offer up their adoration. This, you are told, is the stone on which the body of our Lord was washed and anointed, and prepared for the tomb.

Turning to the left, we came to a round stone let into the pavement, with a canopy of ornamental iron-work over it Here the Virgin Mary is said to have stood when the body of our Saviour was taken down from the cross.

Leaving this, we entered the circular space immediately under the great dome, which is about eighty feet in diameter, and is surrounded by eighteen large square piers, which support the front of a broad gallery. Formerly this circular gallery was supported by white marble pillars: but the church was burnt down about twenty years ago, through the negligence of a drunken Greek monk, who set a light to some parts of the woodwork, and then endeavoured to put out the flames by throwing aqua vitæ upon them, which he mistook for water.

The Chapel of the Sepulchre stands under the centre of the dome. It is a small oblong house of stone, rounded at one end, where there is an altar for the Coptic and Abyssinian Christians. At the other end it is square, and has a platform of marble in front, which is ascended by a flight of steps, and has a low parapet wall and a seat on each side. The chapel contains two rooms. Taking off our shoes and turbans, we entered a low narrow door, and went into a chamber, in the centre of which stands a block of polished marble. On this stone sat the angel who announced the blessed tidings of the resurrection.

From this room, which has a small round window on each side, we passed through another low door into the inner chamber, which contains the Holy Sepulchre itself, which, however, is not visible, being concealed by an altar of white marble. It is said to be a long narrow excavation like a grave or the interior of a sarcophagus hewed out of the rock just beneath the level of the ground. Six rows of lamps of silver gilt, twelve in each row, hang from the ceiling, and are kept perpetually burning. The tomb occupies nearly one-half of the sepulchral chamber, and extends from one end of it to the other on the right side of the door as you enter; a space of three feet wide and rather more than six feet long in front of it being all that remains for the accommodation of the pilgrims, so that not more than three or four can be admitted at a time.

Leaving this hallowed spot, we were conducted first to the place where our Lord appeared to Mary Magdalen, and then to the Chapel of the Latins, where a part of the pillar of flagellation is preserved.

The Greeks have possession of the choir of the church, which is opposite the door of the Holy Sepulchre. This part of the building is of great size, and is magnificently decorated with gold and carving and stiff pictures of the saints. In the centre is a globe of black marble on a pedestal, under which they say the head of Adam was found; and you are told also that this is the exact centre of the globe; the Greeks having thus transferred to Jerusalem, from the temple of Apollo at Delphi, the absurd notions of the pagan priests of antiquity relative to the form of the earth.

Returning towards the door of the church, and leaving it on our right hand, we ascended a flight of about twenty steps, and found ourselves in the Chapel of the Cross on Mount Calvary. At the upper end of this chapel is an altar, on the spot where the crucifixion took place, and under it is the hole into which the end of the cross was fixed: this is surrounded with a glory of silver gilt, and on each side of it, at the distance of about six feet, are the holes in which the crosses of the two thieves stood. Near to these is a long rent in the rock, which was opened by an earthquake at the time of the crucifixion. Although the three crosses appear to have stood very near to each other, yet, from the manner in which they are placed, there would have been room enough for them, as the cross of our Saviour stands in front of the other two.

Leaving this chapel we entered a kind of vault under the stairs, in which the rent of the rock is again seen: it extends from the ceiling to the floor, and has every appearance of having been caused by some convulsion of nature, and not formed by the hands of man. Here were formerly the tombs of Godfrey de Bouillon and Baldwin his brother, who were buried beneath the cross for which they fought so valiantly: but these tombs have lately been destroyed by the Greeks, whose detestation of everything connected with the Latin Church exceeds their aversion to the Mahometan creed. In the sacristy of the Latin monks we were shown the sword and spurs of Godfrey de Bouillon; the sword is apparently of the age assigned to it: it is double-edged and straight, with a cross-guard.[11]

In another part of the church is a small dismal chapel, in the floor of which are several ancient tombs; one of them is said to be the sepulchre of Joseph of Arimathea. Of the antiquity of these tombs there cannot be the slightest doubt; and their being here forms the best argument for the authenticity of the Holy Sepulchre itself, as it shows that this was formerly a place of burial, notwithstanding its situation in the centre of the ancient city, contrary to the almost universal practice of the ancients, whose sepulchres are always found some short distance from their cities; indeed, among the Egyptians, whose manners seem to have been followed in many respects by the Jews, it was a law that no one should be buried in the cultivated grounds, but their tombs were excavated in the rocks of the desert, that the agricultural and other daily pursuits of the living might not interfere with the repose of the dead. It is mentioned in the Bible that Christ was led out to be crucified;

but it is not quite clear from the passage whether he was led out of the city of Jerusalem itself, or only from the city of David on Mount Sion, which appears to have been the citadel and place of residence of the Roman governor. If so, the site of the Holy Sepulchre may be the true one; and, in common with all other pilgrims, I am inclined to hope that the tomb now pointed out may really be the sepulchre of Christ.

Descending a flight of steps from the body of the church, we entered the subterranean chapel of St. Helena, below which is another vault, in which the true cross is said to have been found. A very curious account of the finding of the cross is to be seen in the black-letter pages of Caxton's 'Golden Legend,' and it has formed the subject of many singular traditions and romantic stories in former days. The history of this famous relic would be tedious were I to narrate it in the obsolete phraseology of the father of English printing, and I will therefore only give a short summary of the legend; although, to those who take an interest in monastic traditions, the accounts given in old books, which were read by our ancestors before the Reformation with all the sober seriousness of undoubting faith, afford a curious instance of the proneness of the human intellect to mistake the shadow for the substance, and to substitute an unbounded veneration for outward observances for the more reasonable acts of spiritual devotion.

In the middle ages, while the worship of our Saviour was completely neglected, the wooden cross upon which he was supposed to have suffered was the object of universal adoration to all sects of Christians; armies fought with religious enthusiasm, not for the faith, but for the relic of the cross; and the traditions regarding it were received as undoubted facts by the heroes of the crusades, the hierarchy of the Church, and all who called themselves Christians, in those iron ages, when with rope and fagot, fire and sword, the fierce piety even of good men sought to enforce the precepts of Him whose advent was heralded with the angels' hymn of "peace on earth and good will towards men."

It is related in the apocryphal Gospel of Nicodemus, that when Adam fell sick he sent his son Seth to the gate of the terrestrial paradise to ask the angel for some drops of the oil of mercy, which distilled from the tree of life, to cure him of his disease; but the angel answered that he could not receive this healing oil until 5500 years had passed away. He gave him, however, a branch of this tree, and it was planted upon Adam's grave. In after ages the tree flourished and waxed exceeding fair, for Adam was buried in Mount Lebanon, not very far from the place near Damascus whence the red earth of which his body was formed by the Creator had been taken. When Balkia, Queen of Abyssinia, came to visit Solomon the King, she worshipped this tree, for she said that thereon should the Saviour of the world be hanged, and that from that time the kingdom of the Jews should cease. Upon hearing this, Solomon commanded that the tree should be cut down and buried in a certain place in Jerusalem, where afterwards the pool of Bethesda was dug, and the angel that had charge of the mysterious tree troubled the water of the pool at certain seasons, and those who first dipped into it were cured of their ailments. As the time of the passion of the Saviour approached, the wood floated on the surface of the water, and of that piece of timber, which was of cedar, the Jews made the upright part of the cross, the cross beam was made of cypress, the piece on which his feet rested was of palm, and the other, on which the superscription was written, was of olive.

After the crucifixion the holy cross and the crosses of the two thieves were thrown into the town ditch, or, according to some, into an old vault which was near at hand,

and they were covered with the refuse and ruins of the city. In her extreme old age the Empress Helena, making a pilgrimage to Jerusalem, threatened all the Jewish inhabitants with torture and death if they did not produce the holy cross from the place where their ancestors had concealed it: and at last an old Jew named Judas, who had been put into prison and was nearly famished, consented to reveal the secret; he accordingly petitioned Heaven, whereupon the earth trembled, and from the fissures in the ground a delicious aromatic odour issued forth, and on the soil being removed the three crosses were discovered; and near the crosses the superscription was also found, but it was not known to which of the three it belonged. However, Macarius, Bishop of Jerusalem, repairing with the Empress to the house of a noble lady who was afflicted with an incurable disease, she was immediately restored to health by touching the true cross; and the body of a young man which was being carried out to burial was brought to life on being laid upon the holy wood. At the sight of these miracles Judas the Jew became a Christian, and was baptized by the name of Quiriacus, to the great indignation of the devil, for, said he, "by the first Judas I gained much profit, but by this one's conversion I shall lose many souls."

It would be endless were I to give the history of all the authenticated relics of the holy cross since those days; but of the three principal pieces one is now, or lately was, at Etchmiazin, in Armenia, the monks of which Church are accused of having stolen it from the Latins of Jerusalem when they were imprisoned by Sultan Suleiman. The second piece is still at Jerusalem, in the hands of the Greeks; and the third, which was sent by the Empress Helena herself to the church of Santa Croce di Gerusalemme at Rome, is now preserved in St. Peter's. There is indeed little reason to doubt that the piece of wood exhibited at Rome is the same that the Empress sent there in the year 326. The feast of the "Invention of the Cross" continues to be celebrated every year on the 3rd of May by an appropriate mass.

Besides the objects which I have mentioned, there is within the church an altar on the spot where Christ is said to have appeared to the Virgin after the resurrection. This completes the list of all the sacred places contained under the roof of the great church of the Holy Sepulchre.

I may remark that all the very ancient specimens of the relics of the true cross are of the same wood, which has a very peculiar half-petrified appearance. I have a relic of this kind; the date of the shrine in which it is preserved being of the date of 1280. I have also a piece of the cross in a more modern setting, which is not of the same wood.

Whether all the hallowed spots within these walls really are the places which the guardians of the church declare them to be, or whether they have been fixed on at random, and consecrated to serve the interested views of a crafty priesthood, is a fact that I shall leave others to determine; however this may be, it is a matter of little consequence to the Christian. The great facts on which the history of the Gospel is founded are not so closely connected with particular spots of earth or sacred buildings as to be rendered doubtful by any mistake in the choice of a locality. The main error on the part of the priests of modern times at Jerusalem arises from an anxiety to prove the actual existence of everything to which any allusion is made by the evangelical historians, not remembering that the lapse of ages and the devastation of successive wars must have destroyed much, and disguised more, which the early disciples could most readily have identified. The mere circumstance that the localities of almost all the events which attended the close of our

Saviour's ministry are crowded into one place, and covered by the roof of a single church, might excite a very justifiable doubt as to the exactness of the topography maintained by the friars of Mount Moriah.

CHAPTER XIV.

The Via Dolorosa—The Houses of Dives and of Lazarus—The Prison of St. Peter—The Site of the Temple of Solomon—The Mosque of Omar—The Hadjr el Sakhara—The Greek Monastery—Its Library—Valuable Manuscripts—Splendid MS. of the Book of Job—Arabic spoken at Jerusalem—Mussulman Theory regarding the Crucifixion—State of the Jews—Richness of their Dress in their own Houses—Beauty of their Women—Their literal Interpretation of Scripture—The Service in the Synagogue—Description of the House of a Rabbi—The Samaritans—Their Roll of the Pentateuch—Arrival of Ibrahim Pasha at Jerusalem.

Except
the Holy Sepulchre, none of the places which are pointed out as sacred within the walls of Jerusalem merit a description, as they have evidently been created by the monks to serve their own purposes. You are shown, for instance, the whole of the Via Dolorosa, the way by which our Saviour passed from the hall of Pilate to Mount Calvary, and the exact seven places where he fell under the weight of the cross: you are shown the house of the rich man and that of Lazarus, both of them Turkish buildings, although, as that story is related in a parable, no real localities ever can have been referred to. Near the house of Lazarus there were several dogs when I passed by, and, on my asking the guide whether they were the descendants of the original dogs in the parable, he said he was not quite sure, but that as to the house there could be no doubt. The prison of St. Peter is also to be seen, but the column on which the cock stood who crowed on his denial of our Lord, as well as the steps by which Christ ascended to the judgment-seat of Pilate, have been carried away to Rome, where they are both to be seen on the hill of St. John Lateran.

The mosque of Omar stands on the site of the ancient Temple of Solomon, which covered the whole of the enclosure which is now the garden of the mosque, a space of about 1500 feet long, and 1000 feet wide. In the centre of this garden is a platform of stone about 600 feet square, on which stands the octagonal building of the mosque itself, the upper part being covered with green porcelain tiles which glitter in the sun: below, the walls are paneled with marble richly worked and of different colours: the dome in the centre has a wide cornice round it, ornamented with sentences from the Koran: the whole has a brilliant and extraordinary appearance, more like a Chinese temple than anything else. This building is called the Acksa el Sakhara, from its containing a piece of rock called the Hadjr el Sakhara, or the locked-up stone, which is the principal object of veneration in the place: it occupies the centre of the mosque, and on it are shown the prints of the angel Gabriel's fingers, who brought it from heaven, and the mark of the Prophet's foot and that of his camel, a singularly good leaper, two more of whose footsteps I have seen in Egypt and Arabia, and I believe there is another at Damascus, the whole journey from Jerusalem to Mecca having been performed in four bounds only, for which remarkable service the camel is to have a place in heaven, where he will enjoy the society of Borak, the prophet's horse, Balaam's ass, Tobit's dog, and the dog of the seven sleepers, whose name was Ketmir, and also the companionship of a certain celebrated fly with whose merits I am unacquainted.

We are told that the stone of the Sakhara fell from heaven at the time when prophecy commenced at Jerusalem. It was employed as a seat by the venerable men to whom that gift was communicated, and, as long as the spirit of vatication continued to enlighten their minds, the slab remained steady for their accommodation; but no sooner was the power of prophecy withdrawn, and the persecuted seers compelled to flee for safety to other lands, than the stone manifested the profoundest sympathy in their fate, and evinced a determination to accompany them in their flight: on which Gabriel the archangel interposed his authority, and prevented the departure of the prophetical chair. He grasped it with his mighty hand and nailed it to its rocky bed by seven brass or golden nails. When any event of great importance to the world takes place the head of one of these nails disappears, and when they are all gone the day of judgment will come. As there are now only three left, the Mahometans believe that the end of all things is not far distant. All those who have faithfully performed their devotions at this celebrated mosque are furnished by the priest with a certificate of their having done so, which is to be buried with them that they may show it to the door-keeper of Paradise as a ticket of admission. I was presented with one of these at Jerusalem, and found another in the desert of Al Arisch, a wondrous piece of good fortune in the estimation of my Mahometan followers, as I was provided with a ticket for a friend, as well as a pass for my own reception among the houris of their Prophet's celestial garden.

The Greek monastery adjoins the church of the Holy Sepulchre. It contains a good library, the iron door of which is opened by a key as large as a horse-pistol. The books are kept in good order, and consist of about two thousand printed volumes in various languages; and about five hundred Greek and Arabic MSS. on paper, which are all theological works. There are also about one hundred Greek manuscripts on vellum: the whole collection is in excellent preservation. One of the eight manuscripts of the Gospels which the library contains has the index and the beginning of each Gospel written in gold letters on purple vellum, and has also some curious illuminations. There is likewise a manuscript of the whole Bible: it is a large folio, and is the only one I ever heard of, excepting the one at the Vatican and that at the British Museum. One of the most beautiful volumes in the library is a large folio of the book of Job. It is a most glorious MS.: the text is written in large letters, surrounded with scholia in a smaller hand, and almost every page contains one or more miniatures representing the sufferings of Job, with ghastly portraits of Bildad the Shuhite and his other pitying friends: this manuscript is of the twelfth century. The rest of the manuscripts consist of the works of the Fathers, copies of the 'Anthologia,' and books for the Church service.

The Arabic language is generally spoken at Jerusalem, though the Turkish is much used among the better class. The inhabitants are composed of people of different nations and different religions, who inwardly despise one another on account of their varying opinions; but, as the Christians are very numerous, there reigns among the whole no small degree of complaisance, as well as an unrestrained intercourse in matters of business, amusement, and even of religion. The Mussulmans, for instance, pray in all the holy places consecrated to the memory of Christ and the Virgin, except the tomb of the Holy Sepulchre, the sanctity of which they do not acknowledge, for they believe that Jesus

Christ did not die, but that he ascended alive into heaven, leaving the likeness of his face to Judas, who was condemned to die for him; and that, as Judas was crucified, it was his body, and not that of Jesus, which was placed in the sepulchre. It is for this reason that the Mussulmans do not perform any act of devotion at the tomb of the Holy Sepulchre, and that they ridicule the Christians who visit and revere it.

The Jews—the "children of the kingdom"—have been cast out, and many have come from the east and the west to occupy their place in the desolate land promised to their fathers. Their quarter is in the narrow valley between the Temple and the foot of Mount Zion. Many of the Jews are rich, but they are careful to conceal their wealth from the jealous eyes of their Mahometan rulers, lest they should be subjected to extortion.

It is remarkable that the Jews who are born in Jerusalem are of a totally different caste from those we see in Europe. Here they are a fair race, very lightly made, and particularly effeminate in manner; the young men wear a lock of long hair on each side of the face, which, with their flowing silk robes, gives them the appearance of women. The Jews of both sexes are exceedingly fond of dress; and, although they assume a dirty and squalid appearance when they walk abroad, in their own houses they are to be seen clothed in costly furs and the richest silks of Damascus. The women are covered with gold, and dressed in brocades stiff with embroidery. Some of them are beautiful; and a girl of about twelve years old, who was betrothed to the son of a rich old rabbi, was the prettiest little creature I ever saw; her skin was whiter than ivory, and her hair, which was as black as jet, and was plaited with strings of sequins, fell in tresses nearly to the ground. She was of a Spanish family, and the language usually spoken by the Jews among themselves is Spanish.

The Jewish religion is now so much encumbered with superstition and the extraordinary explanations of the Bible in the Talmud, that little of the original creed remains. They interpret all the words of Scripture literally, and this leads them into most absurd mistakes. On the morning of the day of the Passover I went into the synagogue under the walls of the Temple, and found it crowded to the very door; all the congregation were standing up, with large white shawls over their heads with the fringes which they were commanded to wear by the Jewish law. They were reading the Psalms, and after I had been there a short time all the people began to hop about and to shake their heads and limbs in a most extraordinary manner; the whole congregation was in motion, from the priest, who was dancing in the reading-desk, to the porter, who capered at the door. All this was in consequence of a verse in the 35th Psalm, which says, "All my bones shall say, Lord, who is like unto thee;" and this was their ludicrous manner of doing so. After the Psalm a crier went round the room, who sold the honour of performing different parts of the service to the highest bidder; the money so obtained is appropriated to the relief of the poor. The sanctuary at the upper end of the room was then opened, and a curtain withdrawn, in imitation of that which separated the Holy of Holies from the body of the Temple. From this place the book of the law was taken: it was contained in a case of embossed silver, and two large silver ornaments were fixed on the ends of the rollers, which stuck out from the top of the case. The Jews, out of reverence, as I presume, touched it with a little bodkin of gold, and, on its being carried to the reading-desk, a silver crown was placed upon it, and a man, supported by two others, one on each side of him, chanted the lesson of the day in a loud voice: the book was then replaced in the sanctuary, and the service concluded. The women are not admitted into the synagogue, but are permitted to view the ceremonies from a grated gallery set apart for them. However, they seldom attend, as it seems they are not accounted equal to the men either in body or soul, and trouble themselves very little with matters of religion.

The house of Rabbi A——, with whom I was acquainted, answered exactly to Sir Walter Scott's description of the dwelling of Isaac of York. The outside of the house and the court-yard indicated nothing but poverty and neglect; but on entering I was surprised at the magnificence of the furniture. One room had a silver chandelier, and a great quantity of embossed plate was displayed on the top of the polished cupboards. Some of the windows were filled with painted glass; and the members of the family, covered with gold and jewels, were seated on divans of Damascus brocade. The Rabbi's little son was so covered with charms in gold cases to keep off the evil eye, that he jingled like a chime of bells when he walked along; and a still younger boy, whom I had never seen before, was on this day exalted to the dignity of wearing trousers, which were of red stuff, embroidered with gold, and were brought in by his nurse and a number of other women in procession, and borne on high before him as he was dragged round the room howling and crying without any nether garment on at all. He was walked round again after his superb trousers were put on, and very uncomfortable he seemed to be, but doubtless the honour of the thing consoled him, and he waddled out into the court with an air of conscious dignity.

The learning of the rabbis is now at a very low ebb, and few of them thoroughly understand the ancient Hebrew tongue, although there are Jews at Jerusalem who speak several languages, and are said to be well acquainted with all the traditions of their fathers, and the mysterious learning of the Cabala.

There is in the Holy Land another division of the children of Israel, the Samaritans, who still keep up a separate form of religion. Their synagogue at Nablous is a mean building, not unlike a poor Mahometan mosque. Within it is a large, low, square chamber, the floor of which is covered with matting. Round a part of the walls is a wooden shelf, on which are laid above thirty manuscript books of the Pentateuch written in the Samaritan character: they possess also a very famous roll or volume of the Pentateuch, which is said to have been written by Abishai the grandson of Aaron. It is contained in a curiously ornamented octagon case of brass about two feet high, on opening which the MS. appears within rolled upon two pieces of wood. It is sixteen inches wide, and must be of great length, as each of the two parts of the roll are four or five inches in diameter. The writing is small and not very distinct, and the MS. is in rather a dilapidated condition. The Samaritan Rabbi Ibrahim Israel, true to his Jewish origin, would not open the case until he had been well paid. He affirmed that in this MS. the blessings were directed to be given from Mount Ebal and the curses from Mount Gherizim. However this may be, in an Arabic translation of the Samaritan Pentateuch, which is in my own collection, the 12th and 13th verses of the 27th chapter of Deuteronomy are the same as the usually received text in other Bibles.

Jerusalem was at this time (1834) under the dominion of the Egyptians, and Ibrahim Pasha arrived shortly after we had established ourselves in the vaulted dungeons of the Latin convent. He took up his abode in a house in the town, and did not maintain any state or ceremony; indeed he had scarcely any guards, and but few servants, so secure did he feel in a country which he had so lately conquered. He received us with great courtesy in his mean lodging, where we found an interpreter who spoke English. I had been promised a letter from Mohammed Ali Pasha to Ibrahim Pasha, but on inquiring I found it had not arrived, and Ibrahim Pasha sent a courier to Jaffa to inquire whether it was lying there; however it did not reach me, and I therefore was not permitted to see the interior of the mosque of Omar, or the great church of the Purification, which stands on the site of the Temple of Solomon, and into which at that time no Christian had penetrated.

CHAPTER XV.

Expedition to the Monastery of St. Sabba—Reports of Arab Robbers—The Valley of Jehoshaphat—The Bridge of Al Sirat—Rugged Scenery—An Arab Ambuscade—A successful Parley—The Monastery of St. Sabba—History of the Saint—The Greek Hermits—The Church—The Iconostasis—The Library—Numerous MSS.—The Dead Sea—The Scene of the Temptation—Discovery—The Apple of the Dead Sea—The Statements of Strabo and Pliny confirmed.

As

we wished to be present at the celebration of Easter by the Greek Church, we remained several weeks at Jerusalem, during which time we made various excursions to the most celebrated localities in the neighbourhood. In addition to the Bible, which almost sufficed us for a guidebook in these sacred regions, we had several books of travels with us, and I was struck with the superiority of old Maundrell's narrative over all the others, for he tells us plainly and clearly what he saw, whilst other travellers so encumber their narratives with opinions and disquisitions, that, instead of describing the country, they describe only what they think about it; and thus little real information as to what there was to be seen or done could be gleaned from these works, eloquent and well written as many of them are; and we continually returned to Maundrell's homely pages for a good plain account of what we wished to know. As, however, I had gathered from various incidental remarks in these books that there was a famous library in the monastery of St. Sabba, in which one might expect to find all the lost classics, whole rows of uncial manuscripts, and perhaps the histories of the Preadamite kings in the autograph of Jemshid, I determined to go and see it.

It was of course necessary for every traveller at Jerusalem to "do his Dead Sea;" and accordingly we made arrangements for an excursion in that direction, which was to include a visit to St. Sabba; for my companion kindly put up with my aberrations, and agreed to linger with me for that purpose on our way to Jericho, although it was at the risk of falling among thieves, for we heard all manner of reports of the danger of the roads, and of a certain truculent Robin Hood sort of person, called Abou Gash, who had just got out of some prison or other.

Abou Gash was vastly popular in this part of the country: everybody spoke well of him, and declared that "he was the mildest-mannered man that ever cut a throat or scuttled ship;" but they all hinted that it might be as well to keep out of his way, and that, when we went cantering about the country, poking our noses into caves, and ruins, and other uncanny places, it would be advisable to keep a "good" look-out. For all this we cared little: so, getting together our merry men, we sallied forth through St. Stephen's gate. A gallant band we were, some five-and-twenty horsemen, well armed in the Egyptian style; with tents and kettles, cocks and hens, and cooks and marmitons, stowed upon the baggage-horses. Great store of good things had we—vino doro di Monte Libano, and hams, to show that we were not Mahometans; and tea, to prove that we were not Frenchmen; and guns to shoot partridges withal, and many other European necessaries.

We tramped along upon the hard rocky ground one after the other, through the Valley of Jehoshaphat; and looked up at the corner of the temple, whence is to spring on the last day, as every sound follower of the Prophet believes, the fearful bridge of Al Sirat, which is narrower than the edge of the sharpest cimeter of Khorassaun, and from which those who without due preparation attempt to pass on their way to the paradise of Mahomet will fall into the unfathomable gulf below. Gradually as we advanced into the valley, through which the brook Kedron, when there is any water in it, flows into the Dead Sea, the scenery became more and more savage, the rocks more precipitous, and the valley narrowed into a deep gorge, the path being sometimes among the broken stones in the bed of the stream, and sometimes rising high above it on narrow ledges of rock.

We rode on for some hours, admiring the wild grandeur of the scenery, for this is the hill country of Judea, and seems almost a chaos of rocks and craggy mountains, broken into narrow defiles, or opening into dreary valleys bare of vegetation, except a few shrubs whose tough roots pierce through the crevices of the stony soil, and find a scanty subsistence in the small portions of earth which the rains have washed from the surface of the rocks above. In one place the pathway, which was not more than two or three feet wide, wound round the corner of a precipitous crag in such a manner that a horseman riding along the giddy way showed so clearly against the sky, that it seemed as if a puff of wind would blow horse and man into the ravine beneath. We were proceeding along this ledge—Fathallah, one of our interpreters, first, I second, and the others following—when we saw three or four Arabs with long bright-barrelled guns slip out of a crevice just before us, and take up their position on the path, pointing those unpleasant-looking implements in our faces. From some inconceivable motive, not of the most heroic nature I fear, my first move was to turn my head round to look behind me; but when I did so, I perceived that some more Arabs had crept out of another cleft behind us, which we had not observed as we passed; and on looking up I saw that from the precipice above us a curious collection of bright barrels and brown faces were taking an observation of our party, while on the opposite side of the gorge, which was perhaps a hundred and fifty yards across, every fragment of rock seemed to have brought forth a man in a white tunic and bare legs, with a yellow handkerchief round his head, and a long gun in his hand, which he pointed towards us.

We had fallen into an ambuscade, and one so cleverly laid that all attempt at resistance was hopeless. The path was so narrow that our horses could not turn, and a precipice within a yard of us, of a hundred feet sheer down, rendered our position singularly uncomfortable. Fathallah's horse came to a stand-still: my horse ran his nose against him and stood still too; and so did all the rest of us. "Well!" said I, "Fathallah, what is this? who are these gentlemen?" "I knew it would be so," quoth Fathallah, "I was sure of it! and in such a cursed place too!—I see how it is, I shall never get home alive to Aleppo!"

After waiting a while, I imagine to enjoy our confusion, one of the Arabs in front took up his parable and said, "Oh! oh! ye Egyptians!" (we wore the Egyptian dress)" what are you doing here, in our country? You are Ibrahim Pasha's men; are you? Say—speak;

what reason have ye for being here? for we are Arabs, and the sons of Arabs; and this is our country, and our land?"

"Sir," said the interpreter with profound respect—for he rode first, and four or five guns were pointed directly at his breast—"Sir, we are no Egyptians; thy servants are men of peace; we are peaceable Franks, pilgrims from the holy city, and we are only going to bathe in the waters of the Jordan, as all pilgrims do who travel to the Holy Land." "Franks!" quoth the Arab; "I know the Franks; pretty Franks are ye! Franks are the fathers of hats, and do not wear guns or swords, or red caps upon their heads, as you do. We shall soon see whether ye are Franks or not. Ye are Egyptians, and servants of Ibrahim Pasha the Egyptian: but now ye shall find that ye are our servants!"

"Oh Sir," exclaimed I in the best Arabic I could muster, "thy servants are men of peace, travellers, antiquaries all of us. Oh Sir, we are Englishmen, which is a sort of Frank—very harmless and excellent people, desiring no evil. We beg you will be good enough to let us pass." "Franks!" retorted the Arab sheick, "pretty Franks! Franks do not speak Arabic, nor wear the Nizam dress! Ye are men of Ibrahim Pasha's; Egyptians, arrant Cairoites (Misseri) are ye all, every one of ye;" and he and all his followers laughed at us scornfully, for we certainly did look very like Egyptians. "We are Franks, I tell you!" again exclaimed Fathallah: "Ibrahim Pasha, indeed! who is he, I should like to know? we are Franks; and Franks like to see everything. We are going to see the monastery of St. Sabba; we are not Egyptians; what care we for Egyptians? we are English, Franks, every one of us, and we only desire to see the monastery of St. Sabba; that is what we are, O Arab, son of an Arab (Arab beni Arab). We are no less than this, and no more; we are Franks, as you are Arabs."

Upon this there ensued a consultation between this son of an Arab and the other sons of Arabs, and in process of time the worthy gentlemen, knowing that it was impossible for us to escape, agreed to take us to the monastery of St. Sabba, which was not far off, and there to hear what we had to say in our defence.

The sheick waved his arm aloft as a signal to his men to raise the muzzle of their guns, and we were allowed to proceed; some of the Arabs walking unconcernedly before us, and the others skipping like goats from rock to rock above us, and on the other side of the valley. They were ten times as numerous as we were, and we should have had no chance with them even on fair ground; but here we were completely at their mercy. We were escorted in this manner the rest of the way, and in half an hour's time we found ourselves standing before the great square tower of the monastery of St. Sabba. The battlements were lined with Arabs, who had taken possession of this strong place, and after a short parley and a clanging of arms within, a small iron door was opened in the wall: we dismounted and passed in; our horses, one by one, were pushed through after us. So there we were in the monastery of St Sabba sure enough; but under different circumstances from what we expected when we set out that morning from Jerusalem.

Fathallah had, however, convinced the sheick of the Arabs that we really were Franks, and not followers of Ibrahim Pasha, and before long we not only were relieved from all fear, but became great friends with the noble and illustrious Abou Somebody, who had taken possession of St. Sabba and the defiles leading to it.

This monastery, which is a very ancient foundation, is built upon the edge of the precipice at the bottom of which flows the brook Kedron, which in the rainy season becomes a torrent. The buildings, which are of immense strength, are supported by buttresses so massive that the upper part of each is large enough to contain a small arched chamber; the whole of the rooms in the monastery are vaulted, and are gloomy and imposing in the extreme. The pyramidical-shaped mass of buildings extends half-way down the rocks, and is crowned above by a high and stately square tower, which commands the small iron gate of the principal entrance. Within there are several small irregular courts connected by steep flights of steps and dark arched passages, some of which are carried through the solid rock.

It was in one of the caves in these rocks that the renowned St. Sabba passed his time in the society of a pet lion. He was a famous anchorite, and was made chief of all the monks of Palestine by Sallustius, Patriarch of Jerusalem, about the year 490. He was twice ambassador to Constantinople to propitiate the Emperors Anastasius the Silent and Justinian; moreover he made a vow never to eat apples as long as he lived. He was born at Mutalasca, near Cæsarea of Cappadocia, in 439, and died in 532, in the ninety-fifth year of his age: he is still held in high veneration by both the Greek and Latin churches. He was the founder of the Laura, which was formerly situated among the clefts and crevices of these rocks, the present monastery having been enclosed and fortified at I do not know what period, but long after the decease of the saint.

The word laura, which is often met with in the histories of the first five centuries after Christ, signifies, when applied to monastic institutions, a number of separate cells, each inhabited by a single hermit or anchorite, in contradistinction to a convent or monastery, which was called a cœnobium, where the monks lived together in one building under the rule of a superior. This species of monasticism seems always to have been a peculiar characteristic of the Greek Church, and in the present day these ascetic observances are upheld only by the Greek, Coptic, and Abyssinian Christians, among whom hermits and quietists, such as waste the body for the improvement of the soul, are still to be met with in the clefts of the rocks and in the desert places of Asia and Africa. They are a sort of dissenters as regards their own Church, for, by the mortifications to which they subject themselves, they rebuke the regular priesthood, who do not go so far, although these latter fast in the year above one hundred days, and always rise to midnight prayer. In the dissent, if such it be, of these monks of the desert there is a dignity and self-denying firmness much to be respected. They follow the tenets of their faith and the ordinances of their religion in a manner which is almost sublime. They are in this respect the very opposite to European dissenters, who are as undignified as they are generally snug and cosy in their mode of life. Here, among the followers of St. Anthony, there are no mock heroics, no turning up of the whites of the eyes and drawing down of the corners of the mouth: they form their rule of life from the ascetic writings of the early fathers of the Church: their self-denial is extreme, their devotion heroic; but yet to our eyes it appears puerile and irrational that men should give up their whole lives to a routine of observances which, although they are hard and stern, are yet so trivial that they appear almost ridiculous.

In one of the courts of the monastery there is a palm-tree, said to be endowed with miraculous properties, which was planted by St. Sabba, and is to be numbered among the few now existing in the Holy Land, for at present they are very rarely to be met with, except in the vale of Jericho and the valley of the Jordan and the Dead Sea, in which localities, in consequence of their being so much beneath the level of the rest of the country, the temperature is many degrees higher than it is elsewhere.

The church is rather large and is very solidly built. There are many ancient frescos painted on the walls, and various early Greek pictures are hung round about: many of these are representations of the most famous saints, and on the feast of each his picture is exposed upon a kind of desk before the iconostasis or wooden partition which divides the church from the sanctuary and the altar, and there it receives the kisses and oblations of all the worshippers who enter the sacred edifice on that day.

The ικονοστασις
is dimly represented in our older churches by the rood-loft and screen which divides the chancel from the nave: it is retained also in Lombardy and in the sees under the Ambrosian rule; but these screens and rood-lofts, which destroy the beauty of a cathedral or any large church, are unknown in the Roman churches. They date their origin from the very earliest ages, when the "discipline of the secret" was observed, and when the ceremonies of the communion were held to be of such a sacred and mysterious nature that it was not permitted to the communicants to reveal what then took place—an incomprehensible custom which led to the propagation of many false ideas and strange rumours as to the Christian observances in the third and fourth centuries, and was one of the causes which led to several of the persecutions of the Church, as it was believed by the heathens that the Christians sacrificed children and committed other abominations for which they deserved extermination; and so prone are the vulgar to give credence to such injurious reports, that the Christians in later ages accused the Jews of the very same practices for which they themselves had in former times been held up to execration.

In one part of the church I observed a rickety ladder leaning against the wall, and leading up to a small door about ten feet from the ground. Scrambling up this ladder, I found myself in the library of which I had heard so much. It was a small square room, or rather a large closet, in the upper part of one of the enormous buttresses which supported the walls of the monastery. Here I found about a thousand books, almost all manuscripts, but the whole of them were works of divinity. One volume in the Bulgarian or Servian language was written in uncial letters; the rest were in Greek, and were for the most part of the twelfth century. There were a great many enormous folios of the works of the fathers, and one MS. of the Octoteuch, or first eight hooks of the Old Testament. It is remarkable how very rarely MSS. of any part of the Old Testament are found in the libraries of Greek monasteries; this was the only MS. of the Octoteuch that I ever met with either before or afterwards in any part of the Levant. There were about a hundred other MSS. on a shelf in the apsis of the church: I was not allowed to examine them, but was assured that they were liturgies and church-books which were used on the various high days during the year.

I was afterwards taken by some of the monks into the vaulted chambers of the great square tower or keep, which stood near the iron door by which we had been admitted. Here there were about a hundred MSS., but all imperfect; I found the 'Iliad' of Homer among them, but it was on paper. Some of these MSS. were beautifully written; they were, however, so imperfect, that in the short time I was there, and pestered as I was by a crowd of gaping Arabs, I was unable to discover what they were.

I was allowed to purchase three MSS., with which the next day I and my companion departed on our way to the Dead Sea, our friend the sheick having, from the moment that he was convinced we were nothing better or worse than Englishmen and sight-seers, treated us with all manner of civility.

On arriving at the Dead Sea I forthwith proceeded to bathe in it, in order to prove the celebrated buoyancy of the water, and was nearly drowned in the experiment, for, not being able to swim, my head got much deeper below the water than I intended. Two ignorant pilgrims, who had joined our party for protection, baptized each other in this filthy water, and sang psalms so loudly and discordantly that we asked them what in the name of wonder they were about, when we discovered that they thought this was the Jordan, and were sorely grieved at their disappointment. We found several shells upon the shore and a small dead fish, but perhaps they had been washed down by the waters of the Jordan or the Kedron: I do not know how this may be.

We wandered about for two or three days in this hot, volcanic, and sunken region, and thence proceeded to Jericho. The mountain of Quarantina, the scene of the forty days' temptation of our Saviour, is pierced all over with the caves excavated by the ancient anchorites, and which look like pigeons' nests. Some of them are in the most extraordinary situations, high up on the face of tremendous precipices. However, I will not attempt to detail the singularities of this wild district; we visited the chief objects of interest, and a big book that I brought from St. Sabba is endeared to my recollections by my having constantly made use of it as a pillow in my tent during our wanderings. It was somewhat hard, undoubtedly; but after a long day's ride it served its purpose very well, and I slept as soundly as if it had been read to me.

At two subsequent periods I visited this region, and purchased seven other MSS. from St Sabba; among them was the Octoteuch of the tenth, if not the ninth, century, which I esteem one of the most rare and precious volumes of my library.

We made a somewhat singular discovery when travelling among the mountains to the east of the Dead Sea, where the ruins of Ammon, Jerash, and Adjeloun well repay the labour and fatigue encountered in visiting them. It was a remarkably hot and sultry day: we were scrambling up the mountain through a thick jungle of bushes and low trees, when I saw before me a fine plum-tree, loaded with fresh blooming plums. I cried out to my fellow-traveller, "Now, then, who will arrive first at the plum-tree?" and as he caught a glimpse of so refreshing an object, we both pressed our horses into a gallop to see which would get the first plum from the branches. We both arrived at the same moment; and, each snatching at a fine ripe plum, put it at once into our mouths; when, on biting it, instead of the cool delicious juicy fruit which we expected, our mouths were filled with a dry bitter dust, and we sat under the tree upon our horses sputtering, and hemming, and doing all we could to be relieved of the nauseous taste of this strange fruit. We then perceived, and to my great delight, that we had discovered the famous apple of the Dead Sea, the existence of which has been doubted and canvassed since the days of Strabo and Pliny, who first described it. Many travellers have given descriptions of other vegetable productions which bear some analogy to the one described by Pliny; but up to this time no one had met with the thing itself, either upon the spot mentioned by the ancient authors, or elsewhere. I brought several of them to England. They are a kind of gall-nut. I found others afterwards upon the plains of Troy, but there can be no doubt whatever that this is the apple of Sodom to which Strabo and Pliny referred. Some of those which I brought to England were given to the Linnæan Society, who published an engraving of them, and a description of their vegetable peculiarities, in their 'Transactions;' but as they omitted to explain the peculiar interest attached to them in consequence of their having been sought for unsuccessfully for above 1500 years, they excited little attention; though, as the evidence of the truth of what has so long been considered as a vulgar fable, they are fairly to be classed among the most curious productions which have been brought from the Holy Land.

CHAPTER XVI.

Church of the Holy Sepulchre—Processions of the Copts—The Syrian Maronites and the Greeks—Riotous Behaviour of the Pilgrims—Their immense numbers—The Chant of the Latin Monks—Ibrahim Pasha—The Exhibition of the Sacred Fire—Excitement of the Pilgrims—The Patriarch obtains the Sacred Fire from the Holy Sepulchre—Contest for the Holy Light—Immense sum paid for the privilege of receiving it first—Fatal Effects of the Heat and Smoke—Departure of Ibrahim Pasha—Horrible Catastrophe—Dreadful Loss of Life among the Pilgrims in their endeavours to leave the Church—Battle with the Soldiers—Our Narrow Escape—Shocking Scene in the Court of the Church—Humane Conduct of Ibrahim Pasha—Superstition of the Pilgrims regarding Shrouds—Scallop Shells and Palm Branches—The Dead Muleteer—Moonlight View of the Dead Bodies—The Curse on Jerusalem—Departure from the Holy City.

It
was on Friday, the 3rd of May, that my companions and myself went, about five o'clock in the evening, to the church of the Holy Sepulchre, where we had places assigned us in the gallery of the Latin monks, as well as a good bed-room in their convent. The church was very full, and the numbers kept increasing every moment. We first saw a small procession of the Copts go round the sepulchre, and after them one of the Syrian Maronites. I then went to bed, and at midnight was awakened to see the procession of the Greeks, which was rather grand. By the rules of their Church they are not permitted to carry any images, and therefore to make up for this they bore aloft a piece of brocade, upon which was embroidered a representation of the body of our Saviour. This was placed in the tomb, and, after some short time, brought out again and carried into the chapel of the Greeks, when the ceremonies of the night ended; for there was no procession of the Armenians, as the Armenian Patriarch had made an address to his congregation, and had, it was said, explained the falsity of the miracle of the holy fire; to the excessive astonishment of his hearers, who for centuries have considered an unshakable belief in this yearly wonder as one of the leading articles of their faith. After the Greek procession I went quietly to bed again, and slept soundly till next morning.

The behaviour of the pilgrims was riotous in the extreme; the crowd was so great that many persons actually crawled over the heads of others, and some made pyramids of men by standing on each others' shoulders, as I have seen them do at Astley's. At one time, before the church was so full, they made a race-course round the sepulchre; and some, almost in a state of nudity, danced about with frantic gestures, yelling and screaming as if they were possessed.

Altogether it was a scene of disorder and profanation which it is impossible to describe. In consequence of the multitude of people and the quantities of lamps, the heat was excessive, and a steam arose which prevented your seeing clearly across the church. But every window and cornice, and every place where a man's foot could rest, excepting the gallery—which was reserved for Ibrahim Pasha and ourselves—appeared to be crammed with people; for 17,000 pilgrims were said to be in Jerusalem, almost the whole of whom had come to the Holy City for no other reason than to see the sacred fire.

After the noise, heat, and uproar which I had witnessed from the gallery that overlooked the Holy Sepulchre, the contrast of the calmness and quiet of my room in the Franciscan convent was very pleasing. The room had a small window which opened upon the Latin choir, where, in the evening, the monks chanted the litany of the Virgin: their fine voices and the beautiful simplicity of the ancient chant made a strong impression upon my mind; the orderly solemnity of the Roman Catholic vespers showing to great advantage when compared with the screams and tumult of the fanatic Greeks.

LITANY OF THE VIRGIN

Sung by the Friars of St. Salvador at Jerusalem.

LITANY OF THE VIRGIN Sung by the Friars of St. Salvador at Jerusalem.Sancta Maria—Ora pro nobis.

Sancta Virgo Virginum—Ora pro nobis.

Impeatrix Reginarum—Ora pro nobis.

Laus sanctarum animarum—Ora pro nobis

Vera salutrix earum—Ora pro nobis.

The next morning a way was made through the crowd for Ibrahim Pasha, by the soldiers with the butt-ends of their muskets, and by the Janissaries with their kourbatches and whips made of a quantity of small rope. The Pasha sat in the gallery, on a divan which the monks had made for him between the two columns nearest to the Greek chapel. They had got up a sort of procession to do him honour, the appearance of which did not add to the solemnity of the scene: three monks playing crazy fiddles led the way, then came the choristers with lighted candles, next two Nizam soldiers with muskets and fixed bayonets; a number of doctors, instructors, and officers tumbling over each other's heels, brought up the rear: he was received by the women, of whom there were thousands in the church, with a very peculiar shrill cry, which had a strange unearthly effect. It was the monosyllable la, la, la, uttered in a shrill trembling tone, which I thought much more like pain than rejoicing. The Pasha was dressed in full trousers of dark cloth, a light lilac-coloured jacket, and a red cap without a turban. When he was seated, the monks brought us some sherbet, which was excellently made; and as our seats were very near the great man, we saw everything in an easy and luxurious way; and it being announced that the Mahomedan Pasha was ready, the Christian miracle, which had been waiting for some time, was now on the point of being displayed.

The people were by this time become furious; they were worn out with standing in such a crowd all night, and as the time approached for the exhibition of the holy fire they could not contain themselves for joy. Their excitement increased as the time for the miracle in which all believed drew near. At about one o'clock the Patriarch went into the ante-chapel of the sepulchre, and soon after a magnificent procession moved out of the Greek chapel. It conducted the Patriarch three times round the tomb; after which he took off his outer robes of cloth of silver, and went into the sepulchre, the door of which was then closed. The agitation of the pilgrims was now extreme: they screamed aloud; and the dense mass of people shook to and fro, like a field of corn in the wind.

image of a bundle of thin wax-candles enclosed in an iron frame.

There is a round hole in one part of the chapel over the sepulchre, out of which the holy fire is given, and up to this the man who had agreed to pay the highest sum for this honour was conducted by a strong guard of soldiers. There was silence for a minute; and then a light appeared out of the tomb, and the happy pilgrim received the holy fire from the Patriarch within. It consisted of a bundle of thin wax-candles, lit, and enclosed in an iron frame to prevent their being torn asunder and put out in the crowd: for a furious battle commenced immediately; every one being so eager to obtain the holy light, that one man put out the candle of his neighbour in trying to light his own. It is said that as much as ten thousand piasters has been paid for the privilege of first receiving the holy fire, which is believed to ensure eternal salvation. The Copts got eight purses this year for the first candle they gave to a pilgrim of their own persuasion.

This was the whole of the ceremony; there was no sermon or prayers, except a little chanting during the processions, and nothing that could tend to remind you of the awful event which this feast was designed to commemorate.

Soon you saw the lights increasing in all directions, every one having lit his candle from the holy flame: the chapels, the galleries, and every corner where a candle could possibly be displayed, immediately appeared to be in a blaze. The people, in their frenzy, put the bunches of lighted tapers to their faces, hands, and breasts, to purify themselves from their sins. The Patriarch was carried out of the sepulchre in triumph, on the shoulders of the people he had deceived, amid the cries and exclamations of joy which resounded from every nook of the immense pile of buildings. As he appeared in a fainting state, I supposed that he was ill; but I found that it is the uniform custom on these occasions to feign insensibility, that the pilgrims may imagine he is overcome with the glory of the Almighty, from whose immediate presence they believe him to have returned.

In a short time the smoke of the candles obscured everything in the place, and I could see it rolling in great volumes out at the aperture at the top of the dome. The smell was terrible; and three unhappy wretches, overcome by heat and bad air, fell from the upper range of galleries, and were dashed to pieces on the heads of the people below. One poor Armenian lady, seventeen years of age, died where she sat, of heat, thirst, and fatigue.

After a while, when he had seen all that was to be seen, Ibrahim Pasha got up and went away, his numerous guards making a line for him by main force through the dense mass of people which filled the body of the church. As the crowd was so immense, we waited for a little while, and then set out all together to return to our convent. I went first and my friends followed me, the soldiers making way for us across the church. I got as far as the place where the Virgin is said to have stood during the crucifixion, when I saw a number of people lying one on another all about this part of the church, and as far as I could see towards the door. I made my way between them as well as I could, till they were so thick that there was actually a great heap of bodies on which I trod. It then suddenly struck me they were all dead! I had not perceived this at first, for I thought they were only very much fatigued with the ceremonies and had lain down to rest themselves there; but when I came to so great a heap of bodies I looked down at them, and saw that sharp, hard appearance of the face which is never to be mistaken. Many of them were quite black with suffocation, and farther on were others all bloody and covered with the brains and entrails of those who had been trodden to pieces by the crowd.

At this time there was no crowd in this part of the church; but a little farther on, round the corner towards the great door, the people, who were quite panic-struck, continued to press forward, and every one was doing his utmost to escape. The guards outside, frightened at the rush from within, thought that the Christians wished to attack them, and the confusion soon grew into a battle. The soldiers with their bayonets killed numbers of fainting wretches, and the walls were spattered with blood and brains of men who had been felled, like oxen, with the butt-ends of the soldiers' muskets. Every one struggled to defend himself or to get away, and in the mêlée all who fell were immediately trampled to death by the rest. So desperate and savage did the fight become, that even the panic-struck and frightened pilgrims appear at last to have been more intent upon the destruction of each other than desirous to save themselves.

For my part, as soon as I perceived the danger I had cried out to my companions to turn back, which they had done; but I myself was carried on by the press till I came near the door, where all were fighting for their lives. Here, seeing certain destruction before me, I made every endeavour to get back. An officer of the Pasha's, who by his star was a colonel or bin bashee, equally alarmed with myself, was also trying to return: he caught hold of my cloak, or bournouse, and pulled me down on the body of an old man who was breathing out his last sigh. As the officer was pressing me to the ground we wrestled together among the dying and the dead with the energy of despair. I struggled with this man till I pulled him down, and happily got again upon my legs—(I afterwards found that he never rose again)—and scrambling over a pile of corpses, I made my way back into the body of the church, where I found my friends, and we succeeded in reaching the sacristy of the Catholics, and thence the room which had been assigned to us by the monks. The dead were lying in heaps, even upon the stone of unction; and I saw full four hundred wretched people, dead and living, heaped promiscuously one upon another, in some places above five feet high. Ibrahim Pasha had left the church only a few minutes before me, and very narrowly escaped with his life; he was so pressed upon by the crowd on all sides, and it was said attacked by several of them, that it was only by the greatest exertions of his suite, several of whom were killed, that he gained the outer court. He fainted more than once in the struggle, and I was told that some of his attendants at last had to cut a way for him with their swords through the dense ranks of the frantic pilgrims. He remained outside, giving orders for the removal of the corpses, and making his men drag out the bodies of those who appeared to be still alive from the heaps of the dead. He sent word to us to remain in the convent till all the dead bodies had been removed, and that when we could come out in safety he would again send to us.

We stayed in our room two hours before we ventured to make another attempt to escape from this scene of horror; and then walking close together, with all our servants round us, we made a bold push and got out of the door of the church. By this time most of the bodies were removed; but twenty or thirty were still lying in distorted attitudes at the foot of Mount Calvary; and fragments of clothes, turbans, shoes, and handkerchiefs, clotted with blood and dirt, were strewed all over the pavement.

In the court in the front of the church, the sight was pitiable: mothers weeping over their children—the sons bending over the dead bodies of their fathers—and one poor woman was clinging to the hand of her husband, whose body was fearfully mangled. Most of the sufferers were pilgrims and strangers. The Pasha was greatly moved by this scene of woe; and he again and again commanded his officers to give the poor people every assistance in their power, and very many by his humane efforts were rescued from death.

I was much struck by the sight of two old men with white beards, who had been seeking for each other among the dead; they met as I was passing by, and it was affecting to see them kiss and shake hands, and congratulate each other on having escaped from death.

When the bodies were removed many were discovered standing upright, quite dead; and near the church door one of the soldiers was found thus standing, with his musket shouldered, among the bodies which reached nearly as high as his head; this was in a corner near the great door on the right side as you come in. It seems that this door had been shut, so that many who stood near it were suffocated in the crowd; and when it was opened, the rush was so great that numbers were thrown down and never rose again, being trampled to death by the press behind them. The whole court before the entrance of the church was covered with bodies laid in rows, by the Pasha's orders, so that their friends might find them and carry them away. As we walked home we saw numbers of people carried out, some dead, some horribly wounded and in a dying state, for they had fought with their heavy silver inkstands and daggers.

In the evening I was not sorry to retire early to rest in the low vaulted room in the strangers' house attached to the monastery of St. Salvador. I was weary and depressed after the agitating scenes of the morning, and my lodging was not rendered more cheerful by there being a number of corpses laid out in their shrouds in the stone court beneath its window. It is thought by these superstitious people that a shroud washed in the fountain of Siloam and blessed at the tomb of our Saviour forms a complete suit of armour for the body of a sinner deceased in the faith, and that clad in this invulnerable panoply he may defy the devil and all his angels. For this reason every pilgrim when journeying has his shroud with him, with all its different parts and bandages complete; and to many they became useful sooner than they expected. A holy candle also forms part of a pilgrim's accoutrements. It has some sovereign virtue, but I do not exactly know what; and they were all provided with several long thin tapers, and a rosary or two, and sundry rosaries and ornaments made of pearl oyster-shells—all which are defences against the powers of darkness. These pearl oyster-shells are, I imagine, the scallop-shell of romance, for there are no scallops to be found here. My companion was very anxious to obtain some genuine scallop-shells, as they form part of his arms; but they, as well as the palm branches, carried home by all palmers on their return from the Holy Land, are as rare here as they are in England. This is the more remarkable, as the medal struck by Vespasian on the subjection of this country represents a woman in an attitude of mourning seated under a palm-tree with the legend "Judæa capta;" so there may have been palms in those days. I was going to say there must have been: but on second thoughts it does not follow that there should have been palms in Judæa, because the Romans put them on a medal, any more than that there should be unicorns in England because we represent them on our coins. However, all this is a digression: we must return to our dead men. There were sixteen or seventeen of them, all stiff and stark, lying in the court, nicely wrapped up in their shrouds, like parcels ready to be sent off to the other world: but at the end of the row lay one man in a brown dress; he was one of the lower class—a muleteer, perhaps, a strong, well-made man; but he was not in a shroud. He had died fighting, and there he lay with his knees drawn up, his right arm above his head, and in his hand the jacket of another man, which could not now be released from his grasp, so tightly had his strong hand been clenched in the death-struggle. This figure took a strong hold on my imagination; there was something wild and ghastly in its appearance, different from the quiet attitude of the other victims of the fight in which I also had been engaged. It put me in mind of all manner of horrible old stories of ghosts and goblins with which my memory was well stored; and I went to bed with my head so occupied by these traditions of gloom and ignorance that I could not sleep, or if I did for awhile, I woke up again and still went on thinking of the old woman of Berkeley, and the fire-king, and the stories in Scott's 'Discovery of Witchcraft,' and the 'Hierarchy of the Blessed Aungelles,' and Caxton's 'Golden Legende'—all books wherein I delighted to pore, till I could not help getting out of bed again to have another look at the ghastly regiment in the court below.

 I leant against the heavy stone mullions of the window, which was barred, but without glass, and gazed I know not how long. There they all were, still and quiet; some in the full moonlight, and some half obscured by the shadow of the buildings. In the morning I had walked with them, living men, such as I was myself, and now how changed they were! Some of them I had spoken to, as they lived in the same court with me, and I had taken an interest in their occupations: now I would not willingly have touched them, and even to look at them was terrible! What little difference there is in appearance between the same men asleep and dead! and yet what a fearful difference in fact, not to themselves only, but to those who still remained alive to look upon them! Whilst I was musing upon these things the wind suddenly arose, the doors and shutters of the half-uninhabited monastery slammed and grated upon their hinges; and as the moon, which had been obscured, again shone clearly on the court below, I saw the dead muleteer with the jacket which he held waving in the air, the grimmest figure I ever looked upon. His face was black from the violence of his death, and he seemed like an evil spirit waving on his ghastly crew; and as the wind increased, the shrouds of some of the dead men fluttered in the night air as if they responded to his call. The clouds, passing rapidly over the moon, east such shadows on the corpses in their shrouds, that I could almost have fancied they were alive again. I returned to bed, and thanked God that I was not also laid out with them in the court below.

 In the morning I awoke at a late hour and looked out into the court; the muleteer and most of the other bodies were removed, and people were going about their business as if nothing had occurred, excepting that every now and then I heard the wail of women lamenting for the dead. Three hundred was the number reported to have been carried out of the gates to their burial-places that morning; two hundred more were badly wounded, many of whom probably died, for there were no physicians or surgeons to attend them, and it was supposed that others were buried in the courts and gardens of the city by their surviving friends; so that the precise number of those who perished was not known.

 When we reflect in what place and to commemorate what event the great multitude of Christian pilgrims had thus assembled from all parts of the world, the fearful visitation which came upon them appears more dreadful than if it had occurred under other circumstances. They had entered the sacred walls to celebrate the most joyful event which is recorded in the Scriptures. By the resurrection of our Saviour was proved not only his triumph over the grave, but the truth of the religion which He taught; and the anniversary of that event has been kept in all succeeding ages as the great festival of the Church. On the morning of this hallowed day throughout the Christian world the bells rang merrily, the altars were decked with flowers, and all men gave way to feelings of exultation and joy; in an hour everything was turned to mourning, lamentation, and woe!

There was a time when Jerusalem was the most prosperous and favoured city of the world; then "all her ways were pleasantness, and all her paths were peace;" "plenteousness was in her palaces;" and "Jerusalem was the joy of the whole earth."

But since the awful crime which was committed there, the Lord has poured out the vials of his wrath upon the once chosen city; dire and fearful have been the calamities which have befallen her in terrible succession for eighteen hundred years. Fury and desolation, hand in hand, have stalked round the precincts of the guilty spot; and Jerusalem has been given up to the spoiler and the oppressor.

The day following the occurrences which have been related, I had a long interview with Ibrahim Pasha, and the conversation turned naturally on the blasphemous impositions of the Greek and Armenian patriarchs, who, for the purposes of worldly gain, had deluded their ignorant followers with the performance of a trick in relighting the candles which had been extinguished on Good Friday with fire which they affirmed to have been sent down from heaven in answer to their prayers. The Pasha was quite aware of the evident absurdity which I brought to his notice, of the performance of a Christian miracle being put off for some time, and being kept in waiting for the convenience of a Mahometan prince. It was debated what punishment was to be awarded to the Greek patriarch for the misfortunes which had been the consequence of his jugglery, and a number of the purses which he had received from the unlucky pilgrims passed into the coffers of the Pasha's treasury. I was sorry that the falsity of this imposture was not publicly exposed, as it was a good opportunity of so doing. It seems wonderful that so barefaced a trick should continue to be practised every year in these enlightened times; but it has its parallel in the blood of St. Januarius, which is still liquefied whenever anything is to be gained by the exhibition of that astonishing act of priestly impertinence. If Ibrahim Pasha had been a Christian, probably this would have been the last Easter of the lighting of the holy fire; but from the fact of his religion being opposed to that of the monks, he could not follow the example of Louis XIV., who having put a stop to some clumsy imposition which was at that time bringing scandal on the Church, a paper was found nailed upon the door of the sacred edifice the day afterwards, on which the words were read—

"De part du roi, défense à Dieu
De faire miracle en ce lieu."

The interference of a Mahometan in such a case as this would only have been held as another persecution of the Christians; and the miracle of the holy fire has continued to be exhibited every year with great applause, and luckily without the unfortunate results which accompanied it on this occasion.

Ibrahim Pasha, though by no means the equal of Mehemet Ali in talents or attainments, was an enlightened man for a Turk. Though bold in battle, he was kind to those who were about him; and the cruelties practised by his troops in the Greek and Syrian wars are to be ascribed more to the system of Eastern warfare than to the savage disposition of their commander.

He was born at Cavalla, in Roumelia, in the year 1789, and died at Alexandria on the 10th of November, 1848. He was the son, according to some, of Mehemet Ali, but, according to others, of the wife of the great Viceroy of Egypt by a former husband. At the age of seventeen he joined his father's army, and in 1816 he commanded the expedition against the Wahabees—a sect who maintained that nothing but the Koran was to be held in any estimation by Mahometans, to the exclusion of all notes, explanations, and commentaries, which have in many cases usurped the authority of the text. They called themselves reformers, and, like King Henry VIII., took possession of the golden water-spouts and other ornaments of the Kaaba, burned the books and destroyed the colleges of the Arabian theologians, and carried off everything they could lay hold of, on religious principles. An eye-witness told me that some of the followers of Abd el Wahab had found a good-sized looking-glass in a house at Sanaa, which they were carrying away with great difficulty through the desert, the porters being guarded by a multitude of half-naked warriors, who had neglected all other plunder in the supposition that they had got hold of the diamond of Jemshid, a pre-Adamite monarch famous in the annals of Arabian history. Some more of these wild people found several bags of doubloons at Mocha, which they conceived to be dollars that had been spoiled somehow, and had turned yellow, for they had never seen any before. A "smart" captain of an American vessel at Jedda, who was consulted on the occasion, kindly gave them one real white dollar for four yellow ones—an arrangement which perfectly satisfied both parties. After three years' campaign, Ibrahim Pasha retook the holy cities of Mecca and Medina; and in December, 1819, he made his triumphant entry into Cairo, when he was invested with the title of Vizir and made Pasha of the Hedjaz by the Sultan—a dignity more exalted than that of the Pasha of Egypt.

In 1824 he commanded the armies of the Sultan, which were sent to put down the rebellion of the Greeks: he sailed from Alexandria with a fleet of 163 vessels, 16,000 infantry, 700 cavalry, and four regiments of artillery. Numerous captives were made in the Morea, and the slave-markets were stocked with Greek women and children who had been captured by the soldiers of the Turkish army. The battle of Navarino, in 1827, ended in the destruction of the Mahometan fleets; and thousands of slaves, who were forced to fight against their intended deliverers, being chained to their guns, sunk with the ships which were destroyed by the cannon of the allied forces of England, France, and Russia.

In 1831 Mehemet Ali undertook to wrest Syria from the Sultan his master. Ibrahim Pasha commanded his army of about 30,000 men, under the tuition, however, of a Frenchman, Colonel Sève, who had denied the Christian faith on Christmas-day, and was afterwards known as Suleiman Pasha. The Egyptian troops soon became masters of the Holy Land; Gaza, Jaffa, Jerusalem, and Acre fell before their victorious arms; and on the 22nd of December, 1832, Ibrahim Pasha, with an army of 30,000 men, defeated 60,000 Turks at Koniah, who had been sent against him by Sultan Mahmoud, under the command of Reschid Pasha.

Ibrahim had advanced as far as Kutayeh, on his way to Constantinople, when his march was stopped by the interference of European diplomacy. The Sultan, having made another effort to recover his dominions in Syria, sent an army against Ibrahim, which was utterly routed at the battle of Negib, on the 24th of June, 1839.

This defeat was principally owing to the Seraskier (the Turkish general) refusing to follow the counsels of Jochmus Pasha, a German officer, who, in distinguished contrast to the unhappy Suleiman, retained the religion of his fathers and the esteem of honest men.

His career was again checked by European policy, which, if it had any right to interfere at all, would have benefited the cause of humanity more by doing so before Egypt was drained of nearly all its able-bodied men, and Syria given up to the horrors of a long and cruel war.

The great powers of England, Austria, Russia, and Prussia now combined to restore the wasted provinces of Syria to the Porte; a fleet menaced the shores of the Holy Land; Acre was attacked, and taken in four hours by the accidental explosion of a powder-magazine, which almost destroyed what remained from former sieges of the habitable portion of the town. Ibrahim Pasha evacuated Syria, and retired to Egypt, where he amused himself with agriculture, and planting trees, always his favourite pursuit: the trees which he had planted near Cairo have already reduced the temperature in their vicinity several degrees.

In 1846 he went to Europe for the benefit of his health, and extended his tour to England, where he was much struck with the industry that pervaded all classes, and its superiority in railways and works of utility to the other countries of Europe. "Yes," said he to me at Mivart's Hotel; "in France there is more fantasia; in England there is more roast beef." I observed that he was surprised at the wealth displayed at one or two parties in some great houses in London at which he was present. Whether he had lost his memory in any degree at that time, I do not know; but on my recalling to him the great danger he had been in at Jerusalem, of which he entertained a very lively recollection, he could not remember the name of the Bey who was killed there, although he was the only person of any rank in his suite, with the exception of Selim Bey Selicdar, his swordbearer, with whom I afterwards became acquainted in Egypt.

In consequence of the infirmities of Mehemet Ali, whose great mind had become unsettled in his old age, Ibrahim was promoted by the present Sultan to the Vice-royalty of Egypt, on the 1st of September, 1848. His constitution, which had long been undermined by hardship, excess, and want of care, gave way at length, and on the 10th of November of the same year his body was carried to the tomb which his father had prepared for his family near Cairo, little thinking at the time that he should live to survive his sons Toussoun, Ismail, and Ibrahim, who have all descended before him to their last abode.

In personal appearance Ibrahim Pasha was a short, broad-shouldered man, with a red face, small eyes, and a heavy though cunning expression of countenance. He was as brave as a lion; his habits and ideas were rough and coarse; he had but little refinement in his composition; but, although I have often seen him abused for his cruelty in European newspapers, I never heard any well-authenticated anecdote of his cruelty, and do not believe that he was by any means of a savage disposition, nor that his troops rivalled in any way the horrors committed in Algeria by the civilized and fraternising French. He was a bold, determined soldier. He had that reverence and respect for his father which is so much to be admired in the patriarchal customs of the East; and it is not every one who has lived for years in the enjoyment of absolute power uncontrolled by the admonitions of a Christian's conscience that could get out of the scrape so well, or leave a better name upon the page of history than that of Ibrahim Pasha.

After the fearful catastrophe in the church of the Holy Sepulchre, the whole host of pilgrims seem to have become panic struck, and every one was anxious to escape front the city. There was a report, too, that the plague had broken out, and we with the rest made instant preparation for our departure. In consequence of the numbers who had perished, there was no difficulty in hiring baggage-horses; and we immediately procured as many as we wanted: tents were loaded on some; beds and packages of all sorts and sizes were tied on others, with but slight regard to balance and compactness; and on the afternoon of the 6th of May we rejoiced to find ourselves once more out of the walls of Jerusalem, and riding at our leisure along the pleasant fields fresh with the flowers of spring, a season charming in all countries, but especially delightful in the sultry climate of the Holy Land.

VIEW OF THE MONASTERY OF SAINT BARLAAM, AT METEORA VIEW OF THE MONASTERY OF SAINT BARLAAM, AT METEORA

MONASTERIES OF THE LEVANT.

PART III.

THE MONASTERIES OF METEORA.

CHAPTER XVII.

Albania—Ignorance at Corfu concerning that Country—Its reported abundance of Game and Robbers—The Disturbed State of the Country—The Albanians—Richness of their Arms—Their free use of them—Comparative Safety of Foreigners—Tragic Fate of a German Botanist—Arrival at Gominitza—Ride to Paramathia—A Night's Bivouac—Reception at Paramathia—Albanian Ladies—Yanina—Albanian Mode of settling a Quarrel—Expected Attack from Robbers—A Body-Guard mounted—Audience with the Vizir—His Views of Criminal Jurisprudence—Retinue of the Vizir—His Troops—Adoption of the European Exercises—Expedition to Berat—Calmness and Self-possession of the Turks—Active Preparations for Warfare—Scene at the Bazaar—Valiant Promises of the Soldiers.

Corfu, Friday, Oct. 31, 1834.—I found I could get no information respecting Albania at Corfu, though the high mountains of Epirus seemed almost to over-hang the island. No one knew anything about it, except that it was a famous place for snipes! It appeared never to have struck traveller or tourist that there was anything in Albania except snipes; whereof one had shot fifteen brace, and another had shot many more, only he did not bring them home, having lost the dead birds in the bushes. There were some woodcocks also, it was generally believed, and some spake of wild boars, but I had not the advantage of meeting with anybody who could specifically assert that he had shot one: and besides these there were robbers in multitudes. As to that point every one was agreed. Of robbers there was no end: and just at this particular time there was a revolution, or rebellion, or pronunciamiento, or a general election, or something of that sort, going on in Albania; for all the people who came over from thence said that the whole country was in a ferment. In fact there seemed to be a general uproar taking place, during which each party of the free and independent mountaineers deemed it expedient to show their steady adherence to their own side of the question by shooting at any one they saw, from behind a stone or a tree, for fear that person might accidentally be a partizan of the opposite faction.

TATAR, OR GOVERNMENT MESSENGER TATAR, OR GOVERNMENT MESSENGER

The Albanians are great dandies about their arms: the scabbard of their yataghan, and the stocks of their pistols, are almost always of silver, as well as their three or four little cartridge boxes, which are frequently gilt, and sometimes set with garnets and coral; an Albanian is therefore worth shooting, even if he is not of another way of thinking from the gentleman who shoots him. As I understood, however, that they did not shoot so much at Franks because they usually have little about them worth taking, and are not good to eat, I conceived that I should not run any great risk; and I resolved, therefore, not to be thwarted in my intention of exploring some of the monasteries of that country. There is another reason also why Franks are seldom molested in the East—every Arab or Albanian knows that if a Frank has a gun in his hand, which he generally has, there are two probabilities, amounting almost to certainties, with respect to that weapon. One is, that it is loaded; and the other that, if the trigger is pulled, there is a considerable chance of its going off. Now these are circumstances which apply in a much slighter degree to the magazine of small arms which he carries about his own person. But, beyond all this, when a Frank is shot there is such a disturbance made about it! Consuls write letters—pashas are stirred up—guards, kawasses, and tatars gallop like mad about the country, and fire pistols in the air, and live at free quarters in the villages; the murderer is sought for everywhere, and he, or somebody else, is hanged to please the consul; in addition to which the population are beaten with thick sticks ad libitum. All this is extremely disagreeable, and therefore we are seldom shot at, the pastime being too dearly paid for.

The last Frank whom I heard of as having been killed in Albania was a German, who was studying botany. He rejoiced in a blue coat and brass buttons, and wandered about alone, picking up herbs and flowers on the mountains, which he put carefully into a tin box. He continued unmolested for some time, the universal opinion being that he was a powerful magician, and that the herbs he was always gathering would enable him to wither up his enemies by some dreadful charm, and also to detect every danger which menaced him. Two or three Albanians had watched him for several days, hiding themselves carefully behind the rocks whenever the philosopher turned towards them; and at last one of the gang, commending himself to all his saints, rested his long gun upon a stone and shot the German through the body. The poor man rolled over, but the Albanian did not venture from his hiding-place until he had loaded his gun again, and then, after sundry precautions, he came out, keeping his eye upon the body, and with his friends behind him, to defend him in case of need. The botanizer, however, was dead enough, and the disappointment of the Albanians was extreme, when they found that his buttons were brass and not gold, for it was the supposed value of these precious ornaments that had incited them to the deed.

I procured some letters of introduction to different persons, sent my English servant and most of my effects to England, and hired a youth to act in the double capacity of servant and interpreter during the journey. One of my friends at Corfu was good enough to procure me the use of a great boat, with I do not know how many oars, belonging to government; and in it I was rowed over the calm bright sea twenty-four miles to Gominitza, where I arrived in five hours. Here I hired three horses with pack-saddles, one for my baggage, one for my servant, and one for myself; and away we went towards

Paramathia, which place we were told was four hours off. Paramathia is said to be built upon the site of Dodona, although the exact situation of the oracle is not ascertained; but some of the finest bronzes extant were found there thirty or forty years ago, part of which went to Russia, and part came into the possession of Mr. Hawkins, of Bignor, in Sussex, where they are still preserved.

Our horses were not very good, and our roads were worse; and we scrambled and stumbled over the rocks, up and down hill, all the afternoon, without approaching, as it seemed to me, towards any inhabited place. It was now becoming dark, and the muleteers said we had six hours more to do; it was then seven o'clock, P.M.; we could see nothing, and were upon the top of a hill, where there were plenty of stones and some low bushes, through which we were making our way vaguely, suiting ourselves as to a path, and turning our faces towards any point of the compass which we thought most agreeable, for it did not appear that any of the party knew the way. We now held a council as to what was best to be done; and as we saw lights in some houses about a mile off, I desired one of the muleteers to go there and see if we could get a lodging for the night. "Go to a house?" said the muleteer, "you don't suppose we could be such fools as to go to a house in Albania, where we know nobody?" "No!" said I, "why not?" "Because we should be murdered, of course," said he; "that is if they thought themselves strong enough to venture to undo their doors and let us in; otherwise they would pretend there was nobody in the house, or fire at us out of the window and set the dogs at us; or——" "Oh!" I replied, "that is quite sufficient; I have no desire to trouble your excellent countrymen, only I don't precisely see what else we are to do just now on the top of this hill. How are they off for wolves in this neighbourhood?" "Why," quoth my friend, "I hope you understand that if anything happens to my horses you are bound to reimburse me: as for ourselves, we are armed, and must take our chance; but I don't think there are many wolves here yet; they don't come down from the mountains quite so soon: though certainly it is getting cold already. But we had better sleep here at all events, and at dawn we shall be able, perhaps, to make out a little better where we have got to." There being nothing else for it, we tied the horses' legs together, and I lay down on a travelling carpet by the side of my servant, under the cover of a bush. Awfully cold it was: the horses trembled and shook themselves every now and then, and held their heads down, and I tried all sorts of postures in hopes of making myself snug, but every change was from bad to worse; I could not get warm any how, and a remarkable fact was, that the more sharp stones I picked out from under the carpet the more numerous and sharper were those that remained: my only comfort was to hear the muleteers rolling about too, and anathematizing the stones most lustily. However, I went to sleep in course of time, and was, as it appeared to me, instantaneously awakened by some one shaking me, and telling me it was four o'clock and time to start. It was still as dark as ever, except that a few stars were visible, and we recommenced our journey, stumbling and scrambling about as we had done before, till we came to a place where the horses stopped of their own accord. This it seemed was a ledge of rock above a precipice, about two hundred feet deep, as I judged by the reflection of the stars in the stream which ran below. The dimness of the light made the place look more dangerous and difficult than perhaps it really was. It seems, however, that we were lucky in finding it, for there was no other way off the hill except by this ledge, which was about twelve feet broad. We got off our horses and led them down; they had probably often been there before, for they made no difficulty about it, and in a few hundred yards, the road becoming better, we mounted again, and after five hours' travelling arrived at Paramathia. Just before entering the place we met a party on foot, armed to the teeth, and all carrying their long guns. One of these gentlemen politely asked me if I had a spare purse about me, or any money which I could turn over to his account; but as I looked very dirty and shabby, and as we were close to the town, he did not press his demand, but only asked by which road I intended to leave it. I told him I should remain there for the present, and as we had now reached the houses, he took his departure, to my great satisfaction.

On inquiring for the person to whom I had a letter of introduction, I found he was a shopkeeper who sold cloth in the bazaar. We accordingly went to his shop and found him sitting among his merchandise. When he had read the letter he was very civil, and shutting up his shop, walked on before us to show me the way to his house. It was a very good one, and the best room was immediately given up to me, two old ladies and three or four young ones being turned out in a most summary manner. One or two of the girls were very pretty, and they all vied with each other in their attentions to their guest, looking at me with great curiosity, and perpetually peeping at me through the curtain which hung over the door, and running away when they thought they were observed.

The prettiest of these damsels had only been married a short time: who her husband was, or where he lived, I could not make out, but she amused me by her anxiety to display her smart new clothes. She went and put on a new capote, a sort of white frock coat, without sleeves, embroidered in bright colours down the seams, which showed her figure to advantage; and then she took it off again, and put on another garment, giving me ample opportunity of admiring its effect. I expressed my surprise and admiration in bad Greek, which, however, the fair Albanian appeared to find no difficulty in understanding. She kindly corrected some of my sentences, and I have no doubt I should have improved rapidly under her care, if she had not always run away whenever she heard any one creaking about on the rickety boards of the ante-room and staircase. The other ladies, who were settling themselves in a large gaunt room close by, kept up an interminable clatter, and displayed such unbounded powers of conversation, that it seemed impossible that any one of them could hear what all the others said; till at last the master of the house came up again, and then there was a lull. He told me that I could not hire horses till the afternoon, and as that would have been too late to start, I determined to remain where I was till the next morning. I passed the day in wandering about the place, and considering whether, upon the whole, the dogs or the men of Paramathia were the most savage: for the dogs looked like wolves, and the men like arrant cut-throats, swaggering about, idle and restless, with their long hair, and guns, and pistols, and yataghans; they have none of the composure of the Turks, who delight to sit still in a coffee-house and smoke their pipes, or listen to a story, which saves them the trouble of thinking or speaking. The Albanians did not scream and chatter as the Arabs do, or as their ladies were doing in the houses, but they lounged about the bazaars listlessly, ready to pick a quarrel with any one, and unable to fix themselves down to any occupation; in short they gave me the idea of being a very poor and proud, and good-for-nothing set of scamps.

November 2nd.—The next morning at five o'clock I was on horseback again, and after riding over stones and rocks, and frequently in the bed of a stream, for fourteen hours, I arrived in the evening at Yanina. I was disappointed with the first view of the place. The town is built on the side of a sloping hill above the lake; and as my route lay over the top of this hill, I could see but little of the town until I was quite among the houses, most of which were in a ruinous condition. The lake itself, with an island in it on which are the ruins of a palace built by the famous Ali Pasha, is a beautiful object; but the mountains by which it is bounded on the opposite side are barren, yet not sufficiently broken to be picturesque. The scene altogether put me in mind of the Lake of Genesareth as seen from its western shore near Tiberias. There is a plain to the north and north-west, which is partially cultivated, but it is inferior in beauty to the plains of Jericho, and there is no river like the Jordan to light up the scene with its quick and sparkling waters as it glistens among the trees in its journey towards the lake.

I went to the house of an Italian gentleman who was the principal physician of Yanina, and who I understood was in the habit of affording accommodation to travellers in his house. He received me with great kindness, and gave me an excellent set of rooms, consisting of a bed room, sitting room, and ante-room, all of them much better than those which I occupied in the hotel at Corfu: they were clean and nicely furnished; and altogether the excellence of my quarters in the dilapidated capital of Albania surprised me most agreeably.

The town appears never to have been repaired since the wars and revolutions which occurred at the time of Ali Pasha's death. The houses resemble those of Greece or southern Italy; they are built, some of stone, and some of wood, with tiled roofs. On the walls of many of them there were vines growing. The bazaars are poor, yet I saw very rich arms displayed in some mean little shops, or stalls, as we should call them; for they are all open, like the booths at a fair. The climate is rainy, and there is no lack of mud in wet weather, and dust when it is dry. The whole place had a miserable appearance, nothing seemed to be going on, and the people have a savage, hang-dog look.

I had a good supper and a good bed, and was awakened the next morning by hearing the servants loud in talk about the news of the day. The subject was truly Albanian. A man who had a shop in the bazaar had quarrelled yesterday with some of his fellow townsmen, and in the night they took him out of his bed and cut him to pieces with their yataghans on the hill above the town. Some people coming by early this morning saw various joints of this unlucky man lying on the ground as they passed.

I occupied myself in looking about the place; and having sent to the palace of the vizir to request an audience, it was fixed for the next day. There was not much to see; but I afforded a subject of uninterrupted discussion to all beholders, as it appeared I was the only traveller who had been there for some time. I went to bed early because I had no books to read, and it was a bore trying to talk Greek to my host's family; but I had not been asleep long before I was awakened by the intelligence that a party of robbers had concealed themselves in the ruins round the house, and that we should probably be attacked. Up we all got, and loaded our guns and pistols: the women kept flying about everywhere, and, when they ran against each other in the dark, screamed wofully, as they took everybody for a robber. We had no lights, that we might not afford good marks for the enemy outside, who, however, kept quiet, and did not shoot at us, although every now and then we saw a man or two creeping about among the ruins. My host, who was armed with a gun of prodigious length, was in a state of great alarm; and, having sent for assistance, twenty soldiers arrived, who kept guard round the house, but would not venture among the ruins. These valiant heroes relieved each other during the night; but, as no robbers made their appearance, I got tired of watching for them, and went quietly to bed again.

November 4th.—At nine o'clock in the morning I paid my respects to the Vizir, Mahmoud Pasha, a man with a long nose, and who altogether bore a great resemblance to Pope Benedict XVI. I stayed some hours with him, talking over Turkish matters; and we got into a brisk argument as to whether England was part of London, or London part of England. He appeared to be a remarkably good-natured man, and took great interest in the affairs of Egypt, from which country I had lately arrived, and asked me numberless questions about Mehemet Ali, comparing his character with that of Ali Pasha, who had built this palace, which was in a very ruinous state, for nothing had been expended to keep it in repair. The hall of audience was a magnificent room, richly decorated with inlaid work of mother-of-pearl and tortoiseshell: the ceiling was gilt, and the windows of Venetian plate-glass, but some of them were broken: the floor was loose and almost dangerous; and two holes in the side walls, which had been made by a cannon-ball, were stopped up with pieces of deal board roughly nailed upon the costly inlaid panels. The divan was of red cloth; and a crowd of men, with their girdles stuck full of arms, stood leaning on their long guns at the bottom of the room, listening to our conversation, and laughing loudly whenever a joke was made, but never coming forward beyond the edge of the carpet.

The Pasha offered to give me an escort, as he said that the country at that moment was particularly unsafe; but at length it was settled that he should give me a letter to the commander of the troops at Mezzovo, who would supply me with soldiers to see me safely to the monasteries of Meteora. When I arose to take my leave, he sent for more pipes and coffee, as a signal for me to remain; in short, we became great friends. Whilst I was with him a pasha of inferior rank came in, and sat on the divan for half an hour without saying a single word or doing anything except looking at me unceasingly. After he had taken his departure we had some sherbet; and at last I got away, leaving the Pasha in great wonderment at the English government paying large sums of money for the transportation of criminals, when cutting off their heads would have been so much more economical and expeditious. Incurring any expense to keep rogues and vagabonds in prison, or to send them away from our own country to be the plague of other lands, appeared to him to be an extraordinary act of folly; and that thieves should be fed and clothed and lodged, while poor and honest people were left to starve, he considered to be contrary to common sense and justice. I laughed at the time at what I thought the curious opinions of the Vizir of Yanina; I have since come to the conclusion that there was some sense in his notions of criminal jurisprudence.

In the afternoon, as I was looking out of the window of my lodging, I saw the Vizir going by with a great number of armed people, and I was told that in the present disturbed state of the country he never went out to take a ride without all these attendants. First came a hundred lancers on horseback, dressed in a kind of European uniform; then two horsemen, each with a pair of small kettle-drums attached to the front of his saddle. They kept up an unceasing pattering upon these drums as they rode along. This is a Tartar or Persian custom; and in some parts of Tartary the dignity of khan is conferred by strapping these two little drums on the back of the person whom the king delighteth to honour; and then the king beats the drums as the new khan walks slowly round the court. Thus a thing is reckoned a great honour in one part of the world which in another is accounted a disgrace; for when a soldier is incorrigible, we drum him out of the regiment, whilst the Tartar khan is drummed into his dignity. After the drummers came a brilliantly dressed company of kawasses, with silver pistols and yataghans; then several trumpeters; and after them the Vizir himself on a fine tall horse; he was dressed in the new Turkish Frank style, with the usual red cap on his head; but he had an immense red cloth cloak sumptuously embroidered with gold, which quite covered him, so that no part of the great man was visible, except his two eyes, his nose, and one of his hands, upon which was a splendid diamond ring. Two grooms walked by the sides of his horse, each with one hand on the back of the saddle. Every one bowed as the Vizir went by; and I became a distinguished person from the moment that he gave me a condescending nod. The procession was closed by a crowd of officers and attendants on horseback in gorgeous Albanian dresses, with silver bridles and embroidered housings. They carried what I thought at first were spears, but I soon discovered that they were long pipes; there was quite a forest of them, of all lengths and sizes. When the Vizir was gone and the dust subsided, I strolled out of the town on foot, when I came upon the troops, who were learning the new European exercise. Seeing a man sitting on a carpet in the middle of the plain, I went up to him and found that he was the colonel and commander of this army; so I smoked a pipe with him, and discovered that he knew about as much of tactics and military manœuvres as I did, only he did not take so much interest in the subject. We therefore continued to smoke the pipe of peace on the carpet of reflection, while the soldiers entangled themselves in all sorts of incomprehensible doublings and counter-marches, till at last the whole body was so much puzzled, that they stood still all of a heap, like a cluster of bees. The captains shouted, and the poor men turned round and round, trod on each other's heels, kicked each other's shins, and did all they could to get out of the scrape, but they only got more into confusion. At last a bright thought struck the colonel, who took his pipe out of his mouth, and gave orders, in the name of the Prophet, that every man should go home in the best way he could. This they accomplished like a party of schoolboys, running and jumping and walking off in small parties towards the town. The officers wiped the perspiration from their foreheads, and strolled off too, some to smoke a pipe under a tree, and some to repose on their divans and swear at the Franks who had invented such extraordinary evolutions.

TURKISH COMMON SOLDIER. TURKISH COMMON SOLDIER.

In the evening, among the other news of the day, I was told that three men had been walking together in the afternoon; one of them bought a melon, and his two companions, who were very thirsty, but had no money, asked him to give them some of it. He would not do so; and, as they worried him about it, he ran into an empty house, and, bolting the door, sat down inside to discuss his purchase in quiet. The other two were determined not to be jockeyed in that manner, and, finding a hole in the door, they peeped through, and were enraged at seeing him eating the melon inside. He jeered them, and said that the melon was excellent; until at last one of them swore he should not eat it all, and, putting his pistol through the hole in the door, shot his friend dead; they then walked away, laughing at their own cleverness in shooting him so neatly through the hole.

November 5th.—The next day I went again to the citadel to see the Vizir, but he could not receive me, as news had arrived that the insurgents or robbers—they had entitled themselves to either denomination—had gathered together in force and laid siege to the town of Berat. There had been a good deal of confusion in Yanina before this, but now it appeared to have arrived at a climax. The courtyard of the citadel was full of horses picketed by their head-and-heel ropes, in long rows; parties of men were, according to their different habits, talking over the events of the day,—the Albanians chattering and putting themselves in attitudes; the Arnaouts or Mahometans of Greek blood boasting of the chivalric feats which they intended to perform; and the grave Turks sitting quietly on the ground, smoking their eternal pipes, and taking it all as easily as if they had nothing to do with it. Both before and since these days I have seen a great deal of the Turks; and though, for many reasons, I do not respect them as a nation, still I cannot help admiring their calmness and self-possession in moments of difficulty and danger. There is something noble and dignified in their quietness on these occasions: I have very rarely seen a Turk discomposed; stately and collected, he sits down and bides his time; but when the moment of action comes, he will rouse himself on a sudden, and become full of fire, animation, and activity. It is then that you see the descendant of those conquerors of the East, whose strong will and fierce courage have given them the command over all the nations of Islam.

Although I could not obtain an audience with the vizir, one of the people who were with me managed to send a message to him that I should be glad of the letter, or firman, which he had promised me, and by which I might command the services of an escort, if I thought fit to do so. This man had influence at court; for he had a friend who was chiboukji to the vizir's secretary, or prime minister—a sly Greek, whose acquaintance I had made two days before. The pipe-bearer, propitiated by a trifling bribe, spoke to his master, and he spoke to the vizir, who promised I should have the letter; and it came accordingly in the evening, properly signed and sealed, and all in heathen Greek, of which I could make out a word here and there; but what it was about was entirely beyond my comprehension.

Whilst waiting the result of these negotiations I had leisure to notice the warlike movements which were going on around me. I saw a train of two or three hundred men on horseback issuing out from the citadel, and riding slowly along the plain in the direction of Berat. They were sent to raise the siege; and other troops were preparing to follow them. As I watched these horsemen winding across the plain in a long line, with the sun glancing upon their arms, they seemed like a great serpent, with its glittering scales, gliding along to seek for its prey; and in some respects the simile would hold good, for this detachment would be the terror of the inhabitants of every district through which it passed. Rapine, violence, and oppression would mark its course; friend and foe would alike be plundered; and the villages which had not been burned by the insurgent klephti would be sacked and ruined by the soldiers of the government.

As I descended from the citadel I passed numerous parties of armed men, all full of excitement about the plunder they would get, and the mighty deeds they would perform; for the danger was a good way off, and they were all brim-full of valour. In the bazaar all was business and bustle: everybody was buying arms. Long guns and silver pistols, all ready loaded, I believe, with fiery-looking flints as big as sandwiches, wrapped up first in a bit of red cloth, and then in a sort of open work of lead or tin, were being handed about; and the spirit of commerce was in full activity. Great was the haggling among the dealers. One man walked off with a mace; another, expecting to perform as mighty deeds as Richard Cœur de Lion, bought an old battle-axe, and swung it about to show how he would cut heads off with it before long. Another champion had included among his warlike accoutrements a curious, ancient-looking silver clock, which dangled by his side from a multitude of chains. It was square in shape, and must have been provided with a strong constitution inside if it could go while it was banged about at every step the man took. This worthy, I imagine, intended to kill time, for his purchase did not seem calculated to cope with any other enemy. He had, however, two or three pistols and daggers in addition to his clock. An oldish, hard-featured man was buying a quantity of that abominably sour, white cheese which is the pride of Albania, and a quantity of black olives, which he was cramming into a pair of old saddle-bags, whilst his horse beside him was quietly munching his corn in a sack tied over his nose. There was a look of calm efficiency about this man, which contrasted strongly with the swaggering air of the crowd around him. He was evidently an old hand; and I observed that he had laid in a stock of ball-cartridges—an article in which but little money was spent by the buyers of yataghans in silver sheaths and silver cartridge-boxes.

"Hallo! sir Frank," cried one or two of these gay warriors, "come out with us to Berat: come and see us fight, and you will see something worth travelling for."

"Ay," said I, "it's all up with the enemy: that's quite certain. They will be in a pretty scrape, to be sure, when you arrive. I would not be one of them for a good deal!"

"Sono molto feroce questi palicari," said my guide.

"Oh! yes, they are terrible fellows!" I replied.

"What does the Frank say?" they asked.

"He says you are terrible fellows."

"Ah! I think we are, indeed. But don't be afraid, Frank; don't be afraid!"

"No," said I, "I won't; and I wish you good luck on your way to Berat and back again."

This night the people had been so much occupied in purchasing the implements of death that I heard no accounts of any new murders. In fact it had been a dull day in that respect; but no doubt they would make up for it before long.

CHAPTER XVIII.

Start for Meteora—Rencontre with a Wounded Traveller—Barbarity of the Robbers—Albanian Innkeeper—Effect of the Turkish Language upon the Greeks—Mezzovo—Interview with the chief Person in the Village—Mount Pindus—Capture by Robbers—Salutary effects of Swaggering—Arrival under Escort at the Robbers' Head-Quarters—Affairs take a favourable turn—An unexpected Friendship with the Robber Chief—The Khan of Malacash—Beauty of the Scenery—Activity of our Guards—Loss of Character—Arrival at Meteora.

November 6th.—I had engaged a tall, thin, dismal-looking man, well provided with pistols, knives, and daggers, as an additional servant, for he was said to know all the passes of the mountains, which I thought might be a useful accomplishment in case I had to avoid the more public roads—or paths, rather—for roads there were none. I purchased a stock of provisions, and hired five horses—three for myself and my men, one for the muleteer, and the other for the baggage, which was well strapped on, that the beast might gallop with it, as it was not very heavy. They were pretty good horses—rough and hardy. Mine looked very hard at me out of the corner of his eye when I got upon his back in the cold grey dawn, as if to find out what sort of a person I was. By means of a stout kourbatch—a sort of whip of rhinoceros hide which they use in Egypt—I immediately gave him all the information he desired; and off we galloped round the back part of the town, and, unquestioned by any one, we soon found ourselves trotting along the plain by the south end of the lake of Yanina. Here the waters from the lake disappear in an extraordinary manner in a great cavern, or pit full of rocks and stones, through which the water runs away into some subterranean channel—a dark and mysterious river, which the dismal-looking man, my new attendant, said came out into the light again somewhere in the Gulph of Arta. Before long we got upon the remains of a fine paved road, like a Roman way, which had been made by Ali Pasha. It was, however, out of repair, having in places been swept away by the torrents, and was an impediment rather than an assistance to travellers. This road led up to the hills; and, having dismounted from my horse, I began scrambling and puffing up the steep side of the mountain, stopping every now and then to regain my breath and to admire the beautiful view of the calm lake and picturesque town of Yanina.

As I was walking in advance of my company, I saw a man above me leading a loaded mule. He was coming down the mountain, carefully picking his way among the stones, and in a loud voice exhorting the mule to be steady and keep its feet, although the mule was much the more sure-footed of the two. As they passed me I was struck with the odd appearance of the mule's burden: it consisted of a bundle of large stones on one side, which served as a counterpoise to a packing-case on the other, covered with a cloth, out of which peeped the head of a man, with his long black hair hanging about a face as pale as marble. The box in which he travelled not being more than four feet and a half long, I supposed he must be a dwarf, and was laughing at his peculiar mode of conveyance. The muleteer, observing from my dress that I was a Frank, stopped his mule, when he came up to me, and asked me if I was a physician, begging me to give my assistance to the man in the box, if I knew anything of surgery, for he had had both his legs cut off by some robbers on the way from Salonica, and he was now taking him to Yanina, in hopes of finding some doctor there to heal his wounds. My laughter was now turned into pity for the poor man, for I knew there was no help for him at Yanina. I could do nothing for him; and the only hope was, as his strength had borne him up so far on his journey, that when he got rest at Yanina the wounds might heal of themselves. After expressing my commiseration for him, and my hopes of his recovery, we parted company; and as I stood looking at the mule, staggering and slipping among the loose atones and rocks in the steep descent, it quite made me wince to think of the pain the unfortunate traveller must be enduring, with the raw stumps of his two legs rubbing and bumping against the end of his short box. I was sorry I had not asked why the robbers had cut off his legs, because, if it was their usual system, it was certainly more than I bargained for. I had pretty nearly made up my mind to be robbed, but had no intention whatever to lose my legs; so I sat down upon a rock, and began calculating probabilities, until my party came up, and I mounted my horse, who gave me another look with his cunning eye. We continued on Ali Pasha's broken road until we reached the summit of the mountain, where we made a short halt, that our horses might regain their wind; and then began our descent, stumbling, and sliding, and scrambling down, until we arrived at the bottom, where there was a miserable khan. In this royal hotel, which was a mere shed, there was nothing to be found except mine host, who had it all to himself. At last he made us some coffee; and while our horses were feeding on our own corn, we sat under the shade of a walnut-tree by the road-side. Our host, having nothing which could be eaten or drank except the coffee, did not know how in the world he could manage to get up a satisfactory bill. I saw this very plainly in his puzzled and thoughtful looks; but at last a bright thought struck him, and he charged a good round sum for the shade of the walnut-tree. Now although I admired his ingenuity, I demurred at the charge, particularly as the walnut-tree did not belong to him. It was a wild tree, which everybody threw stones at as he passed by, to bring down the nuts:—

"Nux ego juncta visæ quae sum due crimine vitæ,
Attamen a cunctis saxibus usque petor."—Ovid.

Little did the unoffending walnut-tree think that its shade would be brought forward as a cause of war; for then arose a fierce contest between Greek oaths and Albanian maledictions, to which Arabic and English lent their aid. Though there were no stones thrown, ten times as many hard words were hurled backwards and forwards as there were walnuts on the tree, showing a facility of expression and a redundance of epithets which would have given a lesson to the most practised ladies of Billingsgate.

When the horses were ready the khangee came up to me in a towering passion, swearing that I should pay for sitting under the tree. "Englishman," said he, "get up and pay me what I demand, or you shall not leave this place, by all that is holy." "Kiupek oglou," said I, without moving from the ground, "Oh, son of a dog! go and get my horse, you chattering magpie!" These few words in the language of the conqueror had a marvellous effect on the khangee. "What does his worship say?" he inquired of the dismal-faced man. "Why, he says you had better go and get his excellency's worship's most respectable horse, if you have any regard for your life: so go! be off! vanish! don't stay there staring at the illustrious traveller. 'Tis lucky for you he doesn't order us to cut you up into cabobs; go and get the horse; and perhaps you'll be paid for your coffee, bad as it was. His excellency is the pasha's, his highness's, most particular intimate friend; and if his highness knew what you had been saying, why, where would you be, O man?" The khangee, who had intended to have had it all his own way, was taken terribly aback at the sound of the Turkish tongue: he speedily put on my horse's bridle, gave his nosebag to the muleteer, tightened up his girths, helped the servants, and was suddenly converted into a humble submissive drudge. The way in which anything Turkish is respected among the conquered races in Syria or in Egypt can scarcely be imagined by those who have not witnessed it.

Leaving the khangee to count his paras and piastres, with which, after all, he was evidently well satisfied, we rode on down the valley by the side of a brawling stream, which we crossed no less than thirty-nine times during our day's journey. Our road lay through a magnificent series of picturesque and savage gorges, between high rocks. Sometimes we rode along the bed of the stream, and sometimes upon a ledge so far above it that it looked like a silver ribbon in the sun. Every now and then we came to a cataract or rapid, where the stream boiled and foamed among the rocks, tossing up its spray, and drowning our voices in its noise. In the course of about eight hours of continual scrambling up and down all sorts of rocks, we found ourselves at another wretched shelty dignified with the name of khan. Here, after a tolerable supper, we all rolled ourselves up in the different corners of a sort of loft, with our arms under our heads, and slept soundly until the morning.

November 7th.—This day we continued along the banks of a stream, in the direction of its source, until it dwindled to a mere rivulet, when we left it and took to the hills at the base of another mountain. We rode some way along a rocky path until, turning round a corner to the left, we found ourselves at the town or village of Mezzovo. As Mahmoud Pasha had supplied me with a firman and letters to the principal persons at the several towns on my route, I looked out my Mezzovo letter, with the intention of asking for an escort of a few soldiers to accompany me through the passes of Mount Pindus, which were reported to be full of robbers and cattiva gente of every sort and kind, the great extent of the underwood of box-trees forming an impenetrable cover for those minions of the moon.

Most of the population of Mezzovo turned out to see the procession of the Milordos Inglesis as it entered the precincts of their ancient city, and defiled into the market-place, in the middle of which was a great tree, under whose shade sat and smoked a circle of grave and reverend seignors, the aristocracy of the place; whereupon, holding the pasha's letter in my hand, I cantered up to them. On seeing me advance towards them, a broad-shouldered good-natured looking man, gorgeously dressed in red velvet, embroidered all over with gold, though something tarnished with the rain and weather, arose and stepped forward to meet me. "Here is a letter," said I, "from his highness Mahmoud Pasha, vizir of Yanina, to the chief personage of Mezzovo, whoever he may be, for there is no name mentioned; so tell me who is the chief person in this city; where is he to be found, for I desire to speak with him?" "You want the chief person of Mezzovo?" replied the broad-shouldered man; "well, I think I am the chief person here, am I not?" he asked of the assembled crowd which had gathered together by this time. "Certainly, malista, oh yes, you are the chief person of Mezzovo undoubtedly," they all cried out. "Very well," said he, "then give me the letter." On my giving it to him, he opened it in a very unceremonious manner; and, before he had half read it, burst into a fit of laughing. "What are you laughing at?" said I: "Is not that the vizir's letter?" "Oh!" said he, "you want guards, do you, to protect you against the robbers, the klephti?" "Yes, I do; but I do not see what there is to laugh at in that. I want some men to go with me to Meteora; if you are the captain or commander here, give me an escort, as I wish to be off at once: it is early now, and I can cross the mountains before dark."

After a pause, he said, "Well, I am the captain; and you shall have men who will protect you wherever you go. You are an Englishman, are you not?" "Yes," I said, "I am." "Well, I like the English; and you particularly." "Thank you," said I: and, after some more conversation, he tore off a slip from the vizir's letter (a very unceremonious proceeding in Albania), and, writing a few lines on it, he said, "Now give this paper to the first soldiers you meet at the foot of Mount Pindus, and all will be right." He then instructed the muleteer which way to go. I took the paper, which was not folded up; but the badly-written Romaic was unintelligible to me, so I put it into my pocket, and away we went, my new friend waving his hand to us as we passed out of the market-place; and we were soon trotting along through the open country towards the hills which shoot out from the base of the great chain of Mount Pindus, a mountain famous for having had Mount Ossa put on the top of it by some of the giants when they were fighting against

Jupiter. As that respected deity got the better of the giants, I presume he put Ossa back again; for which I felt very much obliged to him, as Pindus seemed quite high enough and steep enough without any addition.

We rode along, getting nearer and nearer to the mountains; and at length we began to climb a steep rocky path on the side of a lofty hill covered with box-trees. This path continued for some distance until we came to a place where there was a ledge so narrow that two horses could not go abreast. Here, as I was riding quietly along, I heard an exclamation in front of "Robbers! robbers!" and sure enough, out of one of the thickets of box-trees, there advanced three or four bright gun-barrels, which were speedily followed by some gentlemen in dirty white jackets and fustanellas; who, in a short and abrupt style of eloquence, commanded us to stand. This of course we were obliged to do; and as I was getting out my pistol, one of the individuals in white presented his gun at me, and upon my looking round to see whether my tall Albanian servant was preparing to support me, I saw him quietly half-cock his gun and sling it back over his shoulder, at the name time shaking his head as much as to say, "It is no use resisting; we are caught; there are too many of them." So I bolted the locks of the four barrels of my pistol carefully, hoping that the bolts would form an impediment to my being shot with my own weapon after I had been robbed of it. The place was so narrow that there were no hopes of running away, and there we sat on horseback, looking silly enough, I dare say. There was a good deal of talking and chattering among the robbers, and they asked the Albanian various questions to which I paid no attention, all my faculties being engrossed in watching the proceedings of the party in front, who were examining the effects in the panniers of the baggage mule. First they pulled out my bag of clothes, and threw it upon the ground; then out came the sugar and the coffee, and whatever else these was. Some of the men had hold of the poor muleteer, and a loud argument was going on between him and his captors. I did not like all this, but my rage was excited to a violent pitch when I saw one man appropriating to his own use the half of a certain fat tender cold fowl, whereof I had eaten the other half with much appetite and satisfaction. "Let that fowl alone, you scoundrel!" said I in good English; "put it down, will you? if you don't, I'll——!" The man, surprised at this address in an unknown tongue, put down the fowl, and looked up with wonder at the explosion of ire which his actions had called forth. "That is right," said I, "my good fellow, it is too good for such a dirty brute as you." "Let us see," said I to the Albanian, "if there is nothing to be done; say I am the King of England's uncle, or grandson, or particular friend, and that if we are hurt or robbed he will send all manner of ships and armies, and hang everybody, and cut off the heads of all the rest. Talk big, O man! and don't spare great words; they cost nothing, and let us see what that will do."

Upon this the Albanian took up his parable and a long parleying ensued, for the robbers were taken aback with the good English in which I had addressed them, and stood still with open mouths to hear what it all meant. In the middle of this row I thought of the paper which had been given me at Mezzovo. "Here," said I, "here is a letter; read it, see what it says." They took the paper and turned it round and round, for they could not read it: first one looked at it and then another; then they looked at the back, but they could make nothing of it Nevertheless, it produced a great effect upon them, for here, as in all other countries of the East, any writing is looked upon by the uneducated people as a mystery, and is held in high respect; and at last they said they would take us to a place where we should find a person capable of reading it. The thing which most provoked me was that the fellows seemed not to have the slightest fear of us; they did not even take the trouble to demand our arms: my much cherished "patent four-barrelled travelling pistol" they evidently considered too small to be dangerous; and I felt it as a kind of personal insult that they deputed only two of their number to convoy us to the residence of the learned person who was to read the letter. They managed matters, however, in a scientific way: the bridles of our horses were turned over their heads and tied each to the horse that went before; one of our captors walked in front and the other behind; but just when I thought an opportunity had arrived to shake off this yoke, I perceived that the whole pass was guarded, and wherever the road was a little wider or turned a corner round a rock or a clump of trees, there were other long guns peeping out from among the bushes, with the bearers of which our two conquerors exchanged pass-words. Thus we marched along, the robber who went first apparently caring nothing about us, but the one in the rear having his gun cocked and ready to shoot any one of us who should turn restive. The road, which ascended rapidly, was rather too dangerous to be agreeable, being a narrow path cut on the side of a very steep mountain; at one time the track lay across a steep slope of blue marl, which afforded the most insecure footing for our horses: all mountain-travellers are aware how much more dangerous this kind of road is than a firm ledge of rock, however narrow.

We had now got very high, and the ground was sprinkled with patches of ice and snow, which rendered the footing insecure; and frequently large masses of the road, disturbed by our passing over it, gave way beneath our feet, and set off bounding and crashing among the box trees until it was broken into powder on the rocks below.

In process of time we got into a cloud which hid everything from us, and going still higher we got above the cloud into a region of broken crags and rocks and pine-trees, among which there was a large wooden house or shed. It seemed all roof, and was made of long spars of trees sloping towards each other, and was very high, long, and narrow. As we approached it several men made their appearance armed at all points, and took our horses from us. At the end of the shed there was a door through which we were conducted into the interior by our two guards, and placed all of a row, with our backs against the wall, on the right side of the entrance. Towards the other end of this sylvan guard-room there was a large fire on the ground, and a number of men sitting round it drinking aqua vitæ out of coffee cups, and talking load and laughing. In the farthest corner I saw a pile of long bright-barrelled guns leaning against the wall, while on the other side of the fire there were some boards on the ground with a mat or carpet over them, whereon a worthy better dressed than the rest was lounging, apart from every one else and half asleep. To him the paper was given, and he leant forward to read it by the light of the blazing fire, for though it was bright sunshine out of doors, the room was quite dark. The captain was evidently a poor scholar, and he spelt and puzzled over every word. At last a thought struck him: shading his eyes with his hand from the glare of the fire he leant forward and peered into the darkness, where we were awaiting his commands. Not distinguishing us, however, he jumped up upon his feet and shouted out "Hallo! where are the gentlemen who brought this letter? What have you done with them?" At the sound of his voice the rest of the party jumped up also, being then first aware that something out of the common had taken place. Some of the palicari ran towards us and were going to seize us, when the captain came forward and in a civil tone said, "Oh, there you are! Welcome, gentlemen; we are very glad to receive you. Make yourselves at home; come near the fire and sit down." I took him at his word and sat down on the boards by the side of the fire, rubbing my hands and making myself as comfortable as possible under the circumstances. My two servants and the muleteer seeing what turn affairs had taken, became of a sudden as loquacious as they had been silent before, and in a short time we were all the greatest friends in the world.

"So," said the captain, or whatever he was, "you are acquainted with our friend at Mezzovo. How did you leave him? I hope he was well?"

"Oh, yes," I said; "we left him in excellent health. What a remarkably pleasing person he is! and how well he looks in his red velvet dress!"

"Have you known him long?" he asked.

"Why, not very long," replied my Albanian; "but my master has the greatest respect for him, and so has he for my master."

"He says you are to take some of our men with you wherever you like," said our host.

"Yes, I know," said the Albanian; "we settled that at Mezzovo, with my master's friend, his Excellency Mr. What's-his-name."

"Well, how many will you take?"

"Oh! five or six will do; that will be as many as we want. We are going to Meteora and then we shall return over the mountains back to Mezzovo, where I hope we shall have the pleasure of meeting your general again."

Whilst we were talking and drinking coffee by the fire, a prodigious bustling and chattering was going on among the rest of the party, and before long five slim, active, dirty-looking young rogues, in white dresses, with long black hair hanging down their backs, and each with a long thin gun, announced that they were ready to accompany us whenever we were ready to start. As we had nothing to keep us in the dark, smoky hovel, we were soon ready to go; and glad indeed was I to be out again in the open air among the high trees, without the immediate prospect of being hanged upon one of them. My party jumped with great alacrity and glee upon their miserable mules and horses; all our belongings, including the half of the cold fowl, were in statu quo; and off we set—our new friends accompanied us on foot. And so delighted was our Caliban of a muleteer at what we all considered a fortunate escape, that he lifted up his voice and gave vent to his feelings in a song. The grand gentleman in red velvet to whom I had presented the Pasha's letter at Mezzovo, was, it seems, himself the captain of the thieves—the very man against whom the Pasha wished to afford us his protection; and he, feeling amused probably at the manner in which we had fallen unawares into his clutches, and being a good-natured fellow (and he certainly looked such), gave us a note to the officer next in command, ordering him to protect us as his friends, and to provide us with an escort. When I say that he of the red velvet was captain of the thieves, it is to be understood, that although his followers did not excel in honesty, as they proceeded to plunder us the moment they had entrapped us in the valley of the box-trees, yet he should more properly be called a guerilla chief in rebellion for the time being against the authorities of the Turkish government, and I being a young Englishman, he good-naturedly gave me his assistance, without which, as I afterwards found, it would have been impossible for me to have travelled with safety through any one of the mountain passes of the Pindus. I was told that this chief, whose name I unfortunately omitted to note down, commanded a large body of men before the city of Berat, and certainly all the ragamuffins whom I met on my way to and from the monasteries of Meteora acknowledged his authority. I heard that soon afterwards he returned to his allegiance under Mahmoud Pasha, for it appears that the outbreak, during which I had inadvertently started for a tour in Albania, did not last long.

Late in the evening we arrived at a small khan something like an out-building to a farmhouse in England; this was the khan of Malacash: it was prettily situated on the banks of the river Peneus, and contained, besides the stable, two rooms, one of which opened upon a kind of verandah or covered terrace. My two servants and I slept on the floor in this room, and the four robbers or guards (as in common civility I ought to term them) in the ante-chamber. I gave them as good a supper as I could, and we became excellent friends. It was almost dark when we arrived at this place, but the next morning when the glorious sun arose I was charmed with the beautiful scenery around us. On both sides banks of stately trees rose above the margin of a rippling stream, and the valley grew wider and wider as we rode on, the stream increasing by the addition of many little rills, and the trees retiring from it, affording us views of grassy plains and romantic dells, first on one side and then on the other. The scenery was most lovely, and in the distance was the towering summit of the great Mount Olympus, famous nowadays for the Greek monasteries which are built upon its sides, and near whose base runs the valley of Tempe, of which we are expressly told in the Latin Grammar that it is a pleasant vale in Thessaly; and if it is more beautiful than the valley of the Peneus, it must be a very pleasant vale indeed.

I was struck with the original manner in which our mountain friends progressed through the country; sometimes they kept with us, but more usually some of them went on one side of the road and some on the other, like men beating for game, only that they made no noise; and on the rare occasions when we met any traveller trudging along the road or ambling on a long-eared mule, they were always among the bushes or on the tops of the rocks, and never showed themselves upon the road. But despite all these vagaries they were always close to us. They were wonderfully active, for although I trotted or galloped whenever the nature of the road rendered it practicable, they always kept up with me, and apparently without exertion or fatigue; and although they were often out of my sight, I believe I was never out of theirs. Altogether I was glad that we were such friends, for, from what I saw of them, they and their associates would have proved very awkward enemies. They were curious wild animals, as slim and as active as cats: their waists were not much more than a foot and a half in circumference, and they appeared to be able to jump over anything; and the thin mocassins of raw hide which they wore enabled them to run or walk without making the slightest noise. In fact, they were agreeable, honest rogues enough, and we got on amazingly well together. I had a way of singing as I rode along for my own particular edification, and from mere joyousness of heart, for the beautiful scenery, and the fine fresh air, and the bright stream delighted me, so I sung away at a great rate; and my horse sometimes put back one of his ears to listen, which I took as a personal compliment: but my robbers did not like this singing.

"Why," they said to the Albanian, "does the Frank sing?"

"It is a way he has," was the reply.

"Well," they said, "this is a wild country; there is no use in courting attention—he had better not sing."

Nevertheless I would not leave off for all that. Cantabit vacuus coram latrone viator; so I went on singing rather louder than before, particularly as I was convinced that my horse had an ear for music; and in this way, after travelling for seven hours, we came within sight of the extraordinary rocks of Meteora.

Just at this time we observed among the trees before us a long string of travellers who appeared to be convoying a train of baggage horses. On seeing us they stopped, and closed their files; and as my thieves had bolted, as usual, into the bushes some time before, my party consisted only of four persons and five horses. As we approached the other party, a tall, well-armed man, with a rifle across his arm, rode forwards and hailed us, asking who we were. We said we were travellers.

"And who were those who left you just now?" said he.

"They are some of our party who have turned off by a short cut to go to Meteora," replied my Albanian.

"What! a short cut on both sides of the road! how is that? I suspect you are not simple travellers."

"Well," he replied, "we do not wish to molest you. Go on your way in peace, and let us pass quietly, for you are by far the larger party."

"Yes," said the man, "but how many have you in the bushes? What are they about there?"

"I don't know what they are about," said he, "but they will not molest you [one of them was peeping over a bush at the back of the party all the while, but they did not see him]; and we, I assure you, are peaceable travellers like yourselves."

Our new acquaintance did not seem at all satisfied, and he and all his party drew up along the path as we passed them, with evident misgivings as to our purpose; and soon afterwards, looking back, we saw them keeping close together and trotting along as fast as their loaded horses would go, some of them looking round at us every now and then till we lost sight of them among the trees.

The proverb says—you shall know a man by his friends, and my character had evidently suffered from the appearance of the company I kept, for the merchants held me as little better than a rogue; there was, however, no time for explanations, and it was with feelings of indignant virtue that I left the forest, and after crossing the river Peneus at a ford, my merry men and I continued our journey along the grassy plain of Meteora.

CHAPTER XIX.

Meteora—The extraordinary Character of its Scenery—Its Caves formerly the Resort of Ascetics—Barbarous Persecution of the Hermits—Their extraordinary Religious Observances—Singular Position of the Monasteries—The Monastery of Barlaam—The difficulty of reaching it—Ascent by a Windlass and Net, or by Ladders—Narrow Escape—Hospitable Reception by the Monks—The Agoumenos, or Abbot—His strict Fast—Description of the Monastery—The Church—Symbolism in the Greek Church—Respect for Antiquity—The Library—Determination of the Abbot not to sell any of the MSS.—The Refectory—Its Decorations—Aërial Descent—The Monastery of Hagios Stephanos—Its Carved Iconostasis—Beautiful View from the

Monastery—Monastery of Agia Triada—Summary Justice at Triada—Monastery of Agia Roserea—Its Lady Occupants—Admission refused.

The scenery of Meteora is of a very singular kind. The end of a range of rocky hills seems to have been broken off by some earthquake or washed away by the Deluge, leaving only a series of twenty or thirty tall, thin, smooth, needle-like rocks, many hundred feet in height; some like gigantic tusks, some shaped like sugar-loaves, and some like vast stalagmites. These rocks surround a beautiful grassy plain, on three sides of which there grow groups of detached trees, like those in an English park. Some of the rocks shoot up quite clean and perpendicularly from the smooth green grass; some are in clusters; some stand alone like obelisks: nothing can be more strange and wonderful than this romantic region, which is unlike anything I have ever seen either before or since. In Switzerland, Saxony, the Tyrol, or any other mountainous region where I have been, there is nothing at all to be compared to these extraordinary peaks.

At the foot of many of the rocks which surround this beautiful grassy amphitheatre, there are numerous caves and holes, some of which appear to be natural, but most of them are artificial; for in the dark and wild ages of monastic fanaticism whole flocks of hermits roosted in these pigeon-holes. Some of these caves are so high up the rocks that one wonders how the poor old gentlemen could ever get up to them; whilst others are below the surface; and the anchorites who burrowed in them, like rabbits, frequently afforded excellent sport to parties of roving Saracens; indeed, hermit-hunting seems to have been a fashionable amusement previous to the twelfth century. In early Greek frescos, and in small, stiff pictures with gold backgrounds, we see many frightful representations of men on horseback in Roman armour, with long spears, who are torturing and slaying Christian devotees. In these pictures the monks and hermits are represented in gowns made of a kind of coarse matting, and they have long beards, and some of them are covered with hair; these I take it were the ones most to be admired, as in the Greek church sanctity is always in the inverse ratio of beauty. All Greek saints are painfully ugly, but the hermits are much uglier, dirtier, and older than the rest; they must have been very fusty people besides, eating roots, and living in holes like rats and mice. It is difficult to understand by what process of reasoning they could have persuaded themselves that, by living in this useless, inactive way, they were leading holy lives. They wore out the rocks with their knees in prayer; the cliffs resounded with their groans; sometimes they banged their breasts with a big stone, for a change; and some wore chains and iron girdles round their emaciated forms; but they did nothing whatever to benefit their kind. Still there is something grand in the strength and constancy of their faith. They left their homes and riches and the pleasures of this world, to retire to these dens and caves of the earth, to be subjected to cold and hunger, pain and death, that they might do honour to their God, after their own fashion, and trusting that, by mortifying the body in this world, they should gain happiness for the soul in the world to come; and therefore peace be with their memory!

On the tops of these rocks in different directions there remain seven monasteries out of twenty-four which once crowned their airy heights. How anything except a bird was to arrive at one which we saw in the distance on a pinnacle of rock was more than we could divine; but the mystery was soon solved. Winding our way upwards, among a labyrinth of smaller rocks and cliffs, by a romantic path which, afforded us from time to time beautiful views of the green vale below us, we at length found ourselves on an elevated platform of rock, which I may compare to the flat roof of a church; while the monastery of Barlaam stood perpendicularly, above us, on the top of a much higher rock, like the tower of this church. Here we fired off a gun, which was intended to answer the same purpose as knocking at the door in more civilized places; and we all strained our necks in looking up at the monastery to see whether any answer would be made to our call. Presently we were hailed by some one in the sky, whose voice came down to us like the cry of a bird; and we saw the face and grey beard of an old monk some hundred feet above us peering out of a kind of window or door. He asked us who we were, and what we wanted, and so forth; to which we replied, that we were travellers, harmless people, who wished to be admitted into the monastery to stay the night; that we had come all the way from Corfu to see the wonders of Meteora, and, as it was now getting late, we appealed to his feelings of hospitality and Christian benevolence.

"Who are those with you?" said he.

"Oh! most respectable people," we answered; "gentlemen of our acquaintance, who have come with us across the mountains from Mezzovo."

The appearance of our escort did not please the monk, and we feared that he would not admit us into the monastery; but at length he let down a thin cord, to which I attached a letter of introduction which I had brought from Corfu; and after some delay a much larger rope was seen descending with a hook at the end to which a strong net was attached. On its reaching the rock on which we stood the net was spread open: my two servants sat down upon it; and the four corners being attached to the hook, a signal was made, and they began slowly ascending into the air, twisting round and round like a leg of mutton hanging to a bottle-jack. The rope was old and mended, and the height from the ground to the door above was, we afterwards learned, 37 fathoms, or 222 feet. When they reached the top I saw two stout monks reach their arms out of the door and pull in the two servants by main force, as there was no contrivance like a turning-crane for bringing them nearer to the landing-place. The whole process appeared so dangerous, that I determined to go up by climbing a series of ladders which were suspended by large wooden pegs on the face of the precipice, and which reached the top of the rock in another direction, round a corner to the right. The lowest ladder was approached by a pathway leading to a rickety wooden platform which overhung a deep gorge. From this point the ladders hung perpendicularly upon the bare rock, and I climbed up three or four of them very soon; but coming to one, the lower end of which had swung away from the top of the one below, I had some difficulty in stretching across from the one to the other; and here unluckily I looked down, and found that I had turned a sort of angle in the precipice, and that I was not over the rocky platform where I had left the horses, but that the precipice went sheer down to so tremendous a depth, that my head turned when I surveyed the distant valley over which I was hanging in the air like a fly on a wall. The monks in the monastery saw me hesitate, and called out to me to take courage and hold on; and, making an effort, I overcame my dizziness, and clambered up to a small iron door, through which I crept into a court of the monastery, where I was welcomed by the monks and the two servants who had been hauled up by the rope. The rest of my party were not admitted; but they bivouacked at the foot of the rocks in a sheltered place, and were perfectly contented with the coffee and provisions which we lowered down to them.

My servants, in high glee at having been hoisted up safe and sound, were busy in arranging my baggage in the room which had been allotted to us, and in making it comfortable: one went to get ready some warm water for a bath, or at any rate for a good splash in the largest tub that could be found; the other made me a snug corner on the divan, and covered it with a piece of silk, and spread my carpet before it; he put my books in a little heap, got ready the things for tea, and hung my arms and cloak, and everything he could lay his hands on, upon the pegs projecting from the wall under the shelf which was fixed all round the room. My European clothes were soon pitched into the most ignominious corner of the divan, and I speedily arrayed myself in the long, loose robes of Egypt, so much more comfortable and easy than the tight cases in which we cramp up our limbs. In short, I forthwith made myself at home, and took a stroll among the courts and gardens of the monastery while dinner or supper, whichever it might be called, was getting ready. I soon stumbled upon the Agoumenos (the lord abbot) of this aërial monastery, and we prowled about together, peeping into rooms, visiting the church, and poking about until it began to get dark; and then I asked him to dinner in his own room; but he could eat no meat, so I ate the more myself, and he made up for it by other savoury messes, cooked partly by my servants and partly by the monks. He was an oldish man. He did not dislike sherry, though he preferred rosoglio, of which I always carried a few bottles with me in my monastic excursions.

The abbot and I, and another holy father, fraternised, and slapped each other on the back, and had another glass or two, or rather cup, for coffee-cups of thin, old porcelain, called fingians, served us for wine-glasses. Then we had some tea, and they filled up their cups with sugar, and ate seaman's biscuits, and little cakes from Yanina, and rahatlokoom, and jelly of dried-grape juice, till it was time to go to bed; when the two venerable monks gave me their blessing and stumbled out of the room; and in a marvellously short space of time I was sound asleep.

November 9th.—The monastery of Barlaam stands on the summit of an isolated rock, on a flat or nearly flat space of perhaps an acre and a half, of which about one-half is occupied by the church and a smaller chapel, the refectory, the kitchen, the tower of the windlass, where you are pulled up, and a number of separate buildings containing offices and the habitations of the monks, of whom there were at this time only fourteen. These various structures surround one tolerably large, irregularly-shaped court, the chief part of which is paved; and there are several other small open spaces. All Greek monasteries are built in this irregular way, and the confused mass of disjointed edifices is usually encircled by a high bare wall; but in this monastery there is no such enclosing wall, as its position effectually prevents the approach of an enemy. On a portion of the flat space which is not occupied by buildings they have a small garden, but it is not cultivated, and there is nothing like a parapet-wall in any direction to prevent your falling over. The place wears an aspect of poverty and neglect; its best days have long gone by; for here, as everywhere else, the spirit of asceticism is on the wane.

diagram of church with four columns

The church has a porch before the door, νάρθηξ

, supported by marble columns, the interior wall of which on each side of the door is painted with representations of the Last Judgment, and the tortures of the condemned, with a liberal allowance of flames and devils. These pictures of the torments of the wicked are always placed outside the body of the church, as typical of the unhappy state of those who are out of its pale: they are never seen within. The interior of this curious old church, which is dedicated to All Saints, has depicted on its walls on all sides portraits of a great many holy personages, in the stiff, conventional, early style. It has four columns within which support the dome; and the altar or holy table, αγια τραπεζα
, is separated from the nave by a wooden screen, called the iconostasis, on which are paintings of the Blessed Virgin, the Redeemer, and many saints. These pictures are kissed by all who enter the church. The iconostasis has three doors in it; one in the centre, before the holy table, and one on each side. The centre one is only a half-door, like an old English buttery hatch, the upper part being screened with a curtain of rich stuff, which, except on certain occasions, is drawn aside, so as to afford a view of the book of the Gospels, in a rich binding, lying upon the holy table beyond. A Greek church has no sacristy; the vestures are usually kept in presses in this space behind the iconostasis, where none but the priests and the deacon, or servant who trims the lamps, are allowed to enter, and they pass in and out by the side doors. The centre door is only used in the celebration of the holy mass. This part of the church is the sanctuary, and is called, in Romaic, αγιο
, Βημο
, or Θημο
. It is typical of the holy of holies of the Temple, and the veil is represented by the curtain which divides it from the rest of the church. Everything is symbolical in the Eastern Church; and these symbols have been in use from the very earliest ages of Christianity. The four columns which support the dome represent the four Evangelists; and the dome itself is the symbol of heaven, to which access has been given to mankind by the glad tidings of the Gospels which they wrote. Part of the mosaic with which the whole interior of the dome was formerly covered in the cathedral of St. Sofia at Constantinople, is to be seen in the four angles below the dome, where the winged figures of the four evangelists still remain. Luckily for the Greek Church their sacred buildings are not under the authority of lay churchwardens—grocers in towns, and farmers in villages—who feel it their duty to whitewash over everything which is old and venerable, and curious, and to oppose the clergyman in order to show their independence.

The Greek church, debased as it is by ignorance and superstition, has still the merit of carefully preserving and restoring all the memorials of its earlier and purer ages. If the fresco painting of a saint is rubbed out or damaged in the lapse of time, it is scrupulously repainted, exactly as it was before, even to the colour of the robe, the aspect of the countenance, and the minutest accessories of the composition. It is this systematic respect for everything which is old and venerable which renders the interior of the ancient Eastern churches so peculiarly interesting. They are the unchanged monuments of primæval days. The Christians who suffered under the persecution of Dioclesian may have knelt before the very altar which we now see, and which was then exactly the same as we now behold it, without any additions or subtractions either in its form or use.

To us Protestants one of the most interesting circumstances connected with these Eastern churches is, that the altar is not called the altar, but the holy table, as with us, and that the Communion is given before it in both kinds. Besides the principal church there is a smaller one, not far from it, which is painted in the same manner as the other. I unfortunately neglected to ascertain the dates of the foundation of these two edifices.

The library contains about a thousand volumes, the far greater part of which are printed books, mostly Venetian editions of ecclesiastical works, but there are some fine copies of Aldine Greek classics. I did not count the number of the manuscripts; they are all books of divinity and the works of the fathers; there may be between one and two hundred of them. I found one folio Bulgarian manuscript which I could not read, and therefore was, of course, particularly anxious to purchase. As I saw it was not a copy of the Gospels, I thought it might possibly be historical: but the monks would not sell it. The only other manuscript of value was a copy of the Gospels, in quarto, containing several miniatures and illuminations of the eleventh century; but with this also they refused to part, so it remains for some more fortunate collector. It was of no use to the monks themselves, who cannot read either Hellenic or ancient Greek; but they consider the books in their library as sacred relics, and preserve them with a certain feeling of awe for their antiquity and incomprehensibility. Our only chance is when some worldly-minded Agoumenos happens to be at the head of the community, who may be inclined to exchange some of the unreadable old books for such a sum of gold or silver as will suffice for the repairs of one of their buildings, the replenishing of the cellar, or some other equally important purpose. At the time of my visit the march of intellect had not penetrated into the heights of the monastery of St. Barlaam, and the good old-fashioned Agoumenos was not to be overcome by any special pleading; so I told him at last that I respected his prejudices, and hoped he would follow the dictates of his conscience equally well in more important matters. The worthy old gentleman therefore pitched the two much-coveted books back into the dusty corner whence he had taken them, and where to a certainty they will repose undisturbed until some other bookworm traveller visits the monastery; and the sooner he comes the better, as mice and mildew are actively at work.

In a room near the library some ancient relics are preserved in silver shrines or boxes, of Byzantine workmanship: they are, however, not of very great antiquity or interest; the shrines are only of sufficient size to contain two skulls and a few bones; the style and execution of the ornaments are also much inferior to many works of the same kind which are met with in ecclesiastical houses.

The refectory is a separate building, with an apsis at the upper end, in which stands a marble table where the sacred bread used by the Greek church is usually placed, and where, I believe, the agoumenos or the bishop dines on great occasions. The walls of this room are also painted: not, however, with the representations of celebrated eaters, but with the likenesses of such thin, famished-looking saints that they seem most inappropriate as ornaments to a dining-room. The kitchen, which stands near the refectory, is a circular building of great antiquity, but the interior being pitch dark when I looked in, and there coming from the door a dusty cold smell, which did not savour of any dainty fare, I did not examine it.

The monks and the abbot had now assembled in the room where the capstan stood. Ten or twelve of them arranged themselves in order at the bars, the net was spread upon the floor, and, having sat down upon it cross-legged, the four corners were gathered up over my head, and attached to the hook at the end of the rope. All being ready, the monks at the capstan took a few steps round, the effect of which was to lift me off the floor and to launch me out of the door right into the sky, with an impetus which kept me swinging backwards and forwards at a fearful rate; when the oscillation had in some measure ceased the abbot and another monk, leaning out of the door, steadied me with their hands, and I was let down slowly and gently to the ground.

When I was disencumbered of the net by my friends the robbers below, I sat down on a stone, and waited while the rope brought down, first my servants, and then the baggage. All this being accomplished without accident, I sent the horses, baggage, and one servant to the great monastery of Meteora, where I proposed to sleep; and, with the other servant and the palicari, started on foot for a tour among the other monasteries.

A delightful walk of an hour and a half brought us to the entrance of the monastery of Hagios Stephanos, to which we gained access by a wooden drawbridge. The rock on which this monastery stands is isolated on three sides, and on the fourth is separated from the mountain by a deep chasm which, at the point where the drawbridge is placed, is not more than twelve feet wide. The interior of this building resembles St. Barlaam, inasmuch as it consists of a confused mass of buildings, surrounding an irregularly-formed court, of which the principal feature is the church. The paintings in it are not so numerous as at St Barlaam, but the iconostasis, or screen before the altar, is most beautifully carved, something in the style of Grinlin Gibbons: the pictures upon it being surrounded with frames of light open work, consisting of foliage, birds, and flowers in alto rilievo, cut out of a light-coloured wood in the most delicate manner. I was told that the whole of this beautiful work had been executed in Russia, and put up here during the reign of Ali Pasha, who had the good policy to protect the Greeks, and by that means to ensure the co-operation of one half of the population of the country.

In this monastery there were thirteen or fourteen monks and several women. On my inquiring for the library, one of the monks, after some demurring, opened a cupboard door; he then unfastened a second door at the back of it which led into a secret chamber, where the books of the monastery were kept. They were in number about one hundred and fifty; but I was disappointed at finding that although thus carefully concealed there was not a single volume amongst them remarkable for its antiquity or for any other cause: in fact, they were not worth the trouble of turning over. The view from this monastery is very fine: at the foot of the rock is the village of Kalabaki, to the east the citadel of Tricala stands above a wide level plain watered by the river which we had followed from its sources in Mount Pindus; beyond this a sea of distant blue hills extends to the foot of Mount Olympus, whose summit, clothed in perpetual snow, towers above all the other mountains. The whole of this region is inhabited by a race of a different origin from the real Albanians: they speak the Wallachian language, and are said to be extremely barbarous and ignorant. Observing that the village of Kalabaki presented a singularly black appearance, I inquired the cause: it had, they said, been recently burned and sacked by the klephti or robbers (some of my friends, perhaps), and the remnant of the inhabitants had taken refuge in the two monasteries of Hagios Nicholas and Agia Mone, which had been deserted by the monks some time before. The poor people in these two impregnable fastnesses were, they told me, so suspicious of strangers and in such a state of alarm, that there was no use in my visiting them, as to a certainty they would not admit me; and as it appeared that everything portable had been removed when the caloyeri (the monks) had departed from their impoverished homes, I gave up the idea.

I then proceeded along a romantic path to the monastery of Agia Triada, and on the way my servants entertained me by an account of what the monks had told them of their admiration of the Pasha of Tricala, whom they considered as a perfect model of a governor; and that it would be a blessing for the country if all other pashas were like him, as then all the roving bands of robbers, who spread terror and desolation through the land, would be cleared away. There is, it seems, a high tower over the gate of the town of Tricala, and when the Pasha caught any people whom he thought worthy of the distinction, he had them taken up to the top of this tower and thrown from it against the city walls, which his provident care had furnished with numerous large iron hooks, projecting about the length of a man's arm, which caught the bodies of the culprits as they fell, and on which they hung on either side of the town gate, affording a pleasing and instructive spectacle to the people who came in to market of a morning.

Agia Triada contains about ten or twelve monks, who pulled me up to the entrance of their monastery with a rope thirty-two fathoms long. This monastery, like the others, resembles a small village, of which the houses stand huddled round the little painted church. Here I found one hundred books, all very musty and very uninteresting. I saw no manuscripts whatever, nor was there anything worthy of observation in the habitation of the impoverished community. Having paid my respects to the grim effigies of the bearded saints upon the chapel walls, I was let down again by the rope, and walked on, still through most romantic scenery, to the monastery of Hagia Roserea.

The rock upon which this monastery stands is about a hundred feet high; it is perfectly isolated, and quite smooth and perpendicular on all sides, and so small that there is only room enough for the various buildings, without leaving any space for a garden. In fact, the buildings, although far from large, cover the whole summit of the rock. When we had shouted and made as much noise as we could for some time, an old woman came out upon a sort of wooden balcony over our heads; another woman followed her, and they began to talk and scream at us both together, so that we could not understand what they said. At last, one of them screaming louder than the other, we found that the monks were all out, and that these two ladies being the only garrison of the place declined the honour of our visit, and would not let down the rope ladder, which was drawn half way up. We used all the arguments we could think of, and told the old gentlewomen that they were the most beautiful creatures in the world, but all to no purpose; they were not to be overcome by our soft speeches, and would not let down the ladder an inch. Finding there were no hopes of getting in, we told them they were the ugliest old wretches in the country, and that we would not come near them if they asked us upon their knees; upon which they screamed and chattered louder than ever, and we walked off in high indignation.

CHAPTER XX.

The great Monastery of Meteora—The Church—Ugliness of the Portraits of Greek Saints—Greek Mode of Washing the Hands—A Monastic Supper—Morning View from the Monastery—The Library—Beautiful MSS.—Their Purchase—The Kitchen—Discussion among the Monks as to the Purchase Money for the MSS.—The MSS. reclaimed—A last Look at their Beauties—Proposed Assault of the Monastery by the Robber Escort.

As the day was drawing to a close we turned our steps towards the great monastery of Meteora, where we arrived just before dark. The vast rock upon which it is built is separated from the end of a projecting line of mountains by a widish chasm, at the bottom of which we found ourselves, after scrambling up a path which wound among masses of rock and huge stones which at some remote period had fallen from above.

Having reached the foot of the precipice under the monastery, we stopped in the middle of this dark chasm and fired a gun, as we had done at the monastery of Barlaam. Presently, after a careful reconnoitring from several long-bearded monks, a rope with a net at the end of it came slowly down to us, a distance of about twenty-five fathoms; and being bundled into the net, I was slowly drawn up into the monastery, where I was lugged in at the window by two of the strongest of the brethren, and after having been dragged along the floor and unpacked, I was presented to the admiring gaze of the whole reverend community, who were assembled round the capstan. This is by far the largest of the convents in this region; it is also in better order than the others, and is inhabited by a greater number of caloyers; I omitted to count their number, but there may have been about twenty: the monastery is, however, calculated to contain three times that number. The buildings both in their nature and arrangement are very similar to those of St. Barlaam, excepting that they are somewhat more extensive, and that there is a faint attempt at cultivating a garden which surrounded three sides of the monastery. Like all the other monasteries, it has no parapet wall.

The church had a large open porch before it, where some of the caloyers sat and talked in the evening; it was painted in fresco of bright colours, with most edifying representations of the tortures and martyrdoms of little ugly saints, very hairy and very holy, and so like the old caloyers themselves, who were discoursing before them, that they might have been taken for their portraits. These Greek monks have a singular love for the devil, and for everything horrible and hideous. I never saw a picture of a well-looking Greek saint anywhere, and yet the earlier Greek artists in their conceptions of the personages of Holy Writ sometimes approached the sublime; and in the miniatures of some of the manuscripts written previous to the twelfth century, which I collected in the Levant, there are figures of surpassing dignity and solemnity: yet in Byzantine and Egyptian art that purity and angelic expression so much to be admired in the works of Beato Angelico, Giovanni Bellini, and other early Italian masters, are not to be found. The more exalted and refined feeling which prompted the execution of those sublime works seems never to have existed in the Greek church, which goes on century after century, even up to the present time, using the same conventional and stiff forms, so that to the unpractised eye there would be considerable difficulty in discovering the difference between a Greek picture of a saint of the ninth century from one of the nineteenth. The agoumenos, a young active man with a good deal of intelligence in his countenance, sent word that the hour of supper was at hand, previously, however, to which I went through the process of washing my hands in, or rather over a Turkish basin with a perforated cover and a little vase in the middle for the piece of fresh-smelling soap in common use, which is so very much better than ours in England that I wonder none has been as yet imported, a venerable monk all the while pouring the water over my hands from a vessel resembling an antique coffee-pot. I then dried my fingers on an embroidered towel, and sat down with the agoumenos and another officer of the monastery before a metal tray covered with various dainty dishes. We three sat upon cushions on the floor, and the tray stood upon a wooden stool turned upside down, according to the usual fashion of the country: no meat had entered into the composition of our feast, but it was very savoury nevertheless, and our fingers were soon in the midst of the most tempting dishes, knives and forks being considered as useless superfluities. When my right hand was anointed with any oleaginous mixture, which it was very frequently indeed, if I wanted to drink, a monk held a silver bowl to my lips and a napkin under my chin, as you serve babies; after which I began again, until with a sigh I was obliged to throw myself back from the tray, and holding my hands aloft, the perforated basin and the coffee-pot made their appearance again. A cup of piping hot coffee concluded the evening's entertainment, and I retired to another room—the guest chamber—which opened upon a narrow court hard by, where all my things had been arranged. A long, thin candle was placed on a small stool in the middle of the floor, and having winked at the long rays which darted out of it for some time, I rolled myself into a comfortable position in the corner, and was asleep before I had settled upon any optical theory to account for them; nor did the dull, monotonous sound of the mallet, which, struck on a suspended board, called the good brethren to midnight prayer, disturb me for more than a moment.

Nov. 10.—Just before the dawn of day I opened the shutters of the unglazed windows of my room and surveyed the scene before me; all still looked grey and cold, and it was only towards the east that the distant outline of the mountains showed clear and distinct against the dark sky. By degrees the clouds, which had slept upon the shoulders of the hills, rose slowly and heavily, whilst the valleys gradually assumed all their soft and radiant beauty. It seemed to me as if I should never tire of gazing at this view. In the course of time, however, breakfast appeared, and having rapidly despatched it, I went to look at the buildings and curiosities.

The church resembles that of St. Barlaam, but is in better order; and the paintings are more brilliant in colour and are more profusely decorated with gold. There is a dome above the centre of the church, and the iconostasis or screen before the altar is ornamented with the usual stiff pictures and carving, but the latter is not to be compared to that in the monastery of St. Stephanos. There were some silver shrines containing relics, but they were not particularly interesting either as to workmanship or antiquity. The most interesting thing is a picture ascribed to St. Luke, which, whatever may be its real history, is evidently a very ancient and curious painting.

The books are preserved in a range of low-vaulted and secret rooms, very well concealed in a sort of mezzanine: the entrance to them is through a door at the back of a cupboard in an outer chamber, in the same way as at St Stephanos. There are about two thousand volumes of very rubbishy appearance, not new enough for the monks to read or old enough for them to sell; in fact, they are almost valueless. I found, however, a few Aldines and Greek books of the sixteenth century, printed in Italy, some of which may be rather rare editions, but I saw none of the fifteenth century. I did not count the number of the manuscripts; there are, however, some hundreds of them, mostly on paper; but, excepting two, they were all liturgies and church books. These two were poems. One appeared to be on some religious subject, the other was partly historical and partly the poetical effusions of St. Athanasius of Meteora. I searched in vain for the manuscripts of Hesiod and Sophocles mentioned by Biornstern; some later antiquarian may, perhaps, have got possession of them and taken them to some country where they will be more appreciated than they were here. After looking over the books on the shelves, the librarian, an old grey-bearded monk, opened a great chest in which things belonging to the church were kept; and here I found ten or twelve manuscripts of the Gospels, all of the eleventh or twelfth century. They were upon vellum, and all, except one, were small quartos; but this one was a large quarto, and one of the most beautiful manuscripts of its kind I have met with anywhere. In many respects it resembled the Codex Ebnerianus in the Bodleian Library at Oxford. It was ornamented with miniatures of the same kind as those in that splendid volume, but they were more numerous and in a good style of art; it was, in fact, as richly ornamented as a Romish missal, and was in excellent preservation, except one miniature at the beginning, which had been partially smeared over by the wet finger of some ancient sloven. Another volume of the Gospels, in a very small, clear hand, bound in a kind of silver filagree of the same date as the book, also excited my admiration. Those who take an interest in literary antiquities of this class are aware of the great rarity of an ornamental binding in a Byzantine manuscript. This must doubtless have been the pocket volume of some royal personage. To my great joy the librarian allowed me to take these two books to the room of the agoumenos, who agreed to sell them to me for I forget how many pieces of gold, which I counted out to him immediately, and which he seemed to pocket with the sincerest satisfaction. Never was any one more welcome to his money, although I left myself but little to pay the expenses of my journey back to Corfu. Such books as these would be treasures in the finest national collection in Europe.

We looked at the refectory, which also resembled that at Barlaam. The kitchen, however, merits a detailed description. This very ancient building, perched upon the extreme edge of the precipice, was square in its plan, with a steep roof of stone, the top of which was open. Within, upon a square platform of stone, there were four columns serving for the support of the roof, which was arched all round, except in the space between the tops of the columns, where it was open to the sky. This platform was the hearth, where the fire was lit, whilst smaller fires of charcoal might be lit all round against the wall, where there were stone dressers for the purpose, so that in fact the building was all chimney and fireplace; and when a great dinner was prepared on a feast-day the principal difficulty must have been to have prevented the cook from being roasted among the other meats. The whole of the arched roof was thickly covered with lumps of soot, the accumulations probably of centuries. The ancient kitchens at Glastonbury and at Stanton Harcourt are constructed a good deal upon the same plan, but this is probably a much earlier specimen of culinary architecture. The porch outside the church is larger than ordinary, and extends, if I remember rightly, along the side of that building which stands in the principal court, and is not, as is usually the case, attached to the end of the church, over the principal door.

Having seen all that was worthy of observation, I was waiting in the court near the door leading to the place where the monks were assembled to lower me down to the earth again. Just as I was ready to start there arose a discussion among them as to the distribution of the money which I had paid for the two manuscripts. The agoumenos wanted to keep it all for himself, or at least for the expenses of the monastery; but the villain of a librarian swore he would have half. The agoumenos said he should not have a farthing, but as the librarian would not give way he offered him a part of the spoil; however, he did not offer him enough, and out of spite and revenge, or, as he protested, out of uprightness of principle, he told all the monks that the agoumenos had pocketed the money which he had received for their property, for that they all had a right to an equal share in these books, as in all the other things belonging to the community. The monks, even the most dunderheaded, were not slow in taking this view of the subject, and all broke out into a clamorous assertion of their rights, every man of them speaking at once. The price I had given was so large that every one of them would have received several pieces of gold each. But no, they said, it was not that, but for the principles of justice that they contended. They did not want the money, no more did the librarian, but they would not suffer their rules to be outraged or their rights to be trampled under foot. In the monasteries of St. Basil all the members of the society had equal rights—they ate in common, they prayed in common, everything was bought and sold for the benefit of the community at large. Tears fell from the eyes of some of the particularly virtuous monks; others stamped upon the ground, and showed a thoroughly rebellious spirit. As for me, I kept aloof, waiting to see what might be the result.

The agoumenos, who was evidently a man of superior abilities, calmly endeavoured to explain. He told the unruly brethren exactly what the sum was for which he had sold the books, and said that the money was not for his own private use, but to be laid out for the benefit of all, in the same way as the ordinary revenues of the monastery, which, he added, would soon prove quite insufficient if so large a portion of them continued to be divided among the individual members. He told them that the monastery was poor and wanted money, and that this large sum would be most useful for certain necessary expenses. But although he used many unanswerable arguments, the old brute of a librarian had completely awakened the spirit of discord, and the ignorant monks were ready to be led into rebellion, by any one and for any reason or none. At last the contest waxed so warm that the sale of the two manuscripts was almost lost sight of, and every one began to quarrel with his neighbour, the entire community being split into various little angry groups, chattering, gesticulating, and wagging their long beards.

After a while the agoumenos, calling my interpreter, said that as the monks would not agree to let him keep the money in the usual way for the use of the monastery, he could have nothing to do with it; and to my great sorrow I was therefore obliged to receive it back, and to give up the two beautiful manuscripts, which I had already looked upon as the chief ornaments of my library in England. The monks all looked sadly downcast at this unexpected termination of their noble defence of their principles, and my only consolation was to perceive that they were quite as much vexed as I was. In fact we felt that we had gained a loss all round, and the old librarian, after walking up and down once or twice with his hands behind his back in gloomy silence, retreated to a hole where he lived, near the library, and I saw no more of him.

My bag was brought forward, and when the books were extracted from it, I sat down on a stone in the court yard, and for the last time turned over the gilded leaves and admired the ancient and splendid illuminations of the larger manuscript, the monks standing round me as I looked at the blue cypress-trees, and green and gold peacocks, and intricate arabesques, so characteristic of the best times of Byzantine art. Many of the pages bore a great resemblance to the painted windows of the earlier Norman cathedrals of Europe.

It was a superb old book: I laid it down upon the stone beside me and placed the little volume with its curious silver binding on the top of it, and it was with a sigh that I left them there with the sun shining on the curious silver ornaments.

Amongst other arguments it had been asserted by some of the monks that nothing could be sold out of the monastery without the leave of the Bishop of Tricala, and, as a forlorn hope, they now proposed that the agoumenos should go to some place in the vicinity where the bishop was said to be, and that, if he gave permission, the two books should be forwarded immediately by a trusty man to the khan of Malacash, where I was to pass the night. I consented to this plan, although I had no hope of obtaining the manuscripts, as in the present unsettled state of the country the bishop would naturally calculate on the probability of the messenger being robbed, and on the improbability of his meeting me at the khan, as it would be absolutely necessary for me to leave the place before sunrise the next day.

All this being arranged I proceeded to the chamber of the windlass, was put into the net, swung out into the air, and let down. They let me down very badly, being all talking and scolding each other; and had I not made use of my hands and feet to keep myself clear of the projecting points of the rock I should have fared badly. To increase my perils, my friends the palicari at the bottom, to testify their joy at my re-appearance, rested their long guns across their knees and fired them off, without the slightest attention to the direction of the barrels, which were all loaded with ball-cartridge: the bullets spattered against the rock close to me, and in the midst of the smoke I came down and was caught in the arms of my affectionate thieves, who bundled me out of my net with many extraordinary screeches of welcome.

When my servants arrived and informed them of our recent disappointment, "What!" cried they, "would they not let you take the books? Stop a bit, we will soon get them for you!" And away they ran to the series of ladders which hung down another part of the precipice: they would have been up in a minute, for they scrambled like cats; but by dint of running after them and shouting we at length got them to come back, and after some considerable expenditure of oaths and exclamations, kicking of horses, and loading of guns and saddle-bags, we found ourselves slowly winding our way back towards the valley of the Peneus.

After all, what an interesting event it would have been, what a standard anecdote in bibliomaniac history, if I had let my friendly thieves have their own way, and we had stormed the monastery, broken open the secret door of the library, pitched the old librarian over the rocks, and marched off in triumph, with a gorgeous manuscript under each arm! Indeed I must say that under such aggravating circumstances it required a great exercise of forbearance not to do so, and in the good old times many a castle has been attacked and many a town besieged and pillaged for much slighter causes of offence than those which I had to complain of.

CHAPTER XXI.

Return Journey—Narrow Escape—Consequences of Singing—Arrival at the Khan of Malacash—Agreeable Anecdote—Parting from the Robbers at Mezzovo—A Pilau—Wet Ride to Paramathia—Accident to the Baggage-Mule—Its wonderful Escape—Novel Costume—A Deputation—Return to Corfu.

We

made our way from the plain and rocks of Meteora by a different path from the one by which we had arrived, and travelled along the north side of the valley of the Peneus; we kept along the side of the hills, which were covered sometimes with forest and sometimes with a kind of jungle or underwood.

During the afternoon of this day, as I was singing away as usual in advance of my party, some one shouted to me from the thicket, but I took no notice of it. However, before I had ridden on many steps a man jumped out of the bush, seized hold of my horse's bridle, and proceeded to draw his pistol from his belt, but luckily the lock had got entangled in the shawl which he wore round his waist. I pushed my horse against him, and in a moment one of us would have been shot; when the appearance of three or four bright gun-barrels in the bushes close by stopped our proceedings. My men now came running up.

"Hallo!" said one of them. "Is that you? You must not attack this gentleman. He is our friend; he is one of us."

"What!" said the man who had stopped me; "Is that you, Mahommed? Is that you, Hassan? What are you doing here? How is this? Is this your friend? I thought he was a Frank."

In short, they explained what kind of brotherhood we had entered into, where we had been, and where we were going, and all about it. I did not understand much of their conversation, and in the midst of it the Albanian came up to me with a reproachful air and told me that they said my being stopped was owing to my singing, and making such a noise. "Why, Sir," he added, "can't you ride quietly, without letting people know where you are? Why can't you do as others do, and be still, like a—"

"Thief," said I.

"Yes, Sir; or like a quiet traveller. In such troublesome times as these, however honest a man may be, he need not try to excite attention."

I felt that the advice was good, and practised it occasionally afterwards.

In seven hours' time we arrived at the khan of Malacash, where I had slept before; and my carpet was spread in my old corner. I heard my companions talking earnestly about something, and on asking what it was, I was told that they could not make out which room it was where the people had been murdered—this room or the outer one.

"How was that?" I inquired.

Why, some time ago, they said, a party of travellers, people belonging to the country, were attacked by robbers at this khan. One of the party, after he had been plundered, had the imprudence to say that he knew who the thieves were. Upon this the gang, after a short consultation, took the party out, one by one, and cut all their throats in the next room; and this was before the present disturbed state of the country. Nevertheless, I slept very soundly, my only sorrow being that no tidings came of the two manuscripts from Meteora.

November 11th.—In our journey of this day we crossed the chain of the Pindus by a different pass from the one by which we had traversed it before; and in the evening we arrived at Mezzovo, where I was lodged by a schoolmaster who had a comfortable house. The ceiling of the room where we sat was hung all over with bunches of dried or rather drying grapes. Here I presented each of my escort with a small bundle of piasters. We had become so much pleased with each other in the few days we had been together, that we had quite an affecting parting. Their chief, the red velvet personage from whom I had received the letter which gained me the pleasure of their company, was gone, it appeared, towards Berat; but they had found some of their companions, with whom they intended to retire to some small place of defence, the name of which I did not make out, where in a few days they expected to be told what they were to do.

"Why won't you come with us?" said they. "Don't go back to live in a confined, stupid town, to sit all day in a house, and look out of the window. Go back with us into the mountains, where we know every pass, every rock, and every waterfall: you should command us; we would get some more men together: we will go wherever you like, and a rare jolly life we will lead."

"Gentlemen," said I, "I take your kind offers as highly complimentary to me; I am proud to think that I have gained so high a place in your estimation. When you see your captain, pray assure him of my friendship, and how much I feel indebted to him for having given me such gallant and faithful guards."

The poor fellows were evidently sorry to leave me: one of them, the most active and gay of the whole party, seemed more than half inclined to cry; so, cordially shaking hands with them before the door of the schoolmaster of Mezzovo, we parted, with expressions of mutual goodwill.

"Thank goodness they are gone!" said the little schoolmaster; "those palicari are all over the country now; some belong to one chief, some to another; some are for Mahmoud Pasha, and some against him; but I don't know which party is the worst; they are all rogues, every one of them, when they have an opportunity—scamps! sad scamps! These are hard times for quiet, peaceably-disposed people. So now, Sir, we will come in, and lock the door, and make up the fire, for the nights are getting cold."

The schoolmaster had a snug fireplace, with a good divan on each side of it, of blue cloth or baize. These divans came close up to the hearth, which, like the divans, was raised two feet above the floor. The good man brought out his little stores of preserves and marmalade. He was an old bachelor, and we soon made ourselves very comfortable, one on each side of the fire. We had a famous pilau, made by my "artist," and the schoolmaster gave us raisins to put in it—not that they are a necessary part of that excellent condiment, but he had not much else to give; so we flavoured the pilau with raisins, as if it had been a lamb, which, by the by, is the prince of Oriental dishes, and, when stuffed with almonds, raisins, pistachio nuts, rice, bread-crumbs, pepper and salt, and well roasted, is a dish to set before a king.

The schoolmaster, judging of me by the company I kept, never suspected my literary pursuits, and was surprised when I asked him if he knew of anything in that line, and assured him that I had no objection to do a little business in the manuscript way. He said he knew of an old merchant who had a great many books, and that to-morrow we would go and see them. Accordingly, the next day we went to see the merchant's house; but his collection was good for nothing; and after returning for an hour or two to the schoolmaster's hospitable mansion, we got into marching order, and defiled off the village green of Mezzovo.

After fording the river thirty-nine times, as we had done before, our jaded steeds at last stood panting under the windows of the doctor at Yanina, whose comfortable house we had left only a few days before. I stayed at Yanina one day, but the Pasha could not see me to hear my account of the protection I had enjoyed from his firman. A messenger had arrived from Constantinople, and the report in the town was that the Pasha would lose his head or his pashalic if he did not put down the disturbances which had arisen in every part of his government. Some said he would escape by bribing the ministers of the Porte; but as I was no politician I did not trouble myself much on the subject His Highness, however, was good enough to send me word that he would give me any assistance that I needed. Accordingly, I asked for a teskéré for post-horses; and the next day galloped in ten hours to Paramathia. All day long the rain poured down in torrents, and I waded through the bed of the swollen stream, which usually served for a high-road, I do not know how many times. I was told the distance was about sixty miles; and it was one of the hardest day's riding I ever accomplished; for there was nothing deserving the name of a road any part of the way; and the entire day was passed in tearing up and down the rocks or wading in the swollen stream. The rain and the cold compelled us and our horses to do our best: in a hot day we could never have accomplished it.

Towards the afternoon, when we were, by computation, about twenty-five miles from Paramathia, as we were proceeding at a trot along a narrow ledge above a stream, the baggage-horse, or mule I think he was, whose halter was tied to the crupper of my horse, suddenly missed his footing, and fell over the precipice. He caught upon the edge with his fore-feet, the halter supported his head, and my horse immediately stopping, leant with all his might against the wall of rock which rose above us, squeezing my left leg between it and the saddle. The noise of the wind and rain, and the dashing of the torrent underneath, prevented my servants hearing my shouts for assistance. I was the last of the party; and I had the pleasure of seeing all my company trotting on, rising in their stirrups, and bumping along the road before me, unconscious of anything having occurred to check their progress towards the journey's end. It was so bad a day that no one thought of anything but getting on. Every man for himself was the order of the day. I could not dismount, because my left leg was squeezed so tightly against the rock, that I every moment expected the bone to snap. My horse's feet were projected towards the edge of the precipice, and in this way he supported the fallen mule, who endeavoured to retain his hold with his chin and his fore-legs. There we were—the mule's eyeballs almost starting out of his head, and all his muscles quivering with the exertion. At last something cracked: the staple in the back of my saddle gave way; off flew the crupper, and I thought at first my horse's tail was gone with it. The baggage-mule made one desperate scrambling effort, but it was of no use, and down he went, over and over among the crashing bushes far beneath, until at length he fell with a loud splash into the waters of the stream. Some of the people hearing the noise made by the falling mule, turned round and came back to see what was the matter; and, horse and men, we all craned our necks over the edge to see what had become of our companion. There he was in the river, with nothing but his head above the water. With some difficulty we made our way down to the edge of the torrent. The mule kept looking at us very quietly all the while till we got close to him, when the muleteer proceeded to assist him by banging him on the head with a great branch of a tree, upon which he took to struggling and scrambling, and at last, to the surprise of all, came out apparently unhurt, at least with no bones broken. The men looked him over, walked him about, gave him a kick or two by way of asking him how he was, and then placing his load upon him again, we pursued our journey.

Before dark we arrived at Paramathia, and went straight to the house where we had been so hospitably received before. We crawled up like so many drowned rats into the upper rooms, where we were met by the whole troop of ladies giggling, screaming, and talking, as if they had never stopped since we left them a week before. When the baggage came to be undone, alas! what a wreck was there! The coffee and the sugar and the shirts had formed an amalgam; mud, shoes, and cambric handkerchiefs all came out together; not a thing was dry. The only consolation was that the beautiful illuminated manuscripts of Meteora had not participated in this dirty deluge.

I was wet to the skin, and my boots were full of water. In this dilemma I asked if our hosts could not lend me something to put on until some of my own clothes could be dried. The ladies were full of pity and compassion; but unfortunately all the men were from home, not having returned from their daily occupations in the bazaar, and their clothes could not be got at. At last the good-humoured young bride, seeing that wherever I stood there was always, in a couple of minutes' time, a puddle upon the floor, entered into an animated consultation with the other ladies, and before long they brought me a shirt, and an immense garment it was, like an English surplice, embroidered in gay colours down the seams. The fair bride contributed the white capote, which I remembered on my former visit, and a girdle. I soon donned this extempore costume. My wet clothes were taken to a great fire, which was lit for the purpose in another room, and I proceeded to dry my hair with a long narrow towel, its ends heavy with gold embroidery, which one of the ladies warmed far me, and twisted round my head in the way usual in the Turkish bath—a method of drying the head well known in most eastern towns, and which saves a great deal of trouble and exertion in rubbing and brushing according to the European method.

I had ensconced myself in the corner of the divan, having nothing else in the way of clothes beyond what I have mentioned, and was employed in looking at one of my feet, which I had stuck out for the purpose, admiring it in all its pristine beauty, for there were no spare slippers to be had, when the curtain was suddenly lifted from over the door, and my servant rushed in and told me with a troubled voice, that the authorities of Paramathia, grieved at their remissness on the former occasion, had presented themselves to compliment me on my arrival in their town, and had brought me a present of tobacco or something, I forget what, in testimony of their anxiety to show their good-will and respect to so distinguished a personage as myself. "Don't let them in!" I exclaimed. "Tell them I will receive them to-morrow. Say anything, but only keep them out." But this was more than my servants could accomplish. My friends at Corfu had sent letters explaining the prodigious honour conferred upon the whole province of Albania by my presence, so that nothing could stop them, and in walked a file of grave elders in long gowns, one or two in stately fur pelisses, which I envied them very much. They took very little notice of me, as I sat screwed up in the corner, and all, ranging themselves upon the divan on the opposite side of the room, sat in solemn silence, looking at me out of the corners of their eyes, whenever they thought they could do so without my perceiving it.

My servant stood in the middle of the room to interpret; and after he had remained there a prodigious while, as it seemed to me, the most venerable of the old gentlemen at last said, "I am Signor Dimitri So-and-so; this is Signor Anastasi So-and-so; this gentleman is uncle to the master of the house; and so on. We are come to pay our respects to the noble and illustrious Englishman who passed through this place before. Pray have the goodness to signify our arrival to his Excellency, and say that we are waiting here to have the honour of offering him our services. Where is the respected milordos?" Although I could not speak Romaic, yet I understood it sufficiently to know what the old gentleman was saying; and great was their surprise and admiration when they found that the unhappy and very insufficiently-clothed little fellow in the corner was the illustrious milordos himself. The said milordos had now to explain how all his baggage had been upset over a precipice, and that he was not exactly prepared to receive so distinguished a party. After mutual apologies, which ended in a good laugh all round, pipes and coffee were brought in. The visit of ceremony was concluded in as dignified a manner as circumstances would permit; and they went away convinced that I must be a very great man in my own country, as I did not get up more than a few inches to salute them, either on their entry or departure—a most undue assumption of dignity on my part which I sincerely regretted, but which the state of my costume rendered absolutely necessary.

November 15th.—The morning of the following day was bright and clear. I procured fresh horses, and galloped in six hours to the sea at Gominiza. A small vessel was riding at anchor near the shore, whose captain immediately closed with the offer of four dollars to carry me over to Corfu. I was soon on board; and, creeping into a small three-cornered hole under the half-deck, to which I gained access by a hatchway about a foot and a half square, I rolled myself up upon some ropes, and fell asleep at once. It seemed as if I had not been asleep an instant, when my servant, putting his head into the square aperture above, said, "Signore siamo qui." "Yes," said I, "but where is that? What! are we really at Corfu?" I popped my head out of the trap, and there we were sure enough—my fatigue of the day before having made me sleep so soundly that I had been perfectly unconscious of the duration of the voyage; and I landed on the quay congratulating myself on having accomplished the most dangerous and most rapid expedition that it ever was my fortune to undertake.

MONASTERIES OF THE LEVANT.
PART IV.

THE MONASTERIES OF MOUNT ATHOS.
THE NORTH WEST SIDE OF THE PROMONTORY OF MOUNT ATHOS, WITH A VIEW OF THE THE MONASTERY OF PANTOCRATORAS THE NORTH WEST SIDE OF THE PROMONTORY OF MOUNT ATHOS, WITH A VIEW OF THE THE MONASTERY OF PANTOCRATORAS
CHAPTER XXII.
Constantinople—The Patriarch's Palace—The Plague, Anecdotes, Superstitions—The Two Jews—Interview with the Patriarch—Ceremonies of Reception—The Patriarch's Misconception as to the Archbishop of Canterbury—He addresses a Firman to the Monks of Mount Athos—Preparations for Departure—The Ugly Greek Interpreter—Mode of securing his Fidelity.

Ihad
been for some time enjoying the hospitality of Lord and Lady Ponsonby at the British palace at Therapia, when I determined to put into execution a project I had long entertained of examining the libraries in the monasteries of Mount Athos. As no traveller had

been there since the days of Dr. Clarke, I could obtain but little information about the place before I left England. But the Archbishop of Canterbury was kind enough to give me a letter to the Patriarch of Constantinople, in which he requested him to furnish me with any facilities in his power in my researches among the Greek monasteries which owned his sway.

Armed with this valuable document, one day in the spring of the year 1837 I started in a caïque with some gentlemen of the embassy, and proceeded to the palace of the Patriarch in the Fanar—a part of Constantinople situated between the ancient city wall and the port so well known by its name of the Golden Horn. The Fanar does not derive its appellation from the word fanar, a lantern or lighthouse, but from the two words fena yer, a bad place; for it is in a low, dirty situation, where only the conquered Greeks were permitted to reside immediately after the conquest of their metropolis by the Sultan Mahommed II. The palace is a large, dilapidated, shabby-looking building, chiefly of wood painted black; it stands in an open court or yard on a steep slope, and looks out over some lower houses to the Golden Horn and the hills of Pera and Galata beyond.[12]

After waiting a little while in a large, dirty ante-room, during which time there was a scuffling and running up and down of priests and deacons, who were surprised and perhaps a little alarmed at a visit from so numerous a company of gentlemen belonging to the British embassy, we were introduced into a large square room furnished with a divan under the windows and down two sides of the chamber. This divan was covered with a rough sacking of grey goats' hair—a stuff which is said not to be susceptible of the plague; and people sitting on it, or on the bare boards, are not considered to be "compromised"—a word of fearful import when that awful pestilence is raging in this neglected city. When any person is compromised, he is obliged to separate from all society, and to place himself in strict quarantine for forty days, at the end of which period, if the fright and anxiety have not brought on the plague, he is received again by his acquaintances. Dealers in oil, and persons who have an open issue on their bodies, are considered secure from the plague as far as they themselves are concerned; but as their clothes will convey the infection, they are as dangerous as others to their neighbours.

There was an old Armenian, who, whether he considered himself invulnerable, or whether poverty and misfortune made him reckless, I do not know; but he set up as a plague-doctor, and visited and touched those who were stricken with the pestilence. When-ever he came down the street, every one would start aside and give him three or four yards' space at least. Sometimes he had men who walked before him and cried to the people to get out of the way. As the old man moved on in his long, dark robes, shunned with such horror by all, the mind was awfully impressed with the fearful nature of the disease; for if the Prince of Darkness himself had made his appearance in the face of day, no one could have shown greater alarm at his approach than they did when the men cried out that the Armenian plague-doctor was coming down the street.

One peculiarity of the disease is the disinclination which is always shown by those who are plague-stricken to confess that they are so, or even to own that they are ill. They invariably conceal it as long as possible; and even when burning with fever and in an agony of pain, they will pretend that they are well, and try to walk about. But this attempt at deception continues for a very short period, for they soon become either delirious or insensible, and generally are unable to move. There is a look about the eye and an expression of anxiety and horror in the face of one who has got the plague which is not to be mistaken nor forgotten by those who have once seen them. One day at Galata I nearly ran against a man who was sitting on the ground on a hand-bier, upon which some Turks were about to carry him away; and the look of the unfortunate man's face haunted me for days. The expression of hopeless despair and agony was indeed but too applicable to his case; they were going to carry him to the plague hospital, from whence I never heard of any one returning. It would have been far more merciful to have shot him at once.

There are many curious superstitions and circumstances connected with the plague. One is, that when the destroying angel enters into a house the dogs of the quarter assemble in the night and howl before the door; and the Greeks firmly believe that the dogs can see the evil spirit of the plague, although it is invisible to human eyes. Some people, however, are said to have seen the plague, its appearance being that of an old woman, tall, thin, and ghastly, and dressed sometimes in black, sometimes in white: she stalks along the streets—glides through the doors of the habitations of the condemned—and walks once round the room of her victim, who is from that moment death-smitten. It is also asserted that, when three small spots make their appearance upon the knee, the patient is doomed—he has got the plague, and his fate is sealed. They are called the pilotti—the pilots and harbingers of death. Some, however, have recovered after these spots have shown themselves.

I had at this time a lodging in a house at Pera, which I occupied when anything brought me to Constantinople from Therapia. On one occasion I was sitting with a gentleman whose filial piety did him much honour, for he had attended his father through the horrors of this illness, and he had died of the plague in his arms, when we heard the dogs baying in an unusual way.[13] On looking out of the window there they were all of a row, seated against the opposite wall, howling mournfully, and looking up at the houses in the moonlight. One dog looked very hard at me, I thought: I did not like it at all, and began to investigate whether I had not some pain or other about me; and this comfortable feeling was not diminished when my friend's Arab servant came into the room and said that another person who lodged in the house was very unwell; it was said that he had had a fell from his horse that morning. The dogs, though we escaped the plague ourselves, were right; the plague had got into one of the houses close to us in the same street; but how many died of it I did not learn.

It was about this time that two Jews—extortioners, poor men, whom consequently nobody cared about—were walking together in a narrow street at Galata, when they both dropped down stricken with the plague: there they lay upon the ground; no one would touch them; and, as the street was extremely narrow, no one could pass that way; it was in effect blocked up by the two unhappy men. They did not die quickly. "The devil was sure of them," the charitable people said, "so he was in no hurry." There they lay a long time—many days; and people called to them, and put their heads round the corner of the street to look at them. Some, tenderer-hearted than the rest, got a long pole from a dyer's shop hard by, and pushed a tub of water to them, and threw them some bread, for no one dared approach them. One Jew was quiet: he ate a little bread and drank some water, and lay still. The other was violent: the pain of his livid swellings drove him wild, and he shouted and raved and twisted about upon the ground. The people looked at him from the corner, and shuddered as they quickly drew back their heads. He died; and the other Jew still lay there, quiet as he was before, close to the quiet corpse of his poor friend. For some time they did not know whether he was dead or not; but at last they found he drank no more water and ate no more bread; so they knew that he had died also. There lay the two bodies in the way, till some one paid a hamal—a Turkish porter—who, being a stanch predestinarian, caring neither for plague, nor Jew, nor Gentile, dead or alive, carried off the two bodies on his back; and then the street was passable again.

The Turks have a touching custom when the plague rages very greatly, and a thousand corpses are carried out daily from Stamboul through the Adrianople gate to the great groves of cypress which rise over the burial-grounds beyond the walls. At times of terror and grief, such as these, the Sheikh Ul Islam causes all the little children to be assembled on a beautiful green bill called the Oc Maidan—the Place of Arrows—and there they bow down upon the ground, and raise their innocent voices in supplication to the Father of Mercy, and implore his compassion on the afflicted city!

But the grey goats' hair divan of the Patriarch's hall of audience has led me a long way from the Patriarch himself, who entered the chamber shortly after our arrival. He appeared to be rather a young man, certainly not more than thirty-five years of age, with a reddish beard, which is uncommon in this country. He was dressed in purple silk robes, like a Greek bishop, and took his seat in the corner of the divan, and said nothing, and stroked his beard as a pasha might have done.

When we had made our "téménahs," that is, salutations, and little bows, c., and were still again, the curtain over the doorway was pushed aside, and various priestly servants, all without shoes, came in, one of them bearing a richly embossed silver tray, on which were disposed small spoons filled with a preserve of lemon-peel; each of us took a spoonful, and returned the spoon to the dish. Then came various servants—as many servants as guests—and one presented to each of us a cut-glass cup with a lid, full of fresh spring-water. Then these disappeared; and others came in bearing pipes to each of us—a separate servant always coming in for each person of the company. After we had smoked our pipes for a short time, a mighty crowd of attendants again entered at the bottom of the room, among whom was one with a tray, which was covered over with a satin shawl or cover as richly embroidered with gold as was possible for its size, and with a deep gold fringe. Another servant took off this covering, and placed it over the left shoulder of the tray-bearer, who stood like a statue all the while. Now appeared a man with a silver censer suspended by three silver chains, and having a coffee-pot standing upon the burning coals within it. Another man took off the cups which were upon the tray, filled them with coffee; and then various servants, each armed with a coffee-cup placed on its silver zarf or saucer, which he held in his left hand with his thumb and forefinger only, strode forward with one accord, and we all at the same moment were presented with our diminutive cup of coffee; the attendants received the empty cups with both hands, and, walking backwards, disappeared as silently as they came. All this is a scene of every-day occurrence in the East, and, with more or less of display, takes place in the house of every person of consideration.

When we had smoked our pipes for awhile, and all the servants had gone away, I presented the letter of the Archbishop of Canterbury. It was received in due form; and, after a short explanatory exordium, was read aloud to the Patriarch, first in English, and then translated into Greek.

"And who," quoth the Patriarch of Constantinople, the supreme head and primate of the Greek Church of Asia—"who is the Archbishop of Canterbury?"

"What?" said I, a little astonished at the question.

"Who," said he, "is this Archbishop?"

"Why, the Archbishop of Canterbury."

"Archbishop of what?" said the Patriarch.

"Canterbury," said I.

"Oh," said the Patriarch. "Ah! yes! and who is he?"

Here all my English friends and myself were taken aback sadly; we had not imagined that the high-priest before us could be ignorant of such a matter as the one in question. The Patriarch of the Greek church, the successor of Gregory Nazianzen, St. John Chrysostom, and the heresiarch Nestorius, seemed not to be aware that there were any other denominations of Christians besides those of his own church and the Church of Rome. But the fact is that the Patriarch of Constantinople is merely the puppet of an intriguing faction of the Greek bankers and usurers of the Fanar, who select for the office some man of straw whom they feel secure they can rule, and whose appointment they obtain by a heavy bribe paid to the Sultan; for the head of the Christian Church is appointed by the Mahomedan Emperor!

We explained, and said that the Archbishop of Canterbury was a man eminent for his great learning and his Christian virtues; that he was the primate and chief of the great reformed Church of England, and a personage of such high degree, that he ranked next to the blood-royal; that from time immemorial the Archbishop of Canterbury was the great dignitary who placed the crown upon the head of our kings—those kings whose power swayed the destinies of Europe and of the world; and that this present Archbishop and Primate had himself placed the crown upon the head of King William IV., and that he would also soon crown our young Queen.

"Well," replied the Patriarch, "but how is that? how can it happen that the head of your Church is only an Archbishop? whereas I, the Patriarch, command other patriarchs, and under them archbishops, archimandrites, and other dignitaries of the Church? How can these things be? I cannot write an answer to the letter of the Archbishop of—of—"

"Of Canterbury," said I.

"Yes! of Canterbury; for I do not see how he who is only an archbishop can by any possibility be the head of a Christian hierarchy; but as you come from the British embassy I will give my letters as you desire, which will ensure your reception into every monastery which acknowledges the supremacy of the orthodox faith of the Patriarch of Constantinople."

He then sent for his secretary, that I might give that functionary my name and designation. The secretary accordingly appeared; and, although there are only six letters in my name, he set it down incorrectly nearly a dozen times, and then went away to his hole in a window, where he wrote curious little memoranda at the Patriarch's dictation, from which he drew up the firman which was sent me a few days afterwards, and which I found of great service in my visits to various monasteries. As few Protestants have been favoured with a document of this sort from the Primate of the Greek Church, I subjoin a translation of it. It will be perceived that it is written much in the style of the epistles of the early patriarchs to the archbishops and bishops of their provinces. To the requisitions contained in this firman it was incumbent upon those to whom it was addressed to pay implicit obedience.[14]

My business being thus happily concluded with this learned personage, we all smoked away again for a short time in tranquil silence; and then the Universal Patriarch—for so he styles himself—clapped his hands, and in swarmed the whole tribe of silent, bare-footed priestly followers, bringing us sherbet in glass cups. Whilst we drank it, their reverences held the saucer under our chins: and when we had had enough, those who chose it wiped their lips and moustaches on a long, narrow towel, richly embroidered at the two ends with gold and bright-coloured silks. I prefer on these occasions my pocket-handkerchief, as the period at which these rich towels are washed is by no means a matter of certainty. We took our leave with the numerous bows and compliments, and went on our way rejoicing.

My preparations for my expedition were soon made. I hired a Greek servant, whom I intended should serve as interpreter and factotum. He was a sharp, active man—as most Greeks are; and he had an intelligent way of doing things, which pleased me; but he was an ugly, thin, little fellow, and his right eye had a curious obliquity of vision, which was not particularly calculated to inspire confidence. As nobody else was to accompany me, I made various inquiries about him, and, although I did not hear any particular harm of him, yet I failed to become acquainted with any good actions of his performance; and as I was going into a country which at that time was almost entirely unknown, and which had moreover an unpleasant celebrity for pirates, klephti, and other sorts of thieves, I felt that the moral character of my new follower was an important consideration; and that if I could prop up his honesty and fidelity by any artificial means, I might not be doing amiss.

In a few days the firman or letter of the patriarch arrived, and I packed my things and got ready to start. Unknown to my servant I had caused a belt of wash-leather to be made, in which were numerous little divisions calculated to hold a good many pieces of gold without their jingling, and it had a long flap which buttoned down over the series of compartments. I had besides a large ostentatious purse, in which was a small sum for the expenses of the journey, and as I wished to have it supposed that I had but little cash, I made my Greek buy various things for me out of his own money. All being ready, we started in a caïque very early in the morning, and went down the Bosphorus from Therapia to Stamboul, where we got on board a steamer. On handing up the things, my servant found that his box, in which were his new clothes and valuables, was missing—his bag only had come. "Good gracious!" said I, "was that the box with two straps?" "Yes," said he, "a handsome brown box, about so large." "Well," said I, "it is a most unfortunate thing; but when I saw that box in my room this morning I locked it up in the closet and told H—— not to give up the key of the door to anybody till I returned to the embassy again. How very unlucky! however, we shall soon be back, and you have biancheria enough in your bag for so short a journey as the one before us." We were soon under way, and passing the Seraglio Point stood down the swift current in the sea of Marmora, our luggage encumbering but a very small space upon the deck.

CHAPTER XXIII.

Coom Calessi—Uncomfortable Quarters—A Turkish Boat and its Crew—Grandeur of the Scenery—Legend of Jason and the Golden Fleece—The Island of Imbros—Heavy

Rain Storm—A Rough Sea—Lemnos—Bad Accommodation—The Old Woman's Mattress and its Contents—Striking View of Mount Athos from the Sea—The Hermit of the Tower.

On
landing at Coom Calessi, the European castle of the Dardanelles, I found that there was no inn or hotel in the place; but it appeared that the British consul, who lived on the top of the hill two miles off, had built a new house in the town for purposes of business, and upon the payment of a perquisite to the Jew who acted as his factotum, I was presently installed in the new house, which, as houses go in this country, was clean and good, but not a scrap of furniture was there in it, not even a pipkin or a casserole—it was as empty as any house could be. I sent my man out into the bazaar and we got some cabobs and yaourt and salad, and various flaps of bread, and managed so far pretty well, and then we went to the port, and after much waste of time and breath I engaged a curious-looking boat belonging to a Turk, who by the by was the only Turkish sailor I ever had anything to do with, as the seamen are generally Greeks; and then I returned to my house to sleep, for we were not to set out on our voyage till sunrise the next morning. The sleeping was a more difficult affair than the dinner, for after the beds at the embassy the boards did seem supernaturally hard; but I spread all my property on the floor, and lying down on it flat on my back, out of compassion to my hips, I got through the night at last.

All men were up and about in the Turkish town of Coom Calessi as soon as the sun tinged the hills of Olympus, and the gay boat in which I was to sail was bounding up and down on the bright transparent waves by the sandy shore. The long-bearded captain sat on a half deck with the tiller under his arm; he neither moved nor said a word when I came on board, and before the god of day arose in his splendour over the famous plains of Troy my little boat was spreading its white wings before the morning wind. Every moment more and more lovely scenes opened to my delighted eyes among the rocky and classic islands of the Archipelago. How fair and beautiful is every part of that most favoured land! how fresh the breezes on that poetic sea! how magnificent the great precipices of the rocky island of Samotraki seemed as they loomed through the decreasing distance in the morning sun! But no words, no painting can describe this glorious region.

I had hired my grave sailors to take me to Lemnos, but the wind did not serve, so we steered for Imbros, where we arrived in the afternoon. My boat was an original-looking vessel to an English eye, with a high bow and stem covered with bright brass; over the rudder there hung a long piece of network ornamented with blue glass beads: flowers and arabesques were carved on the boards at each end of the vessel, which had one low mast with a single sail. It is the national belief in England that ugliness is the necessary concomitant of utility, but for my own part I confess that I delight in redundant ornament, and I liked my old boat the better and was convinced that it did not sail a bit the worse because it was pleasing to the eye.

We rowed away towards Imbros, and passed in our course a curious line of waves, which looked like a straight whirlpool, if such an epithet may be used; for where the mighty stream of the Dardanelles poured forth into the Egean Sea, the two waters did not immediately mix together, but rolled the one over the other in a long line which seemed as if it would suck down into its snaky vortex anything which approached it. It was not dangerous, however, for we rowed along it and across it; but still it had a look about it which made me feel rather glad than sorry when we had lost sight of its long, straight, curling line of waves.

As I sat in my beautifully-shaped and ornamented boat, which looked like those represented in antique sculptures, with its high stem and lofty prow, I thought how little changed things were in these latitudes since the brave Captain Jason passed this way in the good ship Argo; and if an old author who wrote on the Hermetic philosophy may be taken as authority, that worthy's errand was much the same as mine; for he maintains that the golden fleece was no golden fleece at all, "for who," says he, like a sensible man, "ever saw a sheep of gold?" But what Jason sought was a famous volume written in golden letters upon the skins of sheep, wherein was described the whole science of alchemy, and that the man who should possess himself of that inestimable volume should conquer the green dragon, and being able by help of the grand magisterium to transmute all metals, and draw from the alembic the precious drops of the elixir vitæ, men and nations and languages would bow down before him as the prince of the pleasures of this world.

In the afternoon we arrived at the island of Imbros. The Turkish pilot would go no farther, for he said there would be a storm. I saw no appearance of the kind, but it was of no use talking to him; he had made up his mind, so we drew the boat up on the sand in a little sheltered bay, and making a tent of the sail, the sailors lit a fire and sat down and smoked their pipes with all that quietness and decorum which is so characteristic of their nation. I wandered about the island, but saw neither man nor habitation. I shot at divers rock-partridges with a rifle and hit none; nevertheless towards evening we cooked up a savoury mess, whereof the old bearded Turk and his grave crew ate also, but sparingly: I then curled myself up in a corner inside the boat under the sail, and took to reading a volume of Sir Walter Scott's poems.

I was deep in his romantic legends when of a sudden there came a roar of thunder and such quick bright flashes of sharp lightning that the mountains seemed on fire. Down came the rain in waterfalls, and in went Walter Scott and all his chivalry into the first safe hiding-place I could find. The crew had got under a projecting rock, and I had the boat to myself; the rain did not come in much, and the rattle of the thunder by degrees died away among the surrounding hills. The rain continued to pour down steadily and the fire on the beach went out, but my berth was snug enough, and the dull monotonous sound of the splashing rain and the dashing of the breakers on the shore soon lulled me to sleep, and I was more comfortable than I had been the night before in the bare, empty house at Coom Calessi.

Very early in the morning I peeped out; the rain was gone and the sun shone brightly; all the Turks were up smoking their eternal pipes, so I asked the old captain when we should be off. "There is too much wind," was his laconic reply. We were in a sheltered place, so we felt no wind, but on the other side of a rocky headland we could see the sea running like a cataract towards the south, although it was as smooth as glass in our bay. We got through breakfast, and for the sake of the partridges I repented that I had brought no shot. At last the men began righting the boat and getting things ready, doing everything as quietly and deliberately as usual, and scarcely saying a word to each other. In course of time the captain sat himself down by the rudder, and beckoning to me with his hand he took the pipe out of his mouth and said "Gel" (come). I came, and away we went smoothly with the help of two or three oars till we rounded the rocky headland, and

then all at once we drifted into the race, and began dancing, and leaping, and staggering before the breeze in a way I never saw before nor since. Like the goats, from whom this sea is said to have been named, we leaped from the summit of one wave to that of the next, and seemed hardly to touch the water. We had up a small sail, and we sat still and steady at the bottom of the vessel. Never had I conceived the possibility of a boat scampering along before the wind at such a rate as this. My man crossed himself. I looked up at the old pilot, but he went on quietly smoking his pipe with his finger on the bowl to keep the ashes from being blown away. It was a marvel to me with what exactness he touched the helm just at the right instant, for it seemed as if we had sixty narrow escapes every minute, but the old man did not stir an inch. Gallantly we dashed, and skipped, and bounded along. What a famous lively little boat it was, yet it was carved and gilt and as pretty as anything could be! We were soon running down the west coast of Lemnos, where the surf was lashing the precipice in fury with an angry roar that resounded far out to sea: then of a sudden we rounded a sharp point and shot into such smooth water so instantaneously that one could scarcely believe that the blue waves of the Holy Sea, Αγιος πελαγος
, as the Greeks call it still, could be the same as the furious and frenzied ocean out of which we had darted like an arrow from a bow.

We had a long row in the hot sun along the sheltered coast till we landed at a rotten wooden pier before the chief city or rather the dirty village of the Lemnians. I had a letter to a gentleman who was sent by a merchant of Constantinople to collect wool upon this island; so to him I bent my way, hooted at by some Lemnian women, the worthy descendants probably of those fair dames who have gained a disagreeable immortality by murdering their husbands. Here it was that Vulcan broke his leg, and no wonder, for a more barren, rocky place no one could have been kicked down into. My friend of the woolpacks, who was a Frenchman, was very kind and civil, only he had nothing to offer me beyond the bare house, like the consul's Jew at the Dardanelles, so I walked about and looked at nothing, which was all there was to see, whilst my servant hired a little square-rigged brig to take me next day to Mount Athos.

After dinner I made inquiries of my host what he had in the way of bed. His answer was specific. There was no bed, no mattress, no divan; sheets were unknown things, and the wool he did not recommend. But at last I was told of a mattress which an old woman next door was possessed of, and which she sometimes let out to strangers; and in an evil hour I sent for it. That treacherous bed and its clean white coverlet will never be forgotten by me. I laid down upon it and in one minute was fast asleep—the next I started up a perfect Marsyas. Never until that day had I any idea of what fleas could do. So simultaneous and well conducted was their attack that I was bitten all over from top to toe at the first assault. They evidently were delighted at the unexpected change of diet from a grim, skinny old woman to a well-fed traveller fresh from the table of the embassy. I examined the white coverlet—it was actually brown with fleas. I threw away my clothes, and taking desperate measures to get rid of some myriads of my assailants, I ran out of the room and put on a dressing-gown in the outer hall, at the window of which I sat down to cool the fever of my blood. I half expected to see the fleas open the door and march in after me, as the rats did after Bishop Hatto on his island in the Rhine; but fortunately the villains did not venture to leave their mattress. There I sat, fanning myself in the night air and bathing my face and limbs in water till the sun rose, when with a doleful countenance I asked my way to a bath. I found one, and went into the hot inner room with nothing on but a towel round my waist and one on my head, as the custom is. There was no one else there, and when the bath man came in he started back with horror, for he thought I had got that most deadly kind of plague which breaks out in an eruption and carries off the patient in a few hours. When it was explained to him how I had fallen into the clutches of these Lemnian fleas, he proceeded to rub me and soap me according to the Turkish fashion, and wonderfully soothing and comforting it was.

As there was a rumour of pirates in these seas, the little brig would not sail till night, and I passed the day dozing in the shade out of doors; when evening came I crept down to the port, went on board, and curled myself up in the hole of a cabin among ropes and sails, and went to sleep at once, and did not wake again till we arrived within a short distance of the most magnificent mountain imaginable, rising in a peak of white marble ten thousand feet straight out of the sea. It was a lovely fresh morning, so I stood with half of my body out of the hatchway enjoying the glorious prospect, and making my toilette with the deck for a dressing-table, to the great admiration of the Greek crew, who were a perfect contrast to my former Turkish friends, for they did nothing but lounge about and chatter, and give orders to each other, every one of them appearing unwilling to do his own share of the work.

GREEK SAILOR. GREEK SAILOR.

We steered for a tall square tower which stood on a projecting marble rock above the calm blue sea at the S.E. corner of the peninsula; and rounding a small cape we turned into a beautiful little port or harbour, the entrance of which was commanded by this tower and by one or two other buildings constructed for defence at the foot of it, all in the Byzantine style of architecture. The quaint half-Eastern half-Norman architecture of the little fortress, my outlandish vessel, the brilliant colours of the sailors' dresses, the rich vegetation and great tufts of flowers which grew in crevices of the white marble, formed altogether one of the most picturesque scenes it was ever my good fortune to behold, and which I always remember with pleasure. We saw no one, but about a mile off there was the great monastery of St. Laura standing above us among the trees on the side of the mountain, and this delightful little bay was, as the sailors told us, the scarricatojo or landing-place for pilgrims who were going to the monastery.

We paid off the vessel, and my things were landed on the beach. It was not an operation of much labour, for my effects consisted principally of an enormous pair of saddle-bags, made of a sort of carpet, and which are called khourges, and are carried by the camels in Arabia; but there was at present mighty little in them: nevertheless, light as they were, their appearance would have excited a feeling of consternation in the mind of the most phlegmatic mule. After a brisk chatter on the part of the whole crew, who, with abundance of gesticulations, all talked at once, they got on board, and towing the vessel out by means of an exceeding small boat, set sail, and left me and my man and the saddle-bags high and dry upon the shore. We were somewhat taken by surprise at this sudden departure of our marine, so we sat upon two stones for a while to think about it. "Well," said I, "we are at Mount Athos; so suppose you walk up to the monastery, and get some mules or monks, or something or other to carry up the saddle-bags. Tell them the celebrated Milordos Inglesis, the friend of the Universal Patriarch, is arrived, and that he kindly intends to visit their monastery; and that he is a great ally of the Sultan's, and of all the captains of all the men of war that come down the Archipelago: and," added I, "make haste now, and let us be up at the monastery lest our friends in the brig there should take it into their heads to come back and cut our throats."

Away he went, and I and the saddle-bags remained below. For some time I solaced myself by throwing stones into the water, and then I walked up the path to look about me, and found a red mulberry-tree with fine ripe mulberries on it, of which I ate a prodigious number in order to pass away the time. As I was studying the Byzantine tower, I thought I saw something peeping out of a loophole near the top of it, and, on looking more attentively, I saw it was the head of an old man with a long grey beard, who was gazing cautiously at me. I shouted out at the top of my voice, "Kalemera sas, ariste, kalemera sas (good day to you, sir); ora kali sas (good morning to you); του δάπομειβομενος

;" he answered in return, "Kalos orizete?" (how do you do?) So I went up to the tower, passed over a plank that served as a drawbridge across a chasm, and at the door of a wall which surrounded the lower buildings stood a little old monk, the same who had been peeping out of the loophole above. He took me into his castle, where he seemed to be living all alone in a Byzantine lean-to at the foot of the tower, the window of his room looking over the port beneath. This room had numerous pegs in the wall, on which were hung dried herbs and simples; one or two great jars stood in the corner, and these and a small divan formed all his household furniture. We began to talk in Romaic, but I was not very strong in that language, and presently stuck fast. He showed me over the tower, which contained several groined vaulted rooms one above another, all empty. From the top there was a glorious view of the islands and the sea. Thought I to myself, this is a real, genuine, unsophisticated live hermit; he is not stuffed like the hermit at Vauxhall, nor made up of beard and blankets like those on the stage; he is a genuine specimen of an almost extinct race. What would not Walter Scott have given for him? The aspect of my host and his Byzantine tower savoured so completely of the days of the twelfth century, that I seemed to have entered another world, and should hardly have been surprised if a crusader in chain-armour had entered the room and knelt down before the hermit's feet The poor old hermit observing me looking about at all his goods and chattels, got up on his divan, and from a shelf reached down a large rosy apple, which he presented to me; it was evidently the best thing he had, and I was touched when he gave it to me. I took a great bite: it was very sour indeed; but what was to be done? I could not bear to vex the old man, so I went on eating a great deal of it, although it brought the tears into my eyes.

We now heard a holloing and shouting, which portended the arrival of the mules, and, bidding adieu to the old hermit of the tower, I mounted a mule; the others were lightly loaded with my effects, and we scrambled up a steep rocky path through a thicket of odoriferous evergreen shrubs, our progress being assisted by the screams and bangs inflicted by several stout acolytes, a sort of lay-brethren, who came down with the animals from the convent.

CHAPTER XXIV.

Monastery of St. Laura—Kind Reception by the Abbot—Astonishment of the Monks—History of the Monastery—Rules of the Order of St. Basil—Description of the Buildings—Curious Pictures of the Last Judgment—Early Greek Paintings; Richness of their Frames and Decorations—Ancient Church Plate—Beautiful Reliquary—The Refectory—The Abbot's Savoury Dish—The Library—The MSS.—Ride to the Monastery of Caracalla—Magnificent Scenery.

We

soon emerged upon a flat piece of ground, and there before us stood the great monastery of

ST. LAURA.

It appeared like an ancient fortress, surrounded with high blank walls, over the tops of which were seen numerous domes and pinnacles, and odd-shaped roofs and cypress-trees, all jumbled together. In some places one of those projecting windows, which are called shahneshin at Constantinople, stood out from the great encircling wall at a considerable height above the ground; and in front of the entrance was a porch in the Byzantine style, consisting of four marble columns, supporting a dome; in this porch stood the agoumenos, backed by a great many of the brethren. My servant had, doubtless, told him what an extraordinarily great personage he was to expect, for he received me with great deference; and after the usual bows and compliments the dark train of Greek monks filed in through the outer and two inner iron gates, in a sort of procession, with which goodly company I proceeded to the church, which stood in the middle of the great court-yard. We went up to the screen of the altar, and there everybody made bows, and said "Kyrie eleison," which they repeated as quickly and in as high a key as they could. We then came out of the church, and the agoumenos, taking me by the hand, led me up divers dark wooden staircases, until we came into a large cheerful room well furnished in the Turkish style, and having one of the projecting windows which I had seen from the outside. In this room, which the agoumenos told me I was to consider as my own, we had coffee. I then presented the letter of the patriarch; he read it with great respect, and said I was welcome to remain in the monastery as long as I liked; and after various compliments given and received he left me; and I found myself comfortably installed in one of the grand—and, as yet, unexplored—monasteries of the famous sanctuary of Mount Athos: better known in the Levant by the appellation of Αγιον Ορος

, or, as the Italian hath it, Monte Santo.

Before long I received visits from divers holy brethren, being those who held offices in the monastery under my lord the agoumenos, and there was no end to the civilities which passed between us. At last they all departed, and towards evening I went out and walked about; those monks whom I met either opening their eyes and mouths, and standing still, or else bowing profoundly and going through the whole series of gesticulations which are practised towards persons of superior rank; for the poor monks never having seen a stranger before, or at least a Frank, did not know what to make of me, and according to their various degrees of intellect treated me with respect or astonishment. But Greek monks are not so ill-mannered as an English mob, and therefore they did not run after me, but only stared and crossed themselves as the unknown animal passed by.

I will now, from the information I received from the monks and my own observation, give the best account I can of this extensive and curious monastery. It was founded by an Emperor Nicephorus, but what particular Nicephorus he was nobody knew. Nicephorus, the treasurer, got into trouble with Charlemagne on one side, and Haroun al Raschid on the other, and was killed by the Bulgarians in 811. Nicephorus Phocas was a great captain, a mighty man of valour; who fought with everybody, and frightened the Caliph at the gates of Bagdad, but did good to no one; and at length became so disagreeable that his wife had him murdered in 969. Nicephorus Botoniates, by the help of Alexius Comnenus, caught and put out the eyes of his rival Nicephorus Bryennius, whose son married that celebrated blue-stocking Anna Comnena. However, Nicephorus Botoniates having quarrelled with Alexius Comnenus, that great man kicked him out and reigned in his stead, and Botoniates took refuge in this monastery, which, as I make out, he had founded some time before. He came here about the year 1081, and took the vows of a kaloyeri, or Greek monk.

πατρηζα πατρηζα

This word kaloyeri means a good old man. All the monks of Mount Athos follow the rule of St. Basil: indeed, all Greek monks are of this order. They are ascetics, and their discipline is most severe: they never eat meat, fish they have on feast-days; but on fast-days, which are above a hundred in the year, they are not allowed any animal substance or even oil; their prayers occupy eight hours in the day, and about two during the night, so that they never enjoy a real night's rest. They never sit down during prayer, but as the services are of extreme length they are allowed to rest their arms on the elbows of a sort of stalls without seats, which are found in all Greek churches, and at other times they lean on a crutch. A crutch of this kind, of silver, richly ornamented, forms the patriarchal staff: it is called the patritza, and answers to the crosier of the Roman bishops. Bells are not used to call the fraternity to prayers, but a long piece of board, suspended by two strings, is struck with a mallet. Sometimes, instead of the wooden board, a piece of iron, like part of the tire of a wheel, is used for this purpose. Bells are rung only on occasions of rejoicing, or to show respect to some great personage, and on the great feasts of the church.

The accompanying sketches will explain the forms of the patriarchal staff, the board, and the iron bar.

τοκμακ, a hammer, in Turkish. τοκμακ, a hammer, in Turkish.

τοκμακ, a hammer, in Turkish.

The latter are called in Romaic σημανδρος

, a word derived from σημασοκτουμαι

, to gather together.

According to Johannes Comnenus, who visited Mount Athos in 1701, and whose works are quoted in Montfaucon, 'Paleographia Græca,' page 452, St. Laura was founded by Nicephorus Phocas, and restored by Neagulus, Waywode of Bessarabia. The buildings consist of a thick and lofty wall of stone, which encompasses an irregular space of ground of between three and four acres in extent; there is only one entrance, a crooked passage defended by three separate iron doors; the front of the building on the side of the entrance extends about five hundred feet. There is no attempt at external architecture, but only this plain wall; the few windows which look out from it belong to rooms which are built of wood and project over the top of the wall, being supported upon strong beams like brackets. At the south-west corner of the building there is a large square tower, which formerly contained a printing-press: but this press was destroyed by the Turkish soldiers during the late Greek revolution; and at the same time they carried off certain old cannons, which stood upon the battlements, but which were more for show than use, for the monks had never once ventured to fire them off during the long period they had been there; and my question, as to when they were brought there originally, was answered by the universal and regular answer of the Levant, "τι εξεβζο

—Qui sa?—who knows?" The interior of the monastery consists of several small courts and two large open spaces surrounded with buildings, which have open galleries of wood or stone before them, by means of which entrance is gained into the various apartments, which now afford lodging for one hundred and twenty monks, and there is room for many more. These two large courts are built without any regularity, but their architecture is exceedingly curious, and in its style closely resembles the buildings erected in Constantinople between the fifth and the twelfth century: a sort of Byzantine, of which St. Marc's in Venice is the finest specimen in Europe. It bears some affinity to the Lombardic or Romanesque, only it is more Oriental in its style; the chapel of the ancient palace of Palermo is more in the style of the buildings on Mount Athos than anything else in Christendom that I remember; but the ceilings of that chapel are regularly arabesque, whereas those on Mount Athos are flat with painted beams, like the Italian basilicas, excepting where they are arched or domed; and in those cases there is little or no mosaic, but only coarse paintings in fresco representing saints in the conventional Greek style of superlative ugliness.

In the centre of each of these two large courts stands a church of moderate size, each of which has a porch with thin marble columns before the door; the interior walls of the porches are covered with paintings of saints and also of the Last Judgment, which, indeed, is constantly seen in the porch of every church. In these pictures, which are often of immense size, the artists evidently took much more pains to represent the uncouthness of the devils than the beauty of the angels, who, in all these ancient frescos, are a very hard-favoured set. The chief devil is very big; he is the hero of the scene, and is always marvellously hideous, with a great mouth and long teeth, with which he is usually gnawing two or three sinners, who, to judge from the expression of his face, must be very nauseous articles of food. He stands up to his middle in a red pool which is intended for fire, and wherein numerous little sinners are disporting themselves like fish in all sorts of attitudes, but without looking at all alarmed or unhappy. On one side of the picture an angel is weighing a few in a pair of scales, and others are capering about in company with some smaller devils, who evidently lead a merry life of it. The souls of the blessed are seated in a row on a long hard bench very high up in the picture; these are all old men with beards; some are covered with hair, others richly clothed, anchorites and princes being the only persons elevated to the bench. They have good stout glories round their heads, which in rich churches are gilt, and in the poorer ones are painted yellow, and look like large straw hats. These personages are severe and grim of countenance, and look by no means comfortable or at home; they each hold a large book, and give you the idea that except for the honour of the thing they would be much happier in company with the wicked little sinners and merry imps in the crimson lake below. This picture of the Last Judgment is as much conventional as the portraits of the saints; it is almost always the same, and a correct representation of a part of it is to be seen in the last print of the rare volume of the Monte Santo di Dio, which contains the three earliest engravings known: it would almost appear that the print must have been copied from one of these ancient Greek frescos. It is difficult to conceive how any one, even in the dark ages, can have been simple enough to look upon these quaint and absurd paintings with feelings of religious awe; but some of the monks of the Holy Mountain do so even now, and were evidently scandalized when they saw me smile. This is, however, only one of the numberless instances in which, owing to the differences of education and circumstances, men look upon the same thing with awe or pity, with ridicule or veneration.[15]

The interior of the principal church in this monastery is interesting from the number of early Greek pictures which it contains, and which are hung on the walls of the apsis behind the altar. They are almost all in silver frames, and are painted on wood; most of them are small, being not more than one or two feet square; the back-ground of all of them is gilt; and in many of them this back-ground is formed of plates of silver or gold. One small painting is ascribed to St. Luke, and several have the frames set with jewels, and are of great antiquity. In front of the altar, and suspended from the two columns nearest to the ικονοστασις

—the screen which, like the veil of the temple, conceals the holy of holies from the gaze of the profane—are two pictures larger than the rest: the one represents our Saviour, the other the Blessed Virgin. Except the faces they are entirely covered over with plates of silver-gilt; and the whole of both pictures, as well as their frames, is richly ornamented with a kind of coarse golden filigree, set with large turquoises, agates, and cornelians. These very curious productions of early art were presented to the monastery by the Emperor Andronicus Paleologus, whose portrait, with that of his Empress, is represented on the silver frame.

The floor of this church, and of the one which stands in the centre of the other court, is paved with rich coloured marbles. The relics are preserved in that division of the church which is behind the altar; their number and value is much less than formerly, as during the revolution, when the Holy Mountain was under the rule of Aboulabout Pasha, he squeezed all he could out of the monks of this and all the other monasteries. However, as no Turk is a match for a Greek, they managed to preserve a great deal of ancient church plate, some of which dates as far back as the days of the Roman emperors, for few of the Christian successors of Constantine failed to offer some little bribe to the saints in order to obtain pardon for the desperate manner in which they passed their lives. Some of these pieces of plate are well worthy the attention of antiquarians, being probably the most ancient specimens of art in goldsmith's work now extant; and as they have remained in the several monasteries ever since the piety of their donors first sent them there, their authenticity cannot be questioned, besides which many of them are extremely magnificent and beautiful.

The most valuable reliquary of St. Laura is a kind of triptic, about eighteen inches high, of pure gold, a present from the Emperor Nicephorus, the founder of the abbey. The front represents a pair of folding-doors, each set with a double row of diamonds (the most ancient specimens of this stone that I have seen), emeralds, pearls, and rubies as large as sixpences. When the doors are opened a large piece of the holy cross, splendidly set with jewels, is displayed in the centre, and the inside of the two doors and the whole surface of the reliquary are covered with engraved figures of the saints stuck full of precious stones. This beautiful shrine is of Byzantine workmanship, and, in its way, is a superb work of art.

The refectory of the monastery is a large square building, but the dining-room which it contains is in the form of a cross, about one hundred feet in length each way; the walls are decorated with fresco pictures of the saints, who vie with each other in the hard-favoured aspect of their bearded faces; they are tall and meagre full-length figures as large as life, each having his same inscribed on the picture. Their chief interest is in their accurate representation of the clerical costume. The dining-tables, twenty-four in number, are so many solid blocks of masonry, with heavy slabs of marble on the top; they are nearly semicircular in shape, with the flat side away from the wall; a wide marble bench runs round the circular part of them in this form. A row of these tables extend down each side of the hall, and at the upper end in a semicircular recess is a high table for the superior, who only dines here on great occasions. The refectory being square on the outside, the intermediate spaces between the arms of the cross are occupied by the bakehouse, and the wine, oil, and spirit cellars; for although the monks eat no meat, they drink famously; and the good St. Basil having flourished long before the age of Paracelsus, inserted nothing in his rules against the use of ardent spirits, whereof the monks imbibe a considerable quantity, chiefly bad arrack; but it does not seem to do them any harm, and I never heard of their overstepping the bounds of sobriety. Besides the two churches in the great courts, which are shaded by ancient cypresses, there are twenty smaller chapels, distributed over different parts of the monastery, in which prayers are said on certain days. The monks are now in a more flourishing condition than they have been for some years; and as they trust to the continuance of peace and order in the dominions of the Sultan, they are beginning to repair the injuries they suffered during the revolution, and there is altogether an air of improvement and opulence throughout the establishment.

I wandered over the courts and galleries and chapels of this immense building in every direction, asking questions respecting those things which I did not understand, and receiving the kindest and most civil attention from every one. In front of the door of the largest church a dome, curiously painted and gilt in the interior, and supported by four columns, protects a fine marble vase ten feet in diameter, with a fountain in it; in this magnificent basin the holy water is consecrated with great ceremony on the feast of the Epiphany.[16]

I was informed that no female animal of any sort or kind is admitted on any part of the peninsula of Mount Athos; and that since the days of Constantine the soil of the Holy Mountain had never been contaminated by the tread of a woman's foot. That this rigid law is infringed by certain small and active creatures who have the audacity to bring their wives and large families within the very precincts of the monastery I soon discovered to my sorrow, and heartily regretted that the stern monastic law was not more rigidly enforced; nevertheless, I slept well on my divan, and the next morning at sunrise received a visit from the agoumenos, who came to wish me good day. After some conversation on other matters, I inquired about the library, and asked permission to view its contents. The agoumenos declared his willingness to show me everything that the monastery contained. "But first," said he, "I wish to present you with something excellent for your breakfast; and from the special good will that I bear towards so distinguished a guest I shall prepare it with my own hands, and will stay to see you eat it; for it is really an admirable dish, and one not presented to all persons." "Well," thought I, "a good breakfast is not a bad thing;" and the fresh mountain-air and the good night's rest had given me an appetite; so I expressed my thanks for the kind hospitality of my lord abbot, and he, sitting down opposite to me on the divan, proceeded to prepare his dish. "This," said he, producing a shallow basin half-full of a white paste, "is the principal and most savoury part of this famous dish; it is composed of cloves of garlic, pounded down, with a certain quantity of sugar. With it I will now mix the oil in just proportions, some shreds of fine cheese [it seemed to be of the white acid kind, which resembles what is called caccia cavallo in the south of Italy, and which almost takes the skin off your fingers, I believe] and sundry other nice little condiments, and now it is completed!" He stirred the savoury mess round and round with a large wooden spoon until it sent forth over room and passage and cell, over hill and valley, an aroma which is not to be described. "Now," said the agoumenos, crumbling some bread into it with his large and somewhat dirty hands, "this is a dish for an emperor! Eat, my friend, my much-respected guest; do not be shy. Eat; and when you have finished the bowl you shall go into the library and anywhere else you like; but you shall go nowhere till I have had the pleasure of seeing you do justice to this delicious food, which, I can assure you, you will not meet with everywhere."

I was sorely troubled in spirit. Who could have expected so dreadful a martyrdom as this? The sour apple of the hermit down below was nothing—a trifle in comparison! Was ever an unfortunate bibliomaniac dosed with such a medicine before? It would have been enough to have cured the whole Roxburghe Club from meddling with libraries and books for ever and ever. I made every endeavour to escape this honour. "My Lord," said I, "it is a fast; I cannot this morning do justice to this delicious viand; it is a fast; I am under a vow. Englishmen must not eat that dish in this month. It would be wrong; my conscience won't permit it, though the odour certainly is most wonderful! Truly an astonishing savour! Let me see you eat it, O agoumenos!" continued I; "for behold, I am unworthy of anything so good." "Excellent and virtuous young man!" said the agoumenos, "no, I will not eat it. I will not deprive you of this treat. Eat it in peace; for know, that to travellers all such vows are set aside. On a journey it is permitted to eat all that is set before you, unless it is meat that is offered to idols. I admire your scruples: but be not afraid, it is lawful. Take it, my honoured friend, and eat it: eat it all, and then we will go into the library." He put the bowl into one of my hands and the great wooden spoon into the other: and in desperation I took a gulp, the recollection of which still makes me tremble. What was to be done? Another mouthful was an impossibility: not all my ardour in the pursuit of manuscripts could give me the necessary courage. I was overcome with sorrow and despair. My servant saved me at last: he said "that English gentlemen never ate such rich dishes for breakfast, from religious feelings, he believed; but he requested that it might be put by, and he was sure I should like it very much later in the day." The agoumenos looked vexed, but he applauded my principles; and just then the board sounded for church. "I must be off, excellent and worthy English lord," said he; "I will take you to the library, and leave you the key. Excuse my attendance on you there, for my presence is required in the church." So I got off better than I expected; but the taste of that ladleful stuck to me for days. I followed the good agoumenos to the library, where he left me to my own devices.

The library is contained in two small rooms looking into a narrow court, which is situated to the left of the great court of entrance. One room leads to the other, and the books are disposed on shelves in tolerable order, but the dust on their venerable heads had not been disturbed for many years, and it took me some time to make out what they were, for in old Greek libraries few volumes have any title written on the back. I made out that there were in all about five thousand volumes, a very large collection, of which about four thousand were printed books; these were mostly divinity, but among them there were several fine Aldine classics and the editio princeps of the Anthologia in capital letters.

The nine hundred manuscripts consisted of six hundred volumes written upon paper and three hundred on vellum. With the exception of four volumes, the former were all divinity, principally liturgies and books of prayer. Those four volumes were Homer's 'Iliad' and Hesiod, neither of which were very old, and two curious and rather early manuscripts on botany, full of rudely drawn figures of herbs. These were probably the works of Dioscorides; they were not in good condition, having been much studied by the monks in former days: they were large, thick quartos. Among the three hundred manuscripts on vellum there were many large folios of the works of St. Chrysostom and other Greek fathers of the church of the eleventh and twelfth centuries, and about fifty copies of the Gospels and the Evangelistarium of nearly the same age. One Evangelistarium was in fine uncial letters of the ninth century; it was a thick quarto, and on the first leaf was an illumination the whole size of the page on a gold background, representing the donor of the book accompanied by his wife. This ancient portrait was covered over with a piece of gauze. It was a very remarkable manuscript. There were one quarto and one duodecimo of the Acts, Epistles, and Apocalypse of the eleventh century, and one folio of the book of Job, which had several miniatures in it badly executed in brilliant colours; this was probably of the twelfth century. These three manuscripts were such volumes as are not often seen in European libraries. All the rest were anthologia and books of prayer, nor did I meet with one single leaf of a classic author on vellum. I went into the library several times, and looked over all the vellum manuscripts very carefully, and I believe that I did not pass by unnoticed anything which was particularly interesting in point of subject, antiquity, or illumination. Several of the copies of the Gospels had their titles ornamented with arabesques, but none struck me as being peculiarly valuable.

The twenty-one monasteries of Mount Athos are subjected to different regulations. In some the property is at the absolute disposal of the agoumenos for the time being, but in the larger establishments (and St. Laura is the second in point of consequence) everything belongs to the monks in common. Such being the case, it was hopeless to expect, in so large a community, that the brethren should agree to part with any of their valuables. Indeed, as soon as I found out how affairs stood within the walls of St. Laura, I did not attempt to purchase anything, as it was not advisable to excite the curiosity of the monks upon the subject; nor did I wish that the report should be circulated in the other convents that I was come to Mount Athos for the purpose of rifling their libraries.

I remained at St. Laura three days, and on a beautiful fresh morning, being provided by the monks with mules and a guide, I left the good agoumenos and sallied forth through the three iron gates on my way to the monastery of Caracalla. Our road lay through some of the most beautiful scenery imaginable. The dark blue sea was on my right at about two miles distance; the rocky path over which I passed was of white alabaster with brown and yellow veins; odoriferous evergreen shrubs were all around me; and on my left were the lofty hills covered with a dense forest of gigantic trees, which extended to the base of the great white marble peak of the mountain. Between our path and the sea there was a succession of narrow valleys and gorges, each one more picturesque than the other;

sometimes we were enclosed by high and dense bushes; sometimes we opened upon forest glades, and every here and there we came upon long and narrow ledges of rock. On one of the narrowest and loftiest of these, as I was trotting merrily along thinking of nothing but the beauty of the hour and the scene, my mule stopped short in a place where the path was about a foot wide, and, standing upon three legs, proceeded deliberately to scratch his nose with the fourth. I was too old a mountain traveller to have hold of the bridle, which was safely belayed to the pack-saddle; I sat still for fear of making him lose his balance, and waited in very considerable trepidation until the mule had done scratching his nose. I was at the time half inclined to think that he knew he had a heretic upon his back, and had made up his mind to send me and himself smashing down among the distant rocks. If so, however, he thought better of it, and before long, to my great contentment, we came to a place where the road had two sides to it instead of one, and after a ride of five hours we arrived before the tall square tower which frowns over the gateway of the monastery of Caracalla.

CHAPTER XXV.

The Monastery of Caracalla—Its beautiful Situation—Hospitable Reception—Description of the Monastery—Legend of its Foundation—The Church—Fine Specimens of Ancient Jewellery—The Library—The Value attached to the Books by the Abbot—He agrees to sell some of the MSS.—Monastery of Philotheo—The Great Monastery of Iveron—History of its Foundation—Its Magnificent Library—Ignorance of the Monks—Superb MSS.—The Monks refute to part with any of the MSS.—Beauty of the Scenery of Mount Athos.

The

monastery of Caracalla

is not so large as St. Laura, and in many points resembles an ancient Gothic castle. It is beautifully situated on a promontory of rock two miles from the sea, and viewed from the lofty ground by which we approached it, the buildings had a most striking effect, with the dark blue sea for a background and the lofty rock of Samotraki looming in the distance, whilst the still more remote mountains of Roumelia closed in the picture. As for the island of Samotraki, it must have been created solely for the benefit of artists and admirers of the picturesque, for it is fit for nothing else. It is high and barren, a congeries of gigantic precipices and ridges. I suppose one can land upon it somewhere, for people live on it who are said to be arrant pirates; but as one passes by it at sea, its interminable ribs of grey rock, with the waves lashing against them, are dreary-looking in the extreme; and it is only when far distant that it becomes a beautiful object.

I sent in my servant as ambassador to explain that the first cousin, once removed, of the Emperor of all the Franks was at the gate, and to show the letter of the Greek patriarch. Incontinently the agoumenos made his appearance at the porch with many expressions of welcome and goodwill. I believe it was longer than the days of his life since a Frank had entered the convent, and I doubt whether he had ever seen one before, for he looked so disappointed when he found that I had no tail or horns, and barring his glorious long beard, that I was so little different from himself. We made many speeches to each other, he in heathen Greek and I in English, seasoned with innumerable bows, gesticulations, and téménah; after which I jumped off my mule and we entered the precincts of the monastery, attended by a long train of bearded fathers who came out to stare at me.

The monastery of Caracalla covers about one acre of ground; it is surrounded with a high strong wall, over which appear roofs and domes; and on the left of the great square tower, near the gate, a range of rooms, built of wood, project over the battlements as at the monastery of St Laura. Within is a large irregular court-yard, in the centre of which stands the church, and several little chapels or rooms fitted up as places of worship are scattered about in different parts of the building among the chambers inhabited by the monks. I found that this was the uniform arrangement in all the monasteries of Mount Athos and in nearly all Greek monasteries in the Levant. This monastery was founded by Caracallos, a Roman: who he was, or when he lived, I do not know; but from its appearance this must be a very ancient establishment. By Roman, perhaps, is meant Greek, for Greece is called Roumeli to this day; and the Constantinopolitans called themselves Romans in the old time, as in Persia and Koordistan the Sultan is called Roomi Padischah, the Roman Emperor, by those whose education and general attainments enable them to make mention of so distant and mysterious a potentate. Afterwards Petrus, Authentes or Waywode of Moldavia, sent his protospaithaire, that is his chief swordsman or commander-in-chief, to found a monastery on the Holy Mountain, and supplied him with a sum of money for the purpose; but the chief swordsman, after expending a very trivial portion of it in building a small tower on the sea-shore, pocketed the rest and returned to court. The waywode having found out what he had been at, ordered his head to be cut off; but he prayed so earnestly to be allowed to keep his head and rebuild the monastery of Caracalla out of his own money, that his master consented. The new church was dedicated to St. Peter and St. Paul, and ultimately the ex-chief swordsman prevailed upon the waywode to come to Caracalla and take the vows. They both assumed the same name of Pachomius, and died in the odour of sanctity. All this, and many more legends, was I told by the worthy agoumenos, who was altogether a most excellent person; but he had an unfortunate habit of selecting the most windy places for detailing them, an open archway, the top of an external staircase, or the parapet of a tower, until at last he chilled my curiosity down to zero. In all his words and acts he constantly referred to brother Joasaph, the second in command, to whose superior wisdom he always seemed to bow, and who was quite the right-hand man of the abbot.

My friend first took me to the church, which is of moderate size, the walls ornamented with stiff fresco pictures of the saints, none of them certainly later than the twelfth century, and some probably very much earlier. There were some relics, but the silver shrines containing them were not remarkable for richness or antiquity. On the altar there were two very remarkable crosses, each of them about six or eight inches long, of carved wood set in gold and jewels of very early and beautiful workmanship; one of them in particular, which was presented to the church by the Emperor John Zimisces, was a most curious specimen of ancient jewellery.

This monastery is one of those over which the agoumenos has absolute control, and he was then repairing one side of the court and rebuilding a set of rooms which had been destroyed during the Greek war.

The library I found to be a dark closet near the entrance of the church; it had been locked up for many years, but the agoumenos made no difficulty in breaking the old-fashioned padlock by which the door was fastened. I found upon the ground and upon some broken-down shelves about four or five hundred volumes, chiefly printed books;

but amongst them, every now and then, I stumbled upon a manuscript: of these there were about thirty on vellum and fifty or sixty on paper. I picked up a single loose leaf of very ancient uncial Greek characters, part of the Gospel of St. Matthew, written in small square letters and of small quarto size. I searched in vain for the volume to which this leaf belonged.

As I had found it impossible to purchase any manuscripts at St. Laura, I feared that the same would be the case in other monasteries; however, I made bold to ask for this single leaf as a thing of small value.

"Certainly!" said the agoumenos, "what do you want it for?"

My servant suggested that, perhaps, it might be useful to cover some jam pots or vases of preserves which I had at home.

"Oh!" said the agoumenos, "take some more;" and, without more ado, he seized upon an unfortunate thick quarto manuscript of the Acts and Epistles, and drawing out a knife cut out an inch thickness of leaves at the end before I could stop him. It proved to be the Apocalypse, which concluded the volume, but which is rarely found in early Greek manuscripts of the Acts: it was of the eleventh century. I ought, perhaps, to have slain the tomecide for his dreadful act of profanation, but his generosity reconciled me to his guilt, so I pocketed the Apocalypse, and asked him if he would sell me any of the other books, as he did not appear to set any particular value upon them.

"Malista, certainly," he replied; "how many will you have? They are of no use to me, and as I am in want of money to complete my buildings I shall be very glad to turn them to some account."

After a good deal of conversation, finding the agoumenos so accommodating, and so desirous to part with the contents of his dark and dusty closet, I arranged that I would leave him for the present, and after I had made the tour of the other monasteries, would return to Caracalla, and take up my abode there until I could hire a vessel, or make some other arrangements for my return to Constantinople. Satisfactory as this arrangement was, I nevertheless resolved to make sure of what I had already got, so I packed them up carefully in the great saddlebags, to my extreme delight. The agoumenos kindly furnished me with fresh mules, and in the afternoon I proceeded to the monastery of

PHILOTHEO,

which is only an hour's ride from Caracalla, and stands in a little field surrounded by the forest. It is distant from the sea about four miles, and is protected, like all the others, by a high stone wall surrounding the whole of the building. The church is curious and interesting; it is ornamented with representations of saints, and holy men in fresco, upon the walls of the interior and in the porch. I could not make out when it was built, but probably before the twelfth century. Arsenius, Philotheus, and Dionysius were the founders, but who they were did not appear. The monastery was repaired, and the refectory enlarged and painted, in the year 1492, by Leontius, ο βασιλευς

Καχετιου

, and his son Alexander. I was shown the reliquaries, but they were not remarkable. The monks said they had no library; and there being nothing of interest in the monastery, I determined to go on. Indeed the expression of the faces of some of these monks was so unprepossessing, and their manners so rude, although not absolutely uncivil, that I did not feel any particular inclination to remain amongst them, so leaving a small donation for the church, I mounted my mule and proceeded on my journey.

In half an hour I came to a beautiful waterfall in a rocky glen embosomed in trees and odoriferous shrubs, the rocks being of white marble, and the flowers such as we cherish in greenhouses in England. I do not know that I ever saw a more charmingly romantic spot. Another hour brought us to the great monastery of

IVERON, or IBERON,

(the Georgian, or Iberian, Monastery.)

This monastic establishment is of great size. It is larger than St. Laura, and might almost be denominated a small fortified town, so numerous are the buildings and courts which are contained within its encircling wall. It is situated near the sea, and in its general form is nearly square, with four or five square towers projecting from the walls. On each of the four sides there are rooms for above two hundred monks. I did not learn precisely how many were then inhabiting it, but I should imagine there were above a hundred. As, however, many of the members of all the religious communities on Mount Athos are employed in cultivating the numerous farms which they possess, it is probable that not more than one-half of the monks are in residence at any one time.

This monastery was founded by Theophania (Theodora?), wife of the Emperor Romanus, the son of Leo Sophos,[17] or the Philosopher, between the years 919 and 922. It was restored by a Prince of Georgia or Iberia, and enlarged by his son, a caloyer. The church is dedicated to the "repose of the Virgin." It has four or five domes, and is of considerable size, standing by itself, as usual, in the centre of the great court, and is ornamented with columns and other decorations of rich marbles, together with the usual fresco paintings on the walls.

The library is a remarkably fine one, perhaps altogether the most precious of all those which now remain on the holy mountain. It is situated over the porch of the church, which appears to be the usual place where the books are kept in these establishments. The room is of good size, well fitted up with bookcases with glass doors, of not very old workmanship. I should imagine that about a hundred years ago, some agoumenos, or prior, or librarian, must have been a reading man; and the pious care which he took to arrange the ancient volumes of the monastery has been rewarded by the excellent state of preservation in which they still remain. Since his time, they have probably remained undisturbed. Every one could see through the greenish uneven panes of old glass that there was nothing but books inside, and therefore nobody meddled with them. I was allowed to rummage at my leisure in this mine of archæological treasure. Having taken up my abode for the time being in a cheerful room, the windows of which commanded a glorious prospect, I soon made friends with the literary portion of the community, which consisted of one thin old monk, a cleverish man, who united to many other offices that of librarian. He was also secretary to my lord the agoumenos, a kind-hearted old gentleman, who seemed to wish everybody well, and who evidently liked much better to sit still on his divan than to regulate the affairs of his convent. The rents, the long lists of tuns of wine and oil, the strings of mules laden with corn, which came in daily from the farms, and all the other complicated details of this mighty cœnobium,—over all these, and numberless other important matters, the thin secretary had full control.

Some of the young monks, demure fat youths, came into the library every now and then, and wondered what I could be doing there, looking over so many books; and they would take a volume out of my hand when I had done with it, and, glancing their eyes over its ancient vellum leaves, would look up inquiringly into my face, saying, "τι ενε ?—what is it?—what can be the use of looking at such old books as these?" They were rather in awe of the secretary, who was evidently, in their opinion, a prodigy of learning and erudition. Some, in a low voice, that they might not be overheard by the wise man, asked me where I came from, how old I was, and whether my father was with me; but they soon all went away, and I turned to, in right good earnest, to look for uncial manuscripts and unknown classic authors. Of these last there was not one on vellum, but on paper there was an octavo manuscript of Sophocles, and a Coptic Psaltery with an Arabic translation—a curious book to meet with on Mount Athos. Of printed books there were, I should think, about five thousand—of manuscripts on paper, about two thousand; but all religious works of various kinds. There were nearly a thousand manuscripts on vellum, and these I looked over more carefully than the rest. About one hundred of them were in the Iberian language: they were mostly immense thick quartos, some of them not less than eighteen inches square, and from four to six inches thick. One of these, bound in wooden boards, and written in large uncial letters, was a magnificent old volume. Indeed all these Iberian or Georgian manuscripts were superb specimens of ancient books. I was unable to read them, and therefore cannot say what they were; but I should imagine that they were church books, and probably of high antiquity. Among the Greek manuscripts, which were principally of the eleventh and twelfth centuries—works of St. Chrysostom, St. Basil, and books for the services of the ritual—I discovered the following, which are deserving of especial mention:—A large folio Evangelistarium bound in red velvet, about eighteen inches high and three thick, written in magnificent uncial letters half an inch long, or even more. Three of the illuminations were the whole size of the page, and might almost be termed pictures from their large proportions: and there were several other illuminations of smaller size in different parts of the book. This superb manuscript was in admirable preservation, and as clean as if it had been new. It had evidently been kept with great care, and appeared to have had some clasps or ornaments of gold or silver which had been torn off. It was probably owing to the original splendour of this binding that the volume itself had been so carefully preserved. I imagine it was written in the ninth century.

Another book, of a much greater age, was a copy of the four Gospels, with four finely-executed miniatures of the evangelists. It was about nine or ten inches square, written in round semiuncial letters in double columns, with not more than two or three words in a line. In some respects it resembled the book of the Epistles in the Bodleian Library at Oxford. This manuscript, in the original black leather binding, had every appearance of the highest antiquity. It was beautifully written and very clean, and was altogether such a volume as is not to be met with every day.

A quarto manuscript of the four Gospels, of the eleventh or twelfth century, with a great many (perhaps fifty) illuminations. Some of them were unfortunately rather damaged.

Two manuscripts of the New Testament, with the Apocalypse.

A very fine manuscript of the Psalms, of the eleventh century, which is indeed about the era of the greater portion of the vellum manuscripts on Mount Athos.

There were also some ponderous and magnificent folios of the works of the fathers of the Church—some of them, I should think, of the tenth century; but it is difficult, in a few hours, to detect the peculiarities which prove that manuscripts are of an earlier date than the twelfth century. I am, however, convinced that very few of them were written after that time.

The paper manuscripts were of all ages, from the thirteenth and fifteenth centuries down to a hundred years ago; and some of them, on charta bombycina, would have appeared very splendid books if they had not been eclipsed by the still finer and more carefully-executed manuscripts on vellum.

Neither my arguments nor my eloquence could prevail on the obdurate monks to sell me any of these books, but my friend the secretary gave me a book in his own handwriting to solace me on my journey. It contained a history of the monastery from the days of its foundation to the present time. It is written in Romaic, and is curious not so much from its subject matter as from the entire originality of its style and manner.

The view from the window of the room which I occupied at Iveron was one of the finest on Mount Athos. The glorious sea, and the towers which command the scaricatojos or landing-places of the different monasteries along the coast, and the superb monastery of Stavroniketa like a Gothic castle perched upon a beetling rock, with the splendid forest for a background, formed altogether a picture totally above my powers to describe. It almost compensated for the numberless tribes of vermin by which the room was tenanted. In fact, the whole of the scenery on Mount Athos is so superlatively grand and beautiful that it is useless to attempt any description.

CHAPTER XXVI.

The Monastery of Stavroniketa—The Library—Splendid MS. of St. Chrysostom—The Monastery of Pantocratoras—Ruinous Condition of the Library—Complete Destruction of the Books—Disappointment—Oration to the Monks—The Great Monastery of Vatopede—Its History—Ancient Pictures in the Church—Legend of the Girdle of the Blessed Virgin—The Library—Wealth and Luxury of the Monks—The Monastery of Sphigmenou—Beautiful Jewelled Cross—The Monastery of Kiliantari—Magnificent MS. in Gold Letters on White Vellum—The Monasteries of Zographon, Castamoneta, Docheirou, and Xenophou—The Exiled Bishops—The Library—Very fine MSS.—Proposals for their Purchase—Lengthened Negotiations—Their successful Issue.

An

hour's ride brought us to the monastery of

STAVRONIKETA,

which is a smaller building than Iveron, with a square tower over the gateway. It stands on a rock overhanging the sea, against the base of which the waves ceaselessly beat. It was to this spot that a miraculous picture of St Nicholas, archbishop of Myra in Lycia, floated over, of its own accord, from I do not know where; and in consequence of this auspicious event, Jeremias, patriarch of Constantinople, founded this monastery, of "the victory of the holy cross," about the year 1522. This is the account given by the monks; but from the appearance and architecture of Stavroniketa, I conceive that it is a much older building, and that probably the patriarch Jeremias only repaired or restored it. However that may be, the monastery is in very good order, clean, and well kept; and I had a comfortable frugal dinner there with some of the good old monks, who seemed a cheerful and contented set.

The library contained about eight hundred volumes, of which nearly two hundred were manuscripts on vellum. Amongst these were conspicuous the entire works of St. Chrysostom, in eight large folio volumes complete; and a manuscript of the Scala Perfectionis in Greek, containing a number of most exquisite miniatures in a brilliant state of preservation. It was a quarto of the tenth or eleventh century, and a most unexceptionable tome, which these unkind monks preferred keeping to themselves instead of letting me have it, as they ought to have done. The miniatures were first-rate works of Byzantine art. It was a terrible pang to me to leave such a book behind. There were also a Psalter with several miniatures, but these were partially damaged; five or six copies of the Gospels; two fine folio volumes of the Menologia, or Lives of the Saints; and sundry ομοιλογο

and books of divinity, and the works of the fathers. On paper there were two hundred more manuscripts, amongst which was a curious one of the Acts and Epistles, full of large miniatures and illuminations exceedingly well done. As it is quite clear that all these manuscripts are older than the time of the patriarch Jeremias, they confirm my opinion that he could not have been the original founder of the monastery.

It is an hour's scramble over the rocks from Stavroniketa to the monastery of
PANTOCRATORAS.

This edifice was built by Manuel and Alexius Comnenus, and Johannes Pumicerius, their brother. It was subsequently repaired by Barbulus and Gabriel, two Wallachian nobles. The church is handsome and curious, and contains several relics, but the reliquaries are not of much beauty, nor of very great antiquity. Among them, however, is a small thick quarto volume about five inches square every way, in the handwriting, as you are told, of St. John of Kalavita. Now St. John of Kalavita was a hermit who died in the year 450, and his head is shown at Besançon, in the church of St. Stephen, to which place it was taken after the siege of Constantinople. Howbeit this manuscript did not seem to me to be older than the twelfth century, or the eleventh at the earliest It is written in a very minute hand, and contains the Gospels, some prayers, and lives of saints, and is ornamented with some small illuminations. The binding is very curious: it is entirely of silver gilt, and is of great antiquity. The back part is composed of an intricate kind of chainwork, which bends when the book is opened, and the sides are embossed with a variety of devices.

On my inquiring for the library, I was told it had been destroyed during the revolution. It had formerly been preserved in the great square tower or keep, which is a grand feature in all the monasteries. I went to look at the place, and leaning through a ruined arch, I looked down into the lower story of the tower, and there I saw the melancholy remains of a once famous library. This was a dismal spectacle for a devout lover of old books—a sort of biblical knight errant, as I then considered myself, who had entered on the perilous adventure of Mount Athos to rescue from the thraldom of ignorant monks those fair vellum volumes, with their bright illuminations and velvet dresses and jewelled clasps, which for so many centuries had lain imprisoned in their dark monastic dungeons. It was indeed a heart-rending sight. By the dim light which streamed through the opening of an iron door in the wall of the ruined tower, I saw above a hundred ancient manuscripts lying among the rubbish which had fallen from the upper floor, which was ruinous, and had in great part given way. Some of these manuscripts seemed quite entire—fine large folios; but the monks said they were unapproachable, for that floor also on which they lay was unsafe, the beams below being rotten from the wet and rain which came in through the roof. Here was a trap ready set and baited for a bibliographical antiquary. I peeped at the old manuscripts, looked particularly at one or two that were lying in the middle of the floor, and could hardly resist the temptation. I advanced cautiously along the boards, keeping close to the wall, whilst every now and then a dull cracking noise warned me of my danger, but I tried each board by stamping upon it with my foot before I ventured my weight upon it. At last, when I dared go no farther, I made them bring me a long stick, with which I fished up two or three fine manuscripts, and poked them along towards the door. When I had safely landed them, I examined them more at my ease, but found that the rain had washed the outer leaves quite clean: the pages were stuck tight together into a solid mass, and when I attempted to open them, they broke short off in square bits like a biscuit. Neglect and damp and exposure had destroyed them completely. One fine volume, a large folio in double columns, of most venerable antiquity, particularly grieved me. I do not know how many more manuscripts there might be under the piles of rubbish. Perhaps some of them might still be legible, but without assistance and time I could not clean out the ruins that had fallen from above; and I was unable to save even a scrap from this general tomb of a whole race of books. I came out of the great tower, and sitting down on a pile of ruins, with a bearded assembly of grave caloyeri round me, I vented my sorrow and indignation in a long oration, which however produced a very slight effect upon my auditory; but whether from their not understanding Italian, or my want of eloquence, is matter of doubt. My man was the only person who seemed to commiserate my misfortune, and he looked so genuinely vexed and sorry that I liked him the better ever afterwards. At length I dismissed the assembly: they toddled away to their siesta, and I, mounted anew upon a stout well-fed mule, bade adieu to the hospitable agoumenos, and was soon occupied in picking my way among the rocks and trees towards the next monastery. In two hours' time we passed the ruins of a large building standing boldly on a hill. It had formerly been a college; and a magnificent aqueduct of fourteen double arches—that is, two rows of arches one above the other—connected it with another hill, and had a grand effect, with long and luxuriant masses of flowers streaming from its neglected walls. In half an hour more I arrived at

VATOPEDE.

This is the largest and richest of all the monasteries of Mount Athos. It is situated on the side of a hill where a valley opens to the sea, and commands a little harbour where three small Greek vessels were lying at anchor. The buildings are of great extent, with several towers and domes rising above the walls: I should say it was not smaller than the upper ward of Windsor Castle. The original building was erected by the Emperor Constantine the Great. That worthy prince being, it appears, much afflicted by the leprosy, ordered a number of little children to be killed, a bath of juvenile blood being considered an excellent remedy. But while they were selecting them, he was told in a vision that if he would become a Christian his leprosy should depart from him: he did so, and was immediately restored to health, and all the children lived long and happily. This story is related by Moses Chorensis, whose veracity I will not venture to doubt.

In the fifth century this monastery was thrown down by Julian the Apostate. Theodosius the Great built it up again in gratitude for the miraculous escape of his son Arcadius, who having fallen overboard from his galley in the Archipelago, was landed safely on this spot through the intercession of the Virgin, to whose special honour the great church was founded: fourteen other chapels within the walls attest the piety of other individuals. In the year 862 the Saracens landed, destroyed the monastery by fire, slew many of the monks, took the treasures and broke the mosaics; but the representation of the Blessed Virgin was indestructible, and still remained safe and perfect above the altar. There was also a well under the altar, into which some of the relics were thrown and afterwards recovered by the community.

About the year 1300 St. Athanasius the Patriarch persuaded Nicholaus and Antonius, certain rich men of Adrianople, to restore the monastery once more, which they did, and taking the vows became monks, and were buried in the narthex or portico of the church. I may here observe that this was the nearest approach to being buried within the church that was permitted in the early times of Christianity, and such is still the rule observed in the Greek Church: altars were, however, raised over the tombs or places of execution of martyrs.

This church contains a great many ancient pictures of small size, most of them having the background overlaid with plates of silver-gilt: two of these are said to be portraits of the Empress Theodora. Two other pictures of larger size and richly set with jewels are interesting as having been brought from the church of St. Sophia at Constantinople, when that city fell a prey to the Turkish arms. Over the doors of the church and of the great refectory there are mosaics representing, if I remember rightly, saints and holy persons. One of the chapels, a separate building with a dome which had been newly repaired, is dedicated to the "Preservation of the Girdle of the Blessed Virgin," a relic which must be a source of considerable revenue to the monastery, for they have divided it into two parts, and one half is sent into Greece and the other half into Asia Minor whenever the plague is raging in those countries, and all those who are afflicted with that terrible disease are sure to be cured if they touch it, which they are allowed to do "for a consideration." On my inquiring how the monastery became possessed of so inestimable a medicine, I was gravely informed that, after the assumption of the Blessed Virgin, St. Thomas went up to heaven to pay her a visit, and there she presented him with her girdle. My informant appeared to have the most unshakeable conviction as to the truth of this history, and expressed great surprise that I had never heard it before.

The library, although containing nearly four thousand printed books, has none of any high antiquity or on any subject but divinity. There are also about a thousand manuscripts, of which three or four hundred are on vellum; amongst these there are three copies of the works of St Chrysostom: they also have his head in the church—that golden mouth out of which proceeded the voice which shook the empire with the thunder of its denunciations. The most curious manuscripts are six rolls of parchment, each ten inches wide and about ten feet long, containing prayers for festivals on the anniversaries of the foundation of certain churches. There were at this time above three hundred monks resident in the monastery; many of these held offices and places of dignity under the agoumenos, whose establishment resembled the court of a petty sovereign prince. Altogether this convent well illustrates what some of the great monastic establishments in England must have been before the Reformation. It covers at least four acres of ground, and contains so many separate buildings within its massive walls that it resembles a fortified town. Everything told of wealth and indolence. When I arrived the lord abbot was asleep; he was too great a man to be aroused; he had eaten a full meal in his own apartment, and he could not be disturbed. His secretary, a thin pale monk, was deputed to show me the wonders of the place, and as we proceeded through the different chapels and enormous magazines of corn, wine, and oil, the officers of the different departments bent down to kiss his hand, for he was high in the favour of my lord the abbot, and was evidently a man not to be slighted by the inferior authorities if they wished to get on and prosper. The cellarer was a sly old fellow with a thin grey beard, and looked as if he could tell a good story of an evening over a flagon of good wine. Except at some of the palaces in Germany I have never seen such gigantic tuns as those in the cellars at Vatopede. The oil is kept in marble vessels of the size and shape of sarcophagi, and there is a curious picture in the entrance room of the oil-store, which represents the miraculous increase in their stock of oil during a year of scarcity, when, through the intercession of a pious monk who then had charge of that department, the marble basins, which were almost empty, overflowed, and a river of fine fresh oil poured in torrents through the door. The frame of this picture is set with jewels, and it appears to be very ancient. The refectory is an immense room; it stands in front of the church and has twenty-four marble tables and seats, and is in the same cruciform shape as that at St. Laura. It has frequently accommodated five hundred guests, the servants and tenants of the abbey, who come on stated days to pay their rents and receive the benediction of the agoumenos. Sixty or seventy fat mules are kept for the use of the community, and a very considerable number of Albanian servants and muleteers are lodged in outbuildings before the great gate. These, unlike their brethren of Epirus, are a quiet, stupid race, and whatever may be their notions of another world, they evidently think that in this there is no man living equal in importance to the great agoumenos of Vatopede, and no earthly place to compare with the great monastery over which he rules.

From Vatopede it requires two hours and a half to ride to the monastery of
SPHIGMENOU,
which is a much smaller establishment. It is said to have been founded by the Empress Pulcheria, sister of the Emperor Theodosius the younger, and if so must be a very ancient building, for the empress died on the 18th of February in the year 453. Her brother Theodosius was known by the title or cognomen of καλλιγραφος
, from the beauty of his writing: he was a protector of the Nestorian and Eutychian heretics, and ended his life on the 20th of October, 460.

This monastery is situated in a narrow valley close to the sea, squeezed in between three little hills, from which circumstance it derives its name of σφιγμενος
, "squeezed together." It is inhabited by thirty monks, who are cleaner and keep their church in better order and neatness than most of their brethren on Mount Athos. Among the relics of the saints, which are the first things they show to the pilgrim from beyond the sea, is a beautiful ancient cross of gold set with diamonds. Diamonds are of very rare occurrence in ancient pieces of jewellery; it is indeed doubtful whether they were

known to the ancients, adamantine being an epithet applied to the hardness of steel, and I have never seen a diamond in any work of art of the Roman or classical era. Besides the diamonds the cross has on the upper end and on the extremities of the two arms three very fine and large emeralds, each fastened on with three gold nails: it is a fine specimen of early jewellery, and of no small intrinsic value.

The library is in a room over the porch of the church: it contains about 1500 volumes, half of which are manuscripts, mostly on paper, and all theological. I met with four copies of the Gospels and two of the Epistles, all the others being books of the church service and the usual folios of the fathers. There was, however, a Russian or Bulgarian manuscript of the four Gospels with an illumination at the commencement of each Gospel. It is written in capital letters, and seemed to be of considerable antiquity. I was disappointed at not finding manuscripts of greater age in so very ancient a monastery as this is; but perhaps it has undergone more squeezing than that inflicted upon it by the three hills. I slept here in peace and comfort.

On the sea-shore not far from Sphigmenou are the ruins of the monastery of St. Basil, opposite a small rocky island in the sea, which I left at this point, and striking up the country arrived in an hour's time at the monastery of

KILIANTARI,

or a thousand lions. This is a large building, of which the ground plan resembles the shape of an open fan. It stands in a valley, and contained, when I entered its hospitable gates, about fifty monks. They preserve in the sacristy a superb chalice, of a kind of bloodstone set in gold, about a foot high and eight inches wide, the gift of one of the Byzantine emperors. This monastery was founded by Simeon, Prince of Servia, I could not make out at what time. In the library they had no great number of books, and what there were were all Russian or Bulgarian: I saw none which seemed to be of great antiquity. On inquiring, however, whether they had not some Greek manuscripts, the Agoumenos said they had one, which he went and brought me out of the sacristy; and this, to my admiration and surprise, was not only the finest manuscript on Mount Athos, but the finest that I had met with in any Greek monastery with the single exception of the golden manuscript of the New Testament at Mount Sinai. It was a 4to. Evangelistarium, written in golden letters on fine white vellum. The characters were a kind of semi-uncial, rather round in their forms, of large size, and beautifully executed, but often joined together and having many contractions and abbreviations, in these respects resembling the Mount Sinai MS. This magnificent volume was given to the monastery by the Emperor Andronicus Comnenus about the year 1184; it is consequently not an early MS., but its imperial origin renders it interesting to the admirers of literary treasures, while the very rare occurrence of a Greek MS. written in letters of gold would make it a most desirable and important acquisition to any royal library; for besides the two above-mentioned there are not, I believe, more than seven or eight MSS. of this description in existence, and of these several are merely fragments, and only one is on white vellum: this is in the library of the Holy Synod at Moscow. Five of the others are on blue or purple vellum, viz., Codex Cottonianus, in the British Museum, Titus C. 15, a fragment of the Gospels; an octavo Evangelistarium at Vienna; a fragment of the books of Genesis and St. Luke in silver letters at Vienna; the Codex Turicensis of part of the Psalms; and six leaves of the Gospels of St. Matthew in silver letters with the initials in gold in the Vatican. There may possibly be others, but I have never heard of them. Latin MSS. in golden letters are much less scarce, but Greek MSS., even those which merely contain two or three pages written in gold letters, are of such rarity that hardly a dozen are to be met with; of these there are three in the library at Parham. I think the Codex Ebnerianus has one or two pages written in gold, and the tables of a gospel at Jerusalem are in gold on deep purple vellum. At this moment I do not remember any more, although doubtless there must be a few of these partially ornamented volumes scattered through the great libraries of Europe.

From Kiliantari, which is the last monastery on the N.E. side of the promontory, we struck across the peninsula, and two hours' riding brought us to

ZOGRAPHOU,

through plains of rich green grass dotted over with gigantic single trees, the scenery being like that of an English pork, only finer and more luxuriant as well as more extensive. This monastery was founded in the reign of Leo Sophos, by three nobles of Constantinople who became monks; and the local tradition is that it was destroyed by the "Pope of Rome." How that happened I know not, but it was rebuilt in the year 1502 by Stephanus, Waywode of Moldavia. It is a large fortified building of very imposing appearance, situated on a steep hill surrounded with trees and gardens overlooking a deep valley which opens on the gulf of Monte Santo. The MSS. here are Bulgarian, and not of early date; they had no Greek MSS. whatever.

From Zographou, following the valley, we arrived at a lower plain on the sea coast, and there we discovered that we had lost our way; we therefore retraced our steps, and turning up among the hills to our left we came in three hours to

CASTAMONETA,

which, had we taken the right road, we might have reached in one. This is a very poor monastery, but it is of great age and its architecture is picturesque: it was originally founded by Constantine the Great. It has no library nor anything particularly well worth mentioning, excepting the original deed of the Emperor Manuel Paleologus, with the sign manual of that potentate written in very large letters in red ink at the bottom of the deed, by which he granted to the monastery the lands which it still retains. The poor monks were much edified by the sight of the patriarchal letter, and when I went away rang the bells of the church tower to do me honour.

At the distance of one hour from hence stands the monastery of

DOCHEIROU.

It is the first to the west of those upon the south-west shore of the peninsula. It is a monastery of great size, with ample room for a hundred monks, although inhabited by only twenty. It was built in the reign of Nicephorus Botoniates, and was last repaired in the year 1578 by Alexander, Waywode of Moldavia. I was very well lodged in this convent, and the fleas were singularly few. The library contained two thousand five hundred volumes, of which one hundred and fifty were vellum MSS. I omitted to note the number of MSS. on paper, but amongst them I found a part of Sophocles and a fine folio of Suidas's Lexicon. Among the vellum MSS. there was a folio in the Bulgarian language, and various works of the fathers. I found also three loose leaves of an Evangelistarium in uncial letters of the ninth century, which had been cut out of some ancient volume, for which I hunted in the dust in vain. The monks gave me these three leaves on my asking for them, for even a few pages of such a manuscript as this are not to be despised.

From Docheirou it is only a distance of half an hour to
XENOPHOU,
which stands upon the sea shore. Here they were building a church in the centre of the great court, which, when it is finished, will be the largest on Mount Athos. Three Greek bishops were living here in exile. I did not learn what the holy prelates had done, but their misdeeds had been found out by the Patriarch, and he had sent them here to rusticate. This monastery is of a moderate size; its founder was St. Xenophou, regarding whose history or the period at which he lived I am unable to give any information, as nobody knew anything about him on the spot, and I cannot find him in any catalogue of saints which I possess. The monastery was repaired in the year 1545 by Danzulas Bornicus and Badulus, who were brothers, and Banus (the Ban) Barbulus, all three nobles of Hungary, and was afterwards beautified by Matthæus, Waywode of Bessarabia.

The library consists of fifteen hundred printed books, nineteen MSS. on paper, eleven on vellum, and three rolls on parchment, containing liturgies for particular days. Of the MSS. on vellum there were three which merit a description. One was a fine 4to. of part of the works of St. Chrysostom, of great antiquity, but not in uncial letters. Another was a 4to. of the four Gospels bound in faded red velvet with silver clasps. This book they affirmed to be a royal present to the monastery; it was of the eleventh or twelfth century, and was peculiar from the text being accompanied by a voluminous commentary on the margin and several pages of calendars, prefaces, c., at the beginning. The headings of the Gospels were written in large plain letters of gold. In the libraries of forty Greek monasteries I have only met with one other copy of the Gospels with a commentary. The third manuscript was an immense quarto Evangelistarium sixteen inches square, bound in faded green or blue velvet, and said to be in the autograph of the Emperor Alexius Comnenus. The text throughout on each page was written in the form of a cross. Two of the pages are in purple ink powdered with gold, and these, there is every reason to suppose, are in the handwriting of the imperial scribe himself; for the Byzantine sovereigns affected to write only in purple, as their deeds and a magnificent MS. in another monastic library, of which I have not given an account in these pages, can testify: the titles of this superb volume are written in gold, covering the whole page. Altogether, although not in uncial letters, it was among the finest Greek MSS. that I had ever seen—perhaps, next to the uncial MSS., the finest to be met with anywhere.

I asked the monks whether they were inclined to part with these three books, and offered to purchase them and the parchment rolls. There was a little consultation among them, and then they desired to be shown those which I particularly coveted. Then there was another consultation, and they asked me which I set the greatest value on. So I said the rolls, on which the three rolls were unrolled, and looked at, and examined, and peeped at by the three monks who put themselves forward in the business, with more pains and curiosity than had probably been ever wasted upon them before. At last they said it was impossible, the rolls were too precious to be parted with, but if I liked to give a good price I should have the rest; upon which I took up the St. Chrysostom, the least valuable of the three, and while I examined it, saw from the corner of my eye the three monks nudging each other and making signs. So I said, "Well, now what will you take for your two books, this and the big one?" They asked five thousand piastres; whereupon, with a look of indignant scorn, I laid down the St. Chrysostom and got up to go away; but after a good deal more talk we retired to the divan, or drawing-room as it may be called, of the monastery, where I conversed with the three exiled bishops. In course of time I was called out into another room to have a cup of coffee. There were my friends the three monks, the managing committee, and under the divan, imperfectly concealed, were the corners of the three splendid MSS. I knew that now all depended on my own tact whether my still famished saddle-bags were to have a meal or not that day, the danger lying between offering too much or too little. If you offer too much, a Greek, a Jew, or an Armenian immediately thinks that the desired object must be invaluable, that it must have some magical properties, like the lamp of Aladdin, which will bring wealth upon its possessor if he can but find out its secret; and he will either ask you a sum absurdly large, or will refuse to sell it at any price, but will lock it up and become nervous about it, and examine it over and over again privately to see what can be the cause of a Frank's offering so much for a thing apparently so utterly useless. On the other hand, too little must not be offered, for it would be an indignity to suppose that persons of consideration would condescend to sell things of trifling value—it wounds their aristocratic feelings, they are above such meannesses. By St. Xenophou, how we did talk! for five mortal hours it went on, I pretending to go away several times, but being always called back by one or other of the learned committee. I drank coffee and sherbet and they drank arraghi; but in the end I got the great book of Alexius Comnenus for the value of twenty-two pounds, and the curious Gospels, which I had treated with the most cool disdain all along, was finally thrown into the bargain; and out I walked with a big book under each arm, bearing with perfect resignation the smiles and scoffs of the three brethren, who could scarcely contain their laughter at the way they had done the silly traveller. Then did the saddlebags begin to assume a more comely and satisfactory form.

After a stirrup cup of hot coffee, perfumed with the incense of the church, the monks bid me a joyous adieu; I responded as joyously: in short every one was charmed, except the mule, who evidently was more surprised than pleased at the increased weight which he had to carry.

CHAPTER XXVII.

The Monastery of Russico—Its Courteous Abbot—The Monastery of Xeropotamo—Its History—High Character of its Abbot—Excursion to the Monasteries of St. Nicholas and St. Dionisius—Interesting Relics—Magnificent Shrine—The Library—The Monastery of St. Paul—Respect shown by the Monks—Beautiful MS.—Extraordinary Liberality and Kindness of the Abbot and Monks—A valuable Acquisition at little Cost—The Monastery of Simopetra—Purchase of MS.—The Monk of Xeropotamo—His Ideas about Women—Excursion to Cariez—The Monastery of Coutloumoussi—The Russian Book-Stealer—History of the Monastery—Its reputed Destruction by the Pope of Rome—The Aga of Cariez—Interview in a Kiosk—The She Cat of Mount Athos.

From
Xenophou I went on to
RUSSICO,
where also they were repairing the injuries which different parts of the edifice had sustained during the late Greek war. The agoumenos of this monastery was a remarkably gentlemanlike and accomplished man; he spoke several languages and ruled over a hun-

dred and thirty monks. They had, however, amongst them all only nine MSS., and those were of no interest. The agoumenos told me that the monastery formerly possessed a MS. of Homer on vellum, which he sold to two English gentlemen some years ago, who were immediately afterwards plundered by pirates, and the MS. thrown into the sea. As I never heard of any Englishman having been at Mount Athos since the days of Dr. Clarke and Dr. Carlysle, I could not make out who these gentlemen were: probably they were Frenchmen, or Europeans of some other nation. However, the idea of the pirates gave me a horrid qualm; and I thought how dreadful it would be if they threw my Alexius Comnenus into the sea; it made me feel quite uncomfortable. This monastery was built by the Empress Catherine the First, of Russia—or, to speak more correctly, repaired by her—for it was originally founded by Saint Lazarus Knezes, of Servia, and the church dedicated to St. Panteleemon the Martyr. A ride of an hour brought me to

XEROPOTAMO,

where I was received with so much hospitality and kindness that I determined to make it my headquarters while I visited the other monasteries, which from this place could readily be approached by sea. I was fortunate in procuring a boat with two men—a sort of naval lay brethren,—who agreed to row me about wherever I liked, and bring me back to Xeropotamo for fifty piastres, and this they would do whenever I chose, as they were not very particular about time, an article upon which they evidently set small value.

This monastery was founded by the Emperor Romanus about the year 920; it was rebuilt by Andronicus the Second in 1320; in the sixteenth century it was thrown down by an earthquake, and was again repaired by the Sultan Selim the First, or at least during his reign—that is, about 1515. It was in a ruinous condition in the year 1701; it was again repaired, and in the Greek revolution it was again dismantled; at the time of my visit they were actively employed in restoring it. Alexander, Waywode of Wallachia, was a great benefactor to this and other monasteries of Athos, which owe much to the piety of the different Christian princes of the Danubian states of the Turkish empire.

The library over the porch of the church, which is large and handsome, contains one thousand printed books and between thirty and forty manuscripts in bad condition. I saw none of consequence: that is to say, nothing except the usual volumes of divinity of the twelfth century. In the church is preserved a large piece of the holy cross richly set with valuable jewels. The agoumenos of Xeropotamo, a man with a dark-grey beard, about sixty years of age, struck me as a fine specimen of what an abbot of an ascetic monastery ought to be; simple and kind, yet clever enough, and learned in the divinity of his church, he set an example to the monks under his rule of devotion and rectitude of conduct; he was not slothful, or haughty, or grasping, and seemed to have a truly religious and cheerful mind. He was looked up to and beloved by the whole community; and with his dignified manner and appearance, his long grey hair, and dark flowing robes, he gave me the idea of what the saints and holy men of old must have been in the early days of Christianity, when they walked entirely in the faith, and—if required to do so—willingly gave themselves up as martyrs to the cause: when in all their actions they were influenced solely by the dictates of their religion. Would that such times would come again! But where every one sets up a new religion for himself, and when people laugh at and ridicule those things which their ignorance prevents them from appreciating, how can we hope for this?

Early in the morning I started from my comfortable couch, and ran scrambling down the hill, over the rolling-stones in the dry bed of the torrent on which the monastery of the "dry river" (ξηροποταμου

—courou chesmé in Turkish) is built. We got into the boat: our carpets, some oranges, and various little stores for a day's journey, which the good monks had supplied us with, being brought down by sundry good-natured lubberly κατακυμενοι

—religions youths—who were delighted at having something to do, and were as pleased as children at having a good heavy praying-carpet to carry, or a basket of oranges, or a cushion from the monastery. They all waited on the shore to see us off, and away we went along the coast. As the sun got up it became oppressively hot, and the first monastery we came abreast of was that of Simopetra, which is perched on the top of a perpendicular rock, five or six hundred feet high at least, if not twice as much. This rather daunted me: and as we thought perhaps to-morrow would not be so hot, I put off climbing up the precipice for the present, and rowed gently on in the calm sea till we came before the monastery of

ST. NICHOLAS,

the smallest of all the convents of Mount Athos. It was a most picturesque building, stuck up on a rock, and is famous for its figs, in the eating of which, in the absence of more interesting matter, we all employed ourselves a considerable time; they were marvellously cool and delicious, and there were such quantities of them. We and the boatmen sat in the shade, and enjoyed ourselves till we were ashamed of staying any longer. I forgot to ask who the founder was. There was no library; in fact, there was nothing but figs; so we got into the boat again, and sweltered on a quarter of an hour more, and then we came to

ST. DIONISIUS.

This monastery is also built upon a rock immediately above the sea; it is of moderate size, but is in good repair. There was a look of comfort about it that savoured of easy circumstances, but the number of monks in it was small. Altogether this monastery, as regards the antiquities it contained, was the most interesting of all. The church, a good-sized building, is in a very perfect state of preservation. Hanging on the wall near the door of entrance was a portrait painted on wood, about three feet square, in a frame of silver-gilt, set with jewels; it represented Alexius Comnenus, Emperor of Trebizonde, the founder of the monastery. He it was, I believe, who built that most beautiful church a little way out of the town of Trebizonde, which is called St. Sofia, probably from its resemblance to the cathedral of Constantinople. He is drawn in his imperial robes, and the portrait is one of the most curious I ever saw. He founded this church in the year 1380; and Neagulus and Peter, Waywodes of Bessarabia, restored and repaired the monastery. There was another curious portrait of a lady; I did not learn who it was: very probably the Empress Pulcheria, or else Roxandra Domna (Domina?), wife of Alexander, Waywode of Wallachia; for both these ladies were benefactors to the convent.

I was taken, as a pilgrim, to the church, and we stood in the middle of the floor before the ικονοστασις

, whilst the monks brought out an old-fashioned low wooden table, upon which they placed the relics of the saints which they presumed we came to adore. Of these some were very interesting specimens of intricate workmanship and superb and precious materials. One was a patera, of a kind of china or paste, made, as I imagine, of a multitude of turquoises ground down together, for it was too large to be of one single turquoise; there is one of the same kind, but of far inferior workmanship, in the treasury of St. Marc. This marvellous dish is carved in very high relief with minute figures or little statues of the saints, with inscriptions in very early Greek. It is set in pure gold, richly worked, and was a gift from the Empress or imperial Princess Pulcheria. Then there was an invaluable shrine for the head of St. John the Baptist, whose bones and another of his heads are in the cathedral at Genoa. St. John Lateran also boasts a head of St John, but that may have belonged to St. John the Evangelist. This shrine was the gift of Neagulus, Waywode or Hospodar of Wallachia: it is about two feet long and two feet high, and is in the shape of a Byzantine church; the material is silver-gilt, but the admirable and singular style of the workmanship gives it a value far surpassing its intrinsic worth. The roof is covered with five domes of gold; on each side it has sixteen recesses, in which are portraits of the saints in niello, and at each end there are eight others. All the windows are enriched in open-work tracery, of a strange sort of Gothic pattern, unlike anything in Europe. It is altogether a wonderful and precious monument of ancient art, the production of an almost unknown country, rich, quaint, and original in its design and execution, and is indeed one of the most curious objects on Mount Athos; although the patera of the Princess Pulcheria might probably be considered of greater value. There were many other shrines and reliquaries, but none of any particular interest.

I next proceeded to the library, which contained not much less than a thousand manuscripts, half on paper and half on vellum. Of those on vellum the most valuable were a quarto Evangelistarium, in uncial letters, and in beautiful preservation; another Evangelistarium, of which three fly-leaves were in early uncial Greek; a small quarto of the Dialogues of St. Gregory, διαλογοι Γρεγοριου του θεολογου
, not in uncial letters, with twelve fine miniatures; a small quarto New Testament, containing the Apocalypse; and some magnificent folios of the Fathers of the eleventh century; but not one classic author. Among the manuscripts on paper were a folio of the Iliad of Homer, badly written, two copies of the works of Dionysius the Areopagite, and a multitude of books for the church-service. Alas! they would part with nothing. The library was altogether a magnificent collection, and for the most part well preserved: they had no great number of printed books. I should imagine that this monastery must, from some fortunate accident, have suffered less from spoliation during the late revolution than any of the others; for considering that it is not a very large establishment, the number of valuable things it contained was quite astonishing.

A quarter of an hour's row brought us to the scaricatojo of
ST. PAUL,
from whence we had to walk a mile and a half up a steep hill to the monastery, where building repairs were going on with great activity. I was received with cheerful hospitality, and soon made the acquaintance of four monks, who amongst them spoke English, French, Italian, and German. Having been installed in a separate bed-room, cleanly furnished in the Turkish style, where I subsequently enjoyed a delightful night's rest, undisturbed by a single flea, I was conducted into a large airy hall. Here, after a very comfortable dinner, the smaller fry of monks assembled to hear the illustrious stranger hold forth in turn to the four wise fathers who spoke unknown tongues. The simple, kind-hearted brethren looked with awe and wonder on the quadruple powers of those lips that uttered

such strange sounds: just as the Peruvians made their reverence to the Spanish horses, whose speech they understood not, and whose manners were beyond their comprehension. It was fortunate for my reputation that the reverend German scholar was of a close and taciturn disposition, since my knowledge of his scraughing language did not extend very far, and when we got to scientific discussion I was very nearly at a stand still; but I am inclined to think that he upheld my dignity to save his own; and as my servant, who never minced matters, had doubtless told them that I could speak ninety other languages, and was besides nephew to most of the crowned heads of Europe, if a phœnix had come in he would have had a lower place assigned him. I found also that in this—as indeed in all the other monasteries—one who had performed the pilgrimage to the Holy Land was looked upon with a certain degree of respect. In short, I found that at last I was amongst a set of people who had the sense to appreciate my merits; so I held up my head, and assumed all the dignified humility of real greatness.

This monastery was founded for Bulgarian and Servian monks by Constantine Biancobano, Hospodar of Wallachia. There was little that was interesting in it, either in architecture or any other walk of art; the library was contained in a small light closet, the books were clean, and ranged in order on the new deal shelves. There was only one Greek manuscript, a duodecimo copy of the Gospels of the twelfth or thirteenth century. The Servian and Bulgarian manuscripts amounted to about two hundred and fifty: of these three were remarkable; the first was a manuscript of the four Gospels, a thick quarto, and the uncial letters in which it was written were three fourths of an inch in height: it was imperfect at the end. The second was also a copy of the Gospels, a folio, in uncial letters, with fine illuminations at the beginning of each Gospel, and a large and curious portrait of a patriarch at the end; all the stops in this volume were dots of gold; several words also were written in gold. It was a noble manuscript. The third was likewise a folio of the Gospels in the ancient Bulgarian language, and, like the other two, in uncial letters. This manuscript was quite full of illuminations from beginning to end. I had seen no book like it anywhere in the Levant. I almost tumbled off the steps on which I was perched on the discovery of so extraordinary a volume. I saw that these books were taken care of, so I did not much like to ask whether they would part with them; more especially as the community was evidently a prosperous one, and had no need to sell any of their goods.

After walking about the monastery with the monks, as I was going away the agoumenos said he wished he had anything which he could present to me as a memorial of my visit to the convent of St Paul. On this a brisk fire of reciprocal compliments ensued, and I observed that I should like to take a book. "Oh! by all means!" he said; "we make no use of the old books, and should be glad if you would accept one." We returned to the library; and the agoumenos took out one at a hazard, as you might take a brick or a stone out of a pile, and presented it to me. Quoth I, "If you don't care what book it is that you are so good as to give me, let me take one which pleases me;" and, so saying, I took down the illuminated folio of the Bulgarian Gospels, and I could hardly believe I was awake when the agoumenos gave it into my hands. Perhaps the greatest piece of impertinence of which I was ever guilty, was when I asked to buy another; but that they insisted upon giving me also; so I took the other two copies of the Gospels mentioned above, all three as free-will gifts. I felt almost ashamed at accepting these two last books; but who could resist it, knowing that they were utterly valueless to the monks, and were not saleable in the bazaar at Constantinople, Smyrna, Salonica, or any neighbouring city? However, before I went away, as a salve to my conscience I gave some money to the church. The authorities accompanied me beyond the outer gate, and by the kindness of the agoumenos mules were provided to take us down to the sea-shore, where we found our clerical mariners ready for us. One of the monks, who wished for a passage to Xeropotamo, accompanied us; and, turning our boat's head again to the north-west, we arrived before long a second time below the lofty rock of

SIMOPETRA.

This monastery was founded by St. Simon the Anchorite, of whose history I was unable to learn anything. The buildings are connected with the side of the mountain by a fine aqueduct, which has a grand effect, perched as it is at so great a height above the sea, and consisting of two rows of eleven arches, one above the other, with one lofty arch across a chasm immediately under the walls of the monastery, which, as seen from this side, resembles an immense square tower, with several rows of wooden balconies or galleries projecting from the walls at a prodigious height from the ground. It was no slight effort of gymnastics to get up to the door, where I was received with many grotesque bows by an ancient porter. I was ushered into the presence of the agoumenos, who sat in a hall, surrounded by a reverend conclave of his bearded and long-haired monks; and after partaking of sweetmeats and water, and a cup of coffee, according to custom, but no pipes—for the divines of Mount Athos do not indulge in smoking—they took me to the church and to the library.

In the latter I found a hundred and fifty manuscripts, of which fifty were on vellum, all works of divinity, and not above ten or twelve of them fine books. I asked permission to purchase three, to which they acceded. These were the 'Life and Works of St. John Climax, Agoumenos of Mount Sinai,' a quarto of the eleventh century; the 'Acts and Epistles,' a noble folio written in large letters, in double columns: a very fine manuscript, the letters upright and not much joined together: at the end is an inscription in red letters, which may contain the date, but it is so faint that I could not make it out. The third was a quarto of the four Gospels, with a picture of an evangelist at the beginning of each Gospel. Whilst I was arranging the payment for these manuscripts, a monk, opening the copy of the Gospels, found at the end a horrible anathema and malediction written by the donor, a prince or king, he said, against any one who should sell or part with this book. This was very unlucky, and produced a great effect upon the monks; but as no anathema was found in either of the two other volumes, I was allowed to take them, and so went on my way rejoicing. They rang the bells at my departure, and I heard them at intervals jingling in the air above me as I scrambled down the rocky mountain. Except Dionisiou, this was the only monastery where the agoumenos kissed the letter of the patriarch and laid it upon his forehead: the sign of reverence and obedience which is, or ought to be, observed with the firmans of the Sultan and other oriental potentates.

From a Sketch by R. Curzon. VIEW OF THE MONASTERY AND AQUEDUCT OF SIMOPETRA, ON MOUNT ATHOS, TAKEN FROM THE SEA SHORE.From a Sketch by R. Curzon.

VIEW OF THE MONASTERY AND AQUEDUCT OF SIMOPETRA, ON MOUNT ATHOS, TAKEN FROM THE SEA SHORE.

The same evening I got back to my comfortable room at Xeropotamo, and did ample justice to a good meagre dinner after the heat and fatigues of the day. A monk had arrived from one of the outlying farms who could speak a little Italian; he was deputed to do the honours of the house, and accordingly dined with me. He was a magnificent-looking man of thirty or thirty-five years of age, with large eyes and long black hair and beard. As we sat together in the evening in the ancient room, by the light of one dim brazen lamp, with deep shades thrown across his face and figure, I thought he would have made an admirable study for Titian or Sebastian del Piombo. In the course of conversation I found that he had learnt Italian from another monk, having never been out of the peninsula of Mount Athos. His parents and most of the other inhabitants of the village where he was born, somewhere in Roumelia—but its name or exact position he did not know—had been massacred during some revolt or disturbance. So he had been told, but he remembered nothing about it; he had been educated in a school in this or one of the other monasteries, and his whole life had been passed upon the Holy Mountain; and this, he said, was the case with very many other monks. He did not remember his mother, and did not seem quite sure that he ever had one; he had never seen a woman, nor had he any idea what sort of things women were, or what they looked like. He asked me whether they resembled the pictures of the Panagia, the Holy Virgin, which hang in every church. Now, those who are conversant with the peculiar conventional representations of the Blessed Virgin in the pictures of the Greek church, which are all exactly alike, stiff, hard, and dry, without any appearance of life or emotion, will agree with me that they do not afford a very favourable idea of the grace or beauty of the fair sex; and that there was a difference of appearance between black women, Circassians, and those of other nations, which was, however, difficult to describe to one who had never seen a lady of any race. He listened with great interest while I told him that all women were not exactly like the pictures he had seen, but I did not think it charitable to carry on the conversation farther, although the poor monk seemed to have a strong inclination to know more of that interesting race of beings from whose society he had been so entirely debarred. I often thought afterwards of the singular lot of this manly and noble-looking monk: whether he is still a recluse, either in the monastery or in his mountain-farm, with its little moss-grown chapel as ancient as the days of Constantine; or whether he has gone out into the world and mingled in its pleasures and its cares.

I arranged with the captain of a small vessel which was lying off Xeropotamo taking in a cargo of wood, that he should give me a passage in two or three days, when he said he should be ready to sail; and in the mean time I purposed to explore the metropolis of Mount Athos, the town of Cariez; and then to go to Caracalla, and remain there till the vessel was ready.

CIRCASSIAN LADY. CIRCASSIAN LADY.

Accordingly, the next morning I set out, the Agoumenos supplying me with mules. The guide did not know how far it was to Cariez, which is situated almost in the centre of the peninsula. I found it was only distant one hour and a half; but as I had not made arrangements to go on, I was obliged to remain there all day. Close to the town is the great monastery of
COUTLOUMOUSSI,

the most regular building on Mount Athos. It contains a large square court with a cloister of stone arches all round it, out of which the cells and chambers open, as they do in a Roman Catholic convent. The church stands in the centre of this quadrangle, and glories in a famous picture of the Last Judgment on the wall of the narthex, or porch, before the door of entrance. The monastery was at this time nearly uninhabited; but, after some trouble, I found one monk, who made great difficulties as to showing me the library, for he said a Russian had been there some time ago, and had borrowed a book which he never returned. However, at last I gained admission by means of that ingenious silver key which opens so many locks.

In a good-sized square room, filled with shelves all round, I found a fine, although neglected, collection of books; a great many of them thrown on the floor in heaps, and covered all over with dust, which the Russian did not appear to have much disturbed when he borrowed the book which had occasioned me so much trouble. There were about six or seven hundred volumes of printed books, two hundred MSS. on paper, and a hundred and fifty on vellum. I was not permitted to examine this library at all to my satisfaction. The solitary monk thought I was a Russian, and would not let me alone, or give me the time I wanted for my researches. I found a multitude of folios and quartos of the works of St. Chrysostom, who seems to have been the principal instructor of the monks of Mount Athos, that is, in the days when they were in the habit of reading—a tedious custom, which they have long since given up by general consent. I met also with an Evangelistarium, a quarto in uncial letters, but not in very fine condition. Two or three other old monks had by this time crept out of their holes, but they would not part with any of their books: that unhappy Russian had filled the minds of the whole brotherhood with suspicion. So we went to the church, which was curious and quaint, as they all are; and as we went through all the requisite formalities before various grim pictures, and showed due respect for the sacred character of a Christian church, they began at last to believe that I was not a Russian; but if they had seen the contents of the saddle-bags which were sticking out bravely on each side of the patient mule at the gate, they would perhaps have considered me as something far worse.

Coutloumoussi was founded by the Emperor Alexius Comnenus, and, having been destroyed by "the Pope of Rome," was restored by the piety of various hospodars and waywodes of Bessarabia. It is difficult to understand what these worthy monks can mean when they affirm that several of their monasteries have been burned and plundered by the Pope. Perhaps in the days of the Crusades some of the rapacious and undisciplined hordes who accompanied the armies of the Cross—not to rescue the holy sepulchre from the power of the Saracens, but for the sake of plunder and robbery—may have been attracted by the fame of the riches of these peaceful convents, and have made the differences in their religion a prbook for sacrilege and rapacity. Thus bands of pirates and brigands in the middle ages may have cloaked their acts of violence under the specious excuse of devotion to the Church of Rome; and so the Pope has acquired a bad name, and is looked upon with terror and animosity by the inhabitants of the monasteries of Mount Athos.

Having seen what I could, I went on to the town of Cariez, if it can properly be called such; for it is difficult to explain what it is. One may perhaps say that what Washington is to the United States, Cariez is to Mount Athos. A few artificers do live there who carve crosses and ornaments in cypress-wood. The principal feature of the place is the great church of Protaton, which is surrounded by smaller buildings and chapels. These I saw at a distance, but did not visit, because I could get no mules, and it was too hot to walk so far. A Turkish aga lives here: he is sent by the Porte to collect the revenue from the monks, and also to protect them from other Turkish visitors. He is paid and provided with food by a kind of rate which is levied on the twenty-one monasteries of αγιον ορος , and is in fact a sort of sheep-dog to the flock of helpless monks who pasture among the trees and rocks of the peninsula. On certain days the Agoumenoi of the monasteries and the high officers of their communities meet at the church of Protaton for the transaction of business and the discussion of affairs. I am sorry I did not see this ancient house of parliament. The rooms in which these synods or convocations are held adjoin the church. Situated at short distances around these principal edifices are numerous small ecclesiastical villas, such as were called cells in England before the Reformation: these are the habitations of the venerable senators when they come up to parliament. Some of them are beautifully situated; for Cariez stands in a fair, open vale, half-way up the side of the mountain, and commands a beautiful view to the north of the sea, with the magnificent island of Samotraki looming superbly in the distance. All around are large orchards and plantations of peach-trees and of various other sorts of fruit-bearing trees in great abundance, and the round hills are clothed with greensward. It is a happy, peaceful-looking place, and in its trim and sunny arbours reminds one of Virgil and Theocritus.

I went to the house of the aga to seek for a habitation, but the aga was asleep; and who was there so bold as to wake a sleeping aga? Luckily he awoke of his own accord; and he was soon informed by my interpreter that an illustrious personage awaited his leisure. He did not care for a monk, and not much for an agoumenos; but he felt small in the presence of a mighty Turkish aga. Nevertheless, he ventured a few hints as usual about the kings and queens who were my first cousins, but in a much more subdued tone than usual; and I was received with that courteous civility and good breeding which is so frequently met with among Turks of every degree. The aga apologised for having no good room to offer me; but he sent out his men to look for a lodging; and in the mean time we went to a kiosk, that is, a place like a large birdcage, with enough roof to make a shade, and no walls to impede the free passage of the air. It was built of wood, upon a scaffold eight or ten feet from the ground, in the corner of a garden, and commanded a fine view of the sea. In one corner of this cage I sat all day long, for there was nowhere else to go to; and the aga sat opposite to me in another corner, smoking his pipe, in which solacing occupation to his great surprise I did not partake. We had cups of coffee and sherbet every now and then, and about every half-hour the aga uttered a few words of compliment or welcome, informing me occasionally that there were many dervishes in the place, "very many dervishes," for so he denominated the monks. Dinner came towards evening. There was meat, dolmas, demir tatlessi, olives, salad, roast meat, and pilau, that filled up some time; and shortly afterwards I retired to the house of the monastery of Russico, a little distance from my kiosk; and there I slept on a carpet on the boards; and at sunrise was ready to continue my journey, as were also the mules. The aga gave me some breakfast, at which repast a cat made its appearance, with whom the day before I had made acquaintance; but now it came, not alone, but accompanied by two kittens. "Ah!" said I to the aga, "how is this? Why, as I live, this is a she cat! a cat feminine! What business has it on Mount Athos? and with kittens too! a wicked cat!"

"Hush!" said the Aga, with a solemn grin; "do not say anything about it. Yes, it must be a she-cat: I allow, certainly, that it must be a she-cat. I brought it with me from Stamboul. But do not speak of it, or they will take it away; and it reminds me of my home, where my wife and children are living far away from me."

TURKISH LADY, IN THE YASHMAK, OR VEIL. TURKISH LADY, IN THE YASHMAK, OR VEIL.

I promised to make no scandal about the cat, and took my leave; and as I rode off I saw him looking at me out of his cage with the cat sitting by his side. I was sorry I could not take aga and cat and all with me to Stamboul, the poor gentleman looked so solitary and melancholy.

CHAPTER XXVIII.

Caracalla—The Agoumenos—Curious Cross—The Nuts of Caracalla—Singular Mode of preparing a Dinner Table—Departure from Mount Athos—Packing of the MSS.—Difficulties of the Way—Voyage to the Dardanelles—Apprehended Attack from Pirates—Return to Constantinople.

It

took me three hours to reach Caracalla, where the agoumenos and Father Joasaph received me with all the hospitable kindness of old friends, and at once installed me in my old room, which looked into the court, and was very cool and quiet. Here I reposed in peace during the hotter hours of the day; and here I received the news that the captain of the vessel which I had hired had left me in the lurch and gone out to sea, having, I suppose, made some better bargain. This caused me some tribulation; but there was nothing to be done but to get another vessel; so I sent back to Xeropotamo, which appeared to be the most frequented part of the coast, to see whether there was any craft there which could be hired.

I employed the next day in wandering about with the agoumenos and Father Joasaph in all the holes and corners of the monastery; the agoumenos telling me interminable legends of the saints, and asking Father Joasaph if they were not true. I looked over the library, where I found an uncial Evangelistarium; a manuscript of Demosthenes on paper, but of some antiquity; a manuscript of Justin (Ιουστινου

) in Greek; and several other manuscripts,—all of which the agoumenos agreed to let me have.

One of the monks had a curiously carved cross set in silver, which he wished to sell; but I told the agoumenos that it was not sufficiently ancient: I added, however, that if I could meet with any ancient cross or shrine or reliquary, I should be delighted to purchase such a thing, and that I would give a good price for it. In the afternoon it struck him suddenly that as he did not care for antiquities, perhaps we might come to an arrangement; and the end of the affair was that he gave me one of the ancient crosses which I had seen when I was there before, and put the one the monk had to sell in its place; certain pieces of gold which I produced rendering this transaction satisfactory to all parties. This most curious and beautiful piece of jewellery has been since engraved, and forms the subject of the third plate in Shaw's 'Dresses and Decorations of the Middle Ages,' London, 1843. It had been presented to the monastery by the Emperor John, whom, from what I was told by the agoumenos, I take to have been John Zimisces. It is one of the most ancient as well as one of the finest relics of its kind now existing in England.

On the evening of the second day my man returned from Xeropotamo with the information that he had found a small Greek brig, and had engaged to give the patron or captain eleven hundred piastres for our passage thence to the Dardanelles the next day, if I could manage to be ready in so short a time. As fortunately I had purchased all the manuscripts which I wished to possess, there was nothing to detain me on Mount Athos; for I had now visited every monastery excepting that of St. Anne, which indeed is not a monastery like the rest, but a mere collection of hermitages or cells at the extreme point of the peninsula, immediately under the great peak of the mountain. I was told that there was nothing there worth seeing; but still I am sorry that I did not make a pilgrimage to so original a community, who it appears live on roots and herbs, and are the most strict of all the ascetics in this strange monastic region.

All of a sudden, as we were walking quietly together, the agoumenos asked me if I knew what was the price of nuts at Constantinople.

"Nuts?" said I.

"Yes, nuts," said he; "hazel-nuts: nuts are excellent things. Have they a good supply of nuts at Constantinople?"

"Well," said I, "I don't know; but I dare say they have. But why, my Lord, do you ask? Why do you wish to know the price of hazel-nuts at Constantinople?"

"Oh!" said the agoumenos, "they do not eat half nuts enough at Stamboul. Nuts are excellent things. They should be eaten more than they are. People say that nuts are unwholesome; but it is a great mistake." And so saying, he introduced me into a set of upper rooms that I had not previously entered, the entire floors of which were covered two feet deep with nuts. I never saw one-hundredth part so many before. The good agoumenos, it seems, had been speculating in hazel-nuts; and a vessel was to come to the little tower of the scaricatojo down below to be freighted with them: they were to produce a prodigious profit, and defray the expense of finishing the new buildings of Caracalla.

"Take some," said he; "don't be afraid; there are plenty. Take some, and taste them, and then you can tell your friends at Constantinople what a peculiar flavour you found in the famous nuts of Athos; and in all Athos every one knows that there are no nuts like those of Caracalla!"

They were capital nuts; but as it was before dinner, and I was ravenously hungry, and my lord the agoumenos had not brought a bottle of sherry in his pocket, I did not particularly relish them. But there had been great talking during the morning between the agoumenos and Pater Joasaph about a famous large fish which was to be cooked for dinner; and, as the important hour was approaching, we adjourned to my sitting room. Father Joasaph was already there, having washed his hands and seated himself on the divan, in order to regulate the proceedings of the lay brother who acted as butler. The preparations for the banquet were made. The lay brother first brought in the table-cloth, which he spread upon the ground in one corner of the room; then he turned the table upside down upon the table-cloth, with its legs in the air: next he brought two immense flagons, one of wine, the other of water; these were made of copper tinned, and were each a foot and a half high; he set them down on the carpet a little way from the table-cloth; and round the table he placed three cushions for the agoumenos, Pater Joasaph, and me; and then he went away to bring the dinner. He soon reappeared, bringing in, with the assistance of another stout catechumen, the whole of the dinner on a large circular tray of well-polished brass called a sinni. This was so formed as to fix on the sticking-up legs of the subverted table, and, with the aid of Pater Joasaph, it was soon all tight and straight. In a great centre-dish there appeared the big fish in a sea of sauce surrounded by a mountainous shore of rice. Round this luxurious centre stood a circle of smaller dishes, olives, caviare, salad (no eggs, because there were no hens), papas yaknesi, and several sweet things. Two cats followed the dinner into the room, and sat down demurely side by side. The fish looked excellent, and had a most savoury smell. I had washed my hands, and was preparing to sit down, when the Father Abbot, who was not thinking of the dinner, took this inopportune moment to begin one of his interminable stories.

"We have before spoken," he said, "of the many kings, princes, and patriarchs who have given up the world and ended their days here in peace. One of the most important epochs in the history of Mount Athos occurred about the year 1336, when a Calabrian monk, a man of great learning though of mean appearance, whose name was Barlaam, arrived on a pilgrimage to venerate the sacred relics of our famous sanctuaries. He found here many holy men, who, having retired entirely from the world, by communing with themselves in the privacy of their own cells, had arrived at that state of calm beatitude and heavenly contemplation, that the eternal light of Mount Tabor was revealed to them."

"Mount Tabor?" said I.

"Yes," said the agoumenos, "the light which had been seen during the time of the Transfiguration by the apostles, and which had always existed there, was seen by those who, after years of solitude and penance and maceration of the flesh, had arrived at that state of abstraction from all earthly things that in their bodies they saw the divine light. They in those good times would sit alone in their chambers with their eyes cast down upon the region of their navel; this was painful at first, both from the fixedness of the attitude required, with the head bent down upon the breast, and from the workings of the mind, which seemed to wander in the regions of darkness and space. At last, when they had persevered in fasting day and night with no change of thought or attitude for many hours, they began to feel a wonderful satisfaction; a ray of joy ineffable would seem to illuminate the brain; and no sooner had the soul discovered the place of the heart than it was involved in a mystic and ethereal light."[18]

"Ah," said I, "really!"

"Now this Barlaam, being a carnal and worldly-minded man, took upon himself to doubt the efficacy of this bodily and mental discipline; it is said that he even ventured to ridicule the venerable fathers who gave themselves up so entirely to the contemplation of the light of Mount Tabor. Not only did he question the merits of these ascetic acts, but, being learned in books, and being endowed with great powers of eloquence and persuasion, he infused doubts into the minds of others of the monks and anchorites of Mount Athos. Arguments were used on both sides; conversations arose upon these subjects; arguments grew into disputations, conversations into controversies, till at last, from the most peaceful and regular of communities, the peninsula of the holy mountain became from one end to the other a theatre of discord, doubt, and difference; the flames of contention were lit up; every thing was unsettled; men knew not what to think; till at last, with general consent, the unhappy intruder was dismissed from all the monasteries; and, flying from the storm of angry words which he had raised on all sides around him, he departed from Mount Athos and retired to the city of Constantinople. There his specious manners, his knowledge of the language of the Latins, and the dissensions he had created in the church, brought him into notice at court; and now not only were the monks of Mount Athos and Olympus divided against each other, but the city was split into parties of theological disputants; clamour and acrimony raged on every side. The Emperor Andronicus, willing to remove the cause of so much contention, and being at the same time surrounded with difficulties on all sides (for the unbelieving Turks, commanded by the fierce Orchan, had with their unnumbered tribes overrun Bithynia and many of the provinces of the Christian emperor), he graciously condescended to give his imperial mandate that the monk Barlaam should [here the two cats became vociferous in their impatience for the fish] be sent on an embassy to the Pope of Rome; he was empowered to enter into negotiations for the settlement of all religious differences between the Eastern and Western churches, on condition that the Latin princes should assist the emperor to drive the Turks back into the confines of Asia. The Emperor Andronicus died from a fever brought on by excitement in defending the cause of the ascetic quietists before a council in his palace. John Paleologus was set aside; and John Cantacuzene, in a desperate endeavour to please all parties, gave his daughter Theodora to Orchan the Emperor of the Osmanlis; and at his coronation the purple buskin of his right leg was fastened on by the Greeks, and that of his left leg by the Latins. Notwithstanding these concessions, the embassy of Barlaam, the most important with which any diplomatic agent was ever trusted, failed altogether from the troubles of the times. The Emperor John Cantacuzene, who celebrated his own acts in an edict beginning with the words 'by my sublime and almost incredible virtue,' gave up the reins of power, and taking the name of Josaph, became a monk of one of the monasteries of the holy mountain, which was then known by the name of the monastery of Mangane, while the monk Barlaam was created Bishop of Gerace, in Italy."

By the time the good abbot had come to the conclusion of his history, the fish was cold and the dinner spoilt; but I thought his account of the extraordinary notions which the monks of those dark ages had formed of the duties of Christianity so curious, that it almost compensated for the calamity of losing the only good dinner which I had seen on Mount Athos.

What a difference it would have made in the affairs of Europe if the embassy of Barlaam had succeeded! The Turks would not have been now in possession of Constantinople; and many points of difference having been mutually conceded by the two great divisions of the church, perhaps the Reformation never would have taken place. The narration of these events was the more interesting to me, as I had it from the lips of a monk who to all intents and purposes was living in the darkness of remote antiquity. His ample robes, his long beard, and the Byzantine architecture of the ancient room in which we sat, impressed his words upon my remembrance; and as I looked upon the eager countenance of the abbot, whose thoughts still were fixed upon the world from which he had retired, while he discoursed of the troubles and discords which had invaded the peaceful glades and quiet solitudes of the holy mountain, I felt that there was no place left on this side of the grave where the wicked cease from troubling or where the weary are at rest. No places, however, that I have seen equal the beauty of the scenery and the calm retired look of the small farmhouses, if they may so be called, which I met with in my rides on the declivities of Mount Athos. These buildings are usually situated on the sides of hills opening on the land which the monastic labourers cultivate; they consist of a small square tower, usually appended to which are one or two little stone cottages, and an ancient chapel, from which the tinkling of the bar which calls the monks to prayer may be heard many times a day echoing softly through the lovely glades of the primæval forest. The ground is covered in some places with anemones and cyclamen; waterfalls are met with at the head of half the valleys, pouring their refreshing waters over marble rocks. If the great mountain itself, which towers up so grandly above the enchanting scenery below, had been carved into the form of a statue of Alexander the Great, according to the project of Lysippus, though a wonderful effort of human labour, it could hardly have added to the beauty of the scene, which is so much increased by the appearance of the monasteries, whose lofty towers and rounded domes appear almost like the palaces we read of in a fairy tale.

The next morning, at an early hour, mules were waiting in the court to carry me across the hills to the harbour below the monastery of Xeropotamo, where the Greek brig was lying which was to convey me and my treasures from these peaceful shores. Emptying out my girdle, I calculated how much, or rather how little money would suffice to pay the expenses of my voyage to the Asiatic castle of the Dardanelles, feeling assured that from thence I could get credit for a passage in the magnificent steamer The Stamboul, which ran between Smyrna and Constantinople. With the reservation of this sum, I gave the agoumenos all my remaining gold, and in return he provided me with an old wooden chest, in which I stowed away several goodly folios; for the saddle-bags, although distended to their utmost limits, did not suffice to carry all the great manuscripts and ponderous volumes that were now added to my store. Turning out the corn from the nosebags of the mules, I put one or two smaller books in each; and, after all, an extra mule was sent for to convey the surplus tomes over the rough and craggy ridge which we were to pass in our journey to the other sea. Although the stories of the agoumenos were too windy and too long, I was sorry to part from him, and I took an affectionate leave also of Pater Joasaph and the two cats. Unfortunately, in the hurry of departure, I left on the divan the MS. of Justin, which I had been trying to decipher, and forgot it when I came away. It was a small thick octavo, on charta bombycina, and was probably kicked into the nearest corner as soon as I evacuated the monastery.

Our ride was a very rough one. We had first to ascend the hill, in some places through deep ravines, and in others through most glorious forests of gigantic trees, mostly planes, with a thick underwood of those aromatic flowering evergreens which so beautifully clothe the hills of Greece and this part of Turkey.

When we had crossed the upper ridge of rock, leaving the peak of Athos towering to the sky on our left, we had to descend the dry bed of a torrent so full of great stones and fallen rocks, that it appeared impossible for anything but a goat to travel on such a road. I got off my mule, and began jumping from one rock to another on the edge of the precipice; but the sun was so powerful, that in a short time I was completely exhausted; and on looking at the mules, I saw that one after another they jumped down so unerringly over chasms and broken rocks, alighting so precisely in the exact place where there was standing-room for their feet, that, after a little consideration, I remounted my mule; and keeping my seat, without holding the bridle, we hopped and skipped from rock to rock down this extraordinary track, until in due time we arrived safely at the sea-shore, close to the mouth of the little river of Xeropotamo. My manuscripts and myself were soon embarked, and with a favouring breeze we stood out into the Gulf of Monte Santo, and had leisure to survey the scenery of this superb peninsula as we glided round the lofty marble rocks and noble forests which formed the background to the strange and picturesque Byzantine monasteries with every one of which we had become acquainted.

Being a little nervous on account of the pirates, of whom I had heard many stories during my sojourn on Mount Athos, I questioned the master of the vessel on this subject. "Oh," said he, "the sea is now very quiet; there have been no pirates about the coast for the last fortnight." This assurance hardly satisfied me. How terrible it would be to see these precious volumes thrown into the sea, like my unhappy precursor's MS. of Homer! It was frightful to think of! We were three days at sea, there being at this fine season very little wind. Once we thought we were chased by a wicked-looking cutter with a large white mainsail, which kept to windward of us; but in the end, after some hours of deadly tribulation, during which I hid the manuscripts as well as I could under all kinds of rubbish in the hold, we descried the stars and stripes of America upon her ensign; so then I pulled all the old books out again. This cutter was, I suppose, a tender to some American man-of-war. On the evening of the third day we found ourselves safe under the guns of Roumeli Calessi, the European castle of the Dardanelles; and, after a good deal of tedious tacking, we got across to the Asiatic castle of Coom Calessi, where I landed with all my treasures. Before long, the Smyrna steamer, The Stamboul, hove in sight, and I took my passage in her to Constantinople.

THE END.

London: Printed by W. Clowes and Son, Stamford Street.

FOOTNOTES:

[1]

Moyah—"water."

[2]

This, the first mosque built at Cairo, is said to have been paid for by Sultan Tayloon with a part of an immense treasure in gold, which he found under a monument called the altar of Pharaoh, on the mountain of Mokattam. This building was destroyed by Tayloon, who founded a mosque upon the spot in the year 873, in honour of Judah, the brother of Joseph, who resorted there to pray when he came to Egypt. This mosque becoming ruined, another was built upon the spot by the Emir El Guyoosh, minister of the Caliph Mostansir, A.D.

1094, which still remains perched on the corner of a rock, which is excavated in various places with ancient tombs.

[3]

A fragment of the Gospel of St. Mark was found in the tomb which was reputed to be his. Damp and age have decayed this precious relic, of which only some small fragments remain; but an exact facsimile of it was made before it was destroyed. This facsimile is now in my possession: it is in Latin, and is written in double columns, on sixteen leaves of vellum, of a large quarto size, and proves that whoever transcribed the original must have been a proficient in the art of writing, for the letters are of great size and excellent formation, and in the style of the very earliest manuscripts.

[4]

See Quarterly Review, vol. lxxvii. p. 43.

[5]

It is perhaps more likely that these beautiful specimens of ancient glass were made in the island of Murano, in the lagunes of Venice, as the manufactories of the Venetians supplied the Mahomedans with many luxuries in the middle ages.

[6]

The only early church in which the columns are continued on the end opposite to the altar, where the doorway is usually situated, is the Cathedral of Messina. The effect is very good, and takes off from the baldness usually observable at that end of a basilica. The early Coptic churches have no porch or narthex, an essential part of an original Greek church.

[7]

This curious old sunken oratory bears a resemblance in many points to the fine church of St. Agnese, at Rome, where the ground has been excavated down to the level of the catacomb in which the holy martyr's body reposes. The long straight flight of steps down to the lower level are also similar in these two very ancient churches, although the Church of Der-el-Adra is poor and mean, whilst that of St. Agnese is a superb edifice, and is famous for being the first basilica in which a gallery is found over the side aisles. This gallery was set apart for the women, as in the oriental churches of St. Sophia at Constantinople, and perhaps, also, of the Holy Sepulchre at Jerusalem.

[8]

It is much to be desired that some competent person should write a small cheap book, with plates or wood-cuts explaining what an early Christian Church was; what the ceremonies, ornaments, vestures, and liturgy were at the time when the Church of our Lord was formally established by the Emperor Constantine: for the numerous well-meaning authors who have written on the restoration of our older churches, appear to me to be completely in the dark. Gothic is NOT Christian architecture—it is Roman Catholic architecture: the vestures of English ecclesiastics are not restorations of early simplicity—they are modern inventions taken from German collegiate dresses which have nothing to do with religion.

[9]

We are perhaps not entirely acquainted with the mechanical powers of the ancients. The seated statue of Rameses II., in the Memnonium at Thebes, a solid block of granite forty or fifty feet high, has been broken to pieces apparently by a tremendous blow. How this can have been accomplished without the aid of gunpowder it is difficult to conjecture.

[10]

For the benefit of the reader I subjoin two of there songs translated from the originals; or rather, I may say, paraphrased: although the first of them has the same rhythm as the original. The notes are but very little, if at all, altered from those which have been frequently sung to me, accompanied by a drum, called a tarabouka, or a long sort of guitar with only two or three strings. It must be observed that the chorus, Amaan, Amaan, Amaan, is generally added to all songs—à discrétion—and that the way this chorus is howled out, is to an European ear the most difficult part to bear of the whole:—

1.

Thine eyes, thine eyes have kill'd me:

With love my heart is torn:
Thy looks with pain have fill'd me:
Amaan, Amaan, Amaan.
2.
Oh gently, dearest! gently,
Approach me not with scorn:
With one sweet look content me:
Amaan, Amaan, Amaan.
3.
That yellow shawl encloses
A form made to adorn
A Peri's bower of roses:
Amaan, Amaan, Amaan.
4.
The snows, the snows are melting
On the hills of Isfahan.
As fair, be as relenting:
Amaan, Amaan, Amaan.
  *   *   *   *   *   *   *

1.
Let not her, whose eyelids sleep,
Imagine I no vigil keep.
Alas! with hope and love I burn:
Ah! do not from thy lover turn!
2.
Patron of lovers, Bedowi!
Ah! give me her I hold most dear;
And I will vow to her, and thee,
The brightest shawl In all Cashmere.
3.
Ah! when I view thy loveliness,
The lustre of thy deep black eye,
My songs but add to my distress!
Let me behold thee once, and die.
4.
Think not that scorn and bitter words
Can make me from my true love sever!
Pierce our hearts, then, with your swords:
The blood of both will flow together.
5.
Fill us the golden bowl with wine;
Give us the ripe and downy peach:
And, in this bower of jessamine,
No sorrows our retreat shall reach.
6.

Masr may boast her lovely girls,
Whose necks are deck'd with pearls and gold:
The gold would fall; the purest pearls
Would blush could they my love behold.
7.
Famed Skanderieh's beauties, too,
On Syria's richest silks recline:
Their rosy lips are sweet, 'tis true;
But can they be compar'd to thine?
8.
Fairest! your beauty comes from Heaven:
Freely the lovely gift was given.
Resist not, then, the high decree—
'Twas fated I should sigh for thee.
This last song is well known upon the Nile by the name of its chorus, Doas ya leili.

[11]

This sword is used by the Reverendissimo, the title given to the superior of the Franciscans, when he confers the order of Knight of the Holy Sepulchre, which is only given to a Roman Catholic of noble birth. The Reverendissimo is also authorised by the Pope to give a flag bearing the Five Crosses of Jerusalem to the captain of any ship who has rendered service to the Catholic religion. These honours were first instituted by the Christian Kings of Jerusalem, but they are now sold by the monks for about forty dollars to any Roman Catholic who likes to pay for them.

[12]

On another occasion some years afterwards, I was waiting in the same place, when I wandered into the new Patriarchal church which opens on this court: while I stood there, a corpse was brought in on a bier, followed by many persons, who I suppose were the relations and friends of the deceased. After the funeral service had been read by a priest, every person in the church went up to the bier and kissed the dead man's hand and forehead: this is the usual custom, and an affecting one to see when friends bid friends a last farewell. But this man had died of some fearful and horrible disease, perhaps the plague, which through this horrid means may have been distributed to half the congregation.

[13]

All eastern cities are infested with troops of half-wild dogs, who act the part of scavengers, and live upon the refuse food which is thrown into the streets.

[14]

Direction.

—"To the blessed Inspectors, Officers, Chiefs, and Representatives of the Holy Community of Monte Santo, and to the Holy Fathers of the same, and of all other sacred convents, our beloved Sons.

"We, Gregorios, Patriarch, Archbishop Universal, Metropolitan of Constantinople, c. c. c.

"Blessed Inspectors, Officers, Superiors, and Representatives of the Community of the Holy Mountain, and other Holy Fathers of the same, and of the other Holy and Venerable Convents subject to our holy universal Throne. Peace be to you.

"The bearer of the present, our patriarchal sheet, the Honourable Robert Curzon, of a noble English family, recommended to us by most worthy and much-honoured persons, intending to travel and wishing to be instructed in the old and new philology, thinks to satisfy his curiosity by repairing to those sacred convents which may have any connexion with his intentions. We recommend his person, therefore, to you all: and we order and require of you, that you not only receive him with every esteem and every possible hospitality, in each and in the several holy convents; but to lend yourselves readily to all his wants and desires, and to give him precise and clear explanations to all his interrogations relative to his philological examinations, obliging yourselves, and lending yourselves, in a manner not only fully to satisfy and content him, but so that he shall approve of and praise your conduct.

"This we desire and require to be executed, rewarding you with the Divine and with our blessing.

"(Signed) Gregorios
, Universal Patriarch.
"Constantinople, 1 (13) July, 1837."

[15]

Ridiculous as these pictorial representations of the Last Judgment appear to us, one of them was the cause of a whole nation's embracing Christianity. Bogoris, king of Bulgaria, having written to Constantinople for a painter to decorate the walls of his palace, a monk named Methodius was sent to him—all knowledge of the arts in those days being confined to the clergy. The king desired Methodius to paint on a certain wall the most terrible picture that he could imagine; and, by the advice of the king's sister, who had embraced Christianity some years before whilst in captivity at Constantinople, the monastic artist produced so fearful a representation of the torments of the condemned in the next world, that it had the effect of converting Bogoris to the Christian faith. In consequence of this event the Patriarch of Constantinople despatched a bishop to Bulgaria, who baptised the king by the name of Michael in the year 865. Before long his loyal subjects, following the example of their sovereign, were converted also; and Christianity from that period became the religion of the land.

[16]

In the early ages of the Greek church the Epiphany was a day of very great solemnity; for not only was the adoration of the Magi celebrated on the 6th of January, but also the changing of the water into wine at the marriage at Cana, the baptism, and even the birth of our Lord. On this day the holy water is blessed in the Greek church, by throwing a small cross into it, or otherwise by holding over it the cross, with a handle attached to it, which is used by the Greek clergy in the act of benediction.

[17]

The Emperor Leo the First was crowned by the Patriarch of Anatolia in the year 459. He is the first prince on record who received his crown from the hands of a bishop.

[18]

Mosheim's 'Ecclesiastical History;' Gibbon.
Plan of the church, the convent of the Pulley.
Plan of the church, the convent of the Pulley.
1. Altar. 6. Two three-quarter columns.

2. Apsis, apparently cut out of the rock. 7. Eight columns.
3. Two Corinthian columns. 8. Dark room cut out of the rock (there is another corresponding to it under the steps).
4. Wooden partitions of lattice-work, about 10 ft. high.   9. Steps leading down into the church.
5. Steps leading up to the sanctuary. 10. Screen before the Altar.

Plan of the church of the The Holy Sepulchre. Plan of the church of the The Holy Sepulchre.

The Holy maltese cross
Sepulchre.

1. Entrance to the Church. 15. Where Mary Magdalene stood.
2. The Stone of Unction. 16. Where our Lord appeared to Mary Magdalene.
3. Where our Saviour was nailed to the Cross. 17. The Pillar of Flagellation.
4. Mount Calvary triple cross 18. Rooms of the Latin Convent.
5. Chapel of the Sacrifice of Isaac. 19. Chapel of the Maronites.
6. Chapel of the Altar of Melchisedec. 20. Chapel of the Georgians.
7. Stairs up to Mount Calvary. 21. Sepulchre of Joseph of Arimathea.
8. Stairs down to the Chapel of St. Helena. 22. Chapel of the Copts.
9. Stairs down to the Chapel of the Invention of the Cross. 23. Chapel of the Jacobites.
10. Place where the three Crosses were discovered. 24. Chapel of the Abyssinians, over which is the Chapel of the Armenians.
11. Chapel of the Division of the Garments.   25. The spot where the Blessed Virgin and St. John stood during the Crucifixion.
12. Prison of our Lord. 26. Steps before the entrance of the Holy Sepulchre.
13. Greek Choir, in it center of the world
, the center of the world; on each side are the Stalls for the Monks. 27. Ante-room to the Holy Sepulchre.

In the center is the stone where the Angel sat;
on either side the two windows from whence the
Holy Fire is delivered to the multitude.
14. Latin Choir. 28. The Iconostasis, or Screen before the Greek Altar, which, as in English Churches, is called the Holy Table—ικονοστασις.

INTERIOR OF THE ABYSSINIAN LIBRARY, IN THE MONASTERY OF SOURIANI ON THE NATRON LAKES.

INTERIOR OF THE ABYSSINIAN LIBRARY, IN THE MONASTERY OF SOURIANI ON THE NATRON LAKES.

Abyssinian monk clothed in leather. The dining table. The blind abbot leaning over the Author. Abyssinian monk. Coptic monk. The books hanging from wooden pegs let into the wall. The Author's Egyptian servants.